The Tao Teh King for Awakening

The Tao Teh King for Awakening

A Practical Commentary on Lao Tzu's Classic Exposition of Taoism

Abbot George Burke
(Swami Nirmalananda Giri)

Light of the Spirit Press
Cedar Crest, New Mexico

Published by
    Light of the Spirit Press
    lightofthespiritpress.com

    Light of the Spirit Monastery
    P. O. Box 1370
    Cedar Crest, New Mexico 87008
    www.ocoy.org

Copyright © 2019 Light of the Spirit Monastery.
All rights reserved.

ISBN-13: 978-1-7331643-1-3
ISBN-10: 1-7331643-1-6

Library of Congress Control Number: 2019948239
Light of the Spirit Press, Cedar Crest, New Mexico

Translation of the Bhagavad Gita used in this book is from
The Bhagavad Gita: The Song of God by Abbot George Burke.
Copyright © 2018 Light of the Spirit Monastery.

Bisac Categories:
REL065000   RELIGION / Taoism
PHI023000   PHILOSOPHY / Taoist

First edition, (October 2019)
04052021

Contents

Preface ix
1. On the Absolute Tao 1
2. The Rise of Relative Opposites 6
3. Action Without Deeds 15
4. The Character of the Tao 19
5. Nature 28
6. The Spirit of the Valley 37
7. Living for Others 42
8. Water 45
9. The Danger of Overweening Success 50
10. Embracing the One 53
11. The Utility of Not-Being 59
12. The Senses 61
13. Praise and Blame 63
14. Prehistoric Origins 65
15. The Wise Ones of Old 69
16. Knowing the Eternal Law 75
17. Rulers 78
18. The Decline of Tao 81
19. Realize the Simple Self 84
20. The World and I 87
21. Manifestations of Tao 91
22. Futility of Contention 93
23. Identification with Tao 100
24. The Dregs and Tumors of Virtue 103
25. The Four Eternal Models 106
26. Heaviness and Lightness 109
27. On Stealing the Light 112
28. Keeping to the Female 124
29. Warning Against Interference 129

30. Warning Against the Use of Force 135
31. Weapons of Evil 140
32. Tao is Like the Sea..144
33. Knowing Oneself 148
34. The Great Tao Flows Everywhere....................154
35. The Peace of Tao...159
36. The Rhythm of Life..161
37. World Peace 164
38. Degeneration..167
39. Unity Through Complements 175
40. The Principle of Reversion...............................179
41. Qualities of the Taoist 181
42. The Violent Man..190
43. The Softest Substance 194
44. Be Content...199
45. Calm Quietude 202
46. Racing Horses 208
47. Pursuit of Knowledge 211
48. Conquering the World by Inaction..................214
49. The People's Hearts..217
50. The Preserving of Life......................................220
51. The Mystic Virtue 223
52. Stealing the Absolute 226
53. Brigandage 231
54. The Individual and the State............................234
55. The Character of the Child..............................237
56. Beyond Honor and Disgrace 241
57. The Art of Government...................................245
58. Unobtrusive Government................................250
59. Be Sparing..254
60. Governing a Big Country 256
61. Big and Small Countries..................................258

62. The Good Man's Treasure 261
63. Difficult and Easy 264
64. Beginning and End 267
65. The Grand Harmony 270
66. The Lords of the Ravines 273
67. The Three Treasures 275
68. The Virtue of Not-Contending 277
69. Camouflage 280
70. They Know Me Not 282
71. Sick-Mindedness 286
72. On Punishment (1) 290
73. On Punishment (2) 293
74. On Punishment (3) 298
75. Punishment (4) 300
76. Hard and Soft 302
77. Bending the Bow 305
78. Nothing Weaker than Water 309
79. Peace Settlements 312
80. The Small Utopia 315
81. The Way of Heaven 319
Glossary 325
About the Author 332
Light of the Spirit Monastery 333
Reading for Awakening 334

PREFACE

It is said that the *Tao Teh King* is the work of the great Chinese sage Lao Tzu. Disgusted with the degeneration of Chinese society, he decided to leave and vanish forever, which he did. But as he was leaving the capital, the warden of the gate asked him to set down his realizations since he would no longer be accessible to truth seekers. He did so, and then went out the gate into the lost pages of human history.

If a person wishes he can immerse himself in the stewpot of scholarly speculation as to who Lao Tze really was, whether he ever existed, and whether he wrote the *Tao Teh King*, or who did. None of this means anything. Taoist masters through the centuries have proved the truth of the *Tao Teh King*, and that is all that matters. For truth seekers it stands as a monument to Truth. Even those who understand it imperfectly will reap great gain from its study.

The text on which this commentary is based for the first eighteen sections is that of James Legge, but from then on that of Lin Yutang. The sections are according to those traditional in the ancient texts of the *Tao Teh King*.

1. On the Absolute Tao

The Tao that can be trodden is not the enduring and unchanging Tao. The name that can be named is not the enduring and unchanging name.

(Conceived of as) having no name, it is the Originator of heaven and earth; (conceived of as) having a name, it is the Mother of all things.

Always without desire we must be found,
If its deep mystery we would sound;
But if desire always within us be,
Its outer fringe is all that we shall see.

Under these two aspects, it is really the same; but as development takes place, it receives the different names. Together we call them the Mystery. Where the Mystery is the deepest is the gate of all that is subtle and wonderful.

(Tao Teh King 1)

The Tao that can be trodden is not the enduring and unchanging Tao. The name that can be named is not the enduring and unchanging name. Like so many of the terms of virtually prehistoric Ancient Wisdom, "Tao" is not easy to translate; it may even be impossible to translate. The best we can do is say that "Tao" means Way. In fact, until the West started talking of "Buddhism" the path outlined by Sakyamuni Buddha was called "the Buddha Way" (Buddha Tao) in the orient. Because of the inseparability of Taoism and Chinese culture (which included philosophy and religion), Taoism flowed in the veins of Chinese Buddhism, however much Buddhist purists might have wished it otherwise. The existence of many Buddhist-Taoist temples in China and abroad make this clear.

What is the Way, the Tao? This opening verse might literally be rendered: "The Way that can be 'wayed'" is not the Way." That is, the way that can be traversed or travelled is not The Way that is the subject of this treatise. This may seem hopeless, but it is not that difficult to unravel. The Way is beyond any concept or experience of space and time. Therefore It cannot be thought of in those terms. In The Way we do not go from one point to another. Not even one step can be take on The Way because It does not exist in space. Similarly, we cannot think of "entering" the Way, because we are always "in" It. Nor can we think of time being spent experiencing or establishing ourselves in The Way, for It transcends time. The Way being utterly transcendent, nothing can be spoken that can convey Its nature or even Its existence.

Having no name, it is the Originator of heaven and earth; having a name, it is the Mother of all things. To say the Tao is One is not really accurate, for to our earthbound minds "one" means a single object; and the Tao can never be an object. We can speak of one apple, but not of one Tao. Yet here we see that a kind of duality or difference can be attributed to the Tao. Actually the duality is only in our own mind, but since we are attempting to at least hint at the truth about the Tao we have to "suspend belief" to do so. So from now on in this section the Tao will be spoken of inaccurately so we can get a somewhat accurate idea of It.

The Tao is both transcendent and immanent. In Its transcendent aspect "having no name" beyond all attributes, forms, or conditionings, It is the Source of heaven and earth, "of all things visible and invisible" as the Nicene Creed says. But in Its immanent aspect, "having a name," It is the nurturing Mother of all things. That is, in Its active, dynamic side which produces the cosmos and evolves it to perfection, along with all those intelligences inhabiting forms within it, It is Mother of All. The symbolic expression "Mother" is used because the child receives its body substance from the mother and is nourished by the mother through her own body in the womb and after birth through breast-feeding. The mother sustains the infant by imparting her own body and life-force to it. In the same way we are inextricably bound up with the Tao as our Eternal Mother. Beginning as an atom of hydrogen, we evolve through all the forms of life and ultimately transcend them all through the agency of the Mother Tao. Nothing is done except through, and essentially by, the Tao. We are the Tao and the Tao is us. As the agent for our union with the Tao, it is the Tao that is our Mother.

Always without desire we must be found, if its deep mystery we would sound; but if desire always within us be, its outer fringe is all that we shall see. The Tao does all things, yet our interior disposition determines our success or failure in coming to knowledge of the unknowable Tao.

In every system that seriously intends for its practitioners to attain the highest knowledge, desire is considered the Great Satan. The Bhagavad Gita gives a great deal of time to the devastations of desire (*kama*) and the need for absolute desirelessness. Buddha spoke vigorously of the need to eradicate desire (*tanha*). The Bible is glaringly silent on the subject since Churchianity's major draw is the promise of the fulfillment of all desires: and the more you have, the more God will be pleased to honor them. (This is called "a precious promise.") "Happy as pigs in mud" seems to be the ideal.

But in *The Aquarian Gospel of Jesus the Christ* the view is quite different and is in complete consonance with the wisdom of Taoism, Hinduism, and Buddhism. Jesus had this to say: "The lower self, the carnal self, the body of desires, is… distorted by the murky ethers of the flesh. The lower self is an illusion, and will pass away;…. The lower self is the embodiment of truth reversed, and so is falsehood manifest" (Aquarian Gospel 8:7-9). "Now spirit loves the pure, the good, the true; the body of desires extols the selfish self; the soul becomes the battle ground between the two" (Aquarian Gospel 9:28. This ninth chapter of the Aquarian Gospel is all about the Tao as presented in Taoist scriptures.) Jesus puts a sharper point on the matter when he says: "The sin lies in the wish, in the desire, not in the act" (Aquarian Gospel 27:16). And: "He who would follow me must give up all cravings" (Aquarian Gospel 66:19).

The Tao Teh King, the Bhagavad Gita, and the Aquarian Gospel are speaking of all desires, not just negative ones, for desire itself is bondage.

Desire is also blinding, so we must become desireless if we would perceive the Tao to any meaningful degree and come to some experience of It. If the condition of desire (that state in which desire can arise) remains within us, within our consciousness, however buried it might be, we can see only the outward manifestations of the Tao: the material and illusive world.

Charles Muller renders the verse this way: "Therefore, always desireless, you see the mystery; ever desiring, you see the manifestations." The point he brings out here is that desire and desirelessness cannot be incidental, just phases, sometimes being in one and sometimes in the other. We must be always desireless. Then we shall perceive the Tao. If we are always desiring, we shall only see Its manifestations, only see the foam of the sea but never the water. There is an implication here that it is a matter of either/or. We are either always desireless or always desiring. There is no in between. This is important, for most people, even though they know it is otherwise, look upon the conscious mind as the totality, and if they are not experiencing something on the conscious level they think it is not taking place. But the subconscious is the incubator of all desires. Even if the stage of the mind-theater is empty, that does not mean there are not plenty of desire-actors in the wings just waiting to emerge. In addition, it is implied that desire and desirelessness are conditions, not just action or inaction. So even if we have no desires formed in either the conscious or subconscious minds, if we are capable of desire, not having transcended the conditions of desire, we are in the state of desire and so "ever desiring."

Under these two aspects, it is really the same; but as development takes place, it receives the different names. The Tao is always one, whether we think of It as manifest or unmanifest. And the same is true of ourselves: whether we desire or not, we, too, are always one. "As development takes place, it receives the different names." Before we begin the process of evolution we are in the state of unity, but only dimly, subliminally. When we enter the realm of evolution we experience duality and become lost in it. After the attainment of illumination we re-enter the Tao-Unity fully able to experience It and function within It. Then if we should descend to the world of duality we shall know it as the Unity and be untouched by its illusions. We shall function as One in the world of Two.

Together we call them the Mystery. The transcendent and the immanent, the One and the Two, the unconditioned and the conditioned known in the Upanishads as Nirguna and Saguna Brahman, God without attributes and with attributes, should be considered together, for "together we call them the Mystery," meaning that we do not accept one and reject the other, claiming that alone to be the Tao.

Where the Mystery is the deepest is the gate of all that is subtle and wonderful. Gates are natural symbols for those points at which we pass from one state of awareness to another, plateaus of our evolution. Jesus spoke more than once of the gateway to the kingdom, which he called "the gate of consciousness" (Aquarian Gospel 143:42). "If you would find the spirit life, the life of man in God, then you must walk a narrow way and enter through a narrow gate. The way is Christ, the gate is Christ, and you must come up by the way of Christ. No man comes unto God but by the Christ," (Aquarian Gospel 129:7-8) the Consciousness that *is* Christ. (Always keep in mind that "Christ" really means Ishwara, the Consciousness that is inherent in all creation as its guide, as well as its source and ultimate dissolution.)

In the depths, in the heart, of the Tao, there is the "gate" from which all things have emanated and to which all things return. At that gate, however, all "thingness" has vanished and only the thinnest of veils remains between us and the Tao. And when we pass through the gate, that veil, too, dissolves and is no more. That is why Jesus said: "The nearer to the kingdom gate you come, more spacious is the room; the multitudes have gone" (Aquarian Gospel 67:8).

2. THE RISE OF RELATIVE OPPOSITES

All in the world know the beauty of the beautiful, and in doing this they have (the idea of) what ugliness is; they all know the skill of the skillful, and in doing this they have (the idea of) what the want of skill is.

So it is that existence and non-existence give birth the one to (the idea of) the other; that difficulty and ease produce the one (the idea of) the other; that length and shortness fashion out the one the figure of the other; that (the ideas of) height and lowness arise from the contrast of the one with the other; that the musical notes and tones become harmonious through the relation of one with another; and that being before and behind give the idea of one following another.

Therefore the sage manages affairs without doing anything, and conveys his instructions without the use of speech.

All things spring up, and there is not one which declines to show itself; they grow, and there is no claim made for their ownership; they go through their processes, and there is no expectation (of a reward for the results). The work is accomplished, and there is no resting in it (as an achievement).

The work is done, but how no one can see; 'Tis this that makes the power not cease to be.

(Tao Teh King 2)

2. The Rise of Relative Opposites

All in the world know the beauty of the beautiful, and in doing this they have [knowledge of] what ugliness is; they all know the skill of the skilful, and in doing this they have [knowledge of] what the want of skill is. Thank you, thank you, Lao Tzu! As a right-brainer growing up in a left-brain society I was often stunned by the absolute stupidity of universally-accepted "truisms" that were as silly as they were erroneous. One of them that chafed me the most was the imbecilic statement that if we were never unhappy we would not know happiness, and variations on that. That is like saying that if we were never hungry we would not know what it was to be well-fed. Or that if we did not know everybody else in the world we would not know our own mother! In religion this foolishness runs amok in the words and writings of those who think that the way to know the truth is to first know untruth, and consequently grind out volume after volume of analysis and denunciation of "heresy" in the delusion that by this way they are expounding "orthodoxy." Since very intelligent people accept and engage in this, the phenomenon is bewildering until we understand that right-brain/left-brain is a very real factor in human thought and behavior.

In relation to spiritual life we must realize that we do not need to go through all kinds of delusions to eventually come to the truth. Nor do we need to first suffer, wander, rebel, deny and go down dead-end byways before turning and seeking conscious union with the Tao. Those who assert that we do are simply trying to cover up their own vagaries as being necessary and therefore somehow acceptable and even worthy. When Jesus said: "Seek ye first the kingdom of God, and his righteousness; and all these things shall be added unto you." (Matthew 6:33), he was speaking the simple facts. If we seek the Tao first then everything we need will come to us automatically. Long before Jesus' counsel, the Mundaka Upanishad (1.1.3) referred to the Tao as "That Which, when known, *everything* is known." For it is the Tao that is "the one thing needful" (Luke 10:42). As the Upanishad also says: "He shining, everything shines." Knowing the Tao, all is known. And knowing It we become one with It.

In Indian philosophy we inevitably come across the idea that everything is dual in relative existence, manifesting as the *dwandwas*, the pairs of opposites such as heat/cold, wet/dry, light/darkness and so forth.

So it is that existence and non-existence give birth the one to (the idea of) the other; that difficulty and ease produce the one (the idea of) the other; that length and shortness fashion out of the one the figure of the other; that (the ideas of) height and lowness arise from the contrast of the one with the other; that the musical notes and tones become harmonious through the relation of one with another; and that being before and behind give the idea of one following another. The meaning here is that one dwandwa instructs us in the existence of the other. The presence gives rise to the concept of the absence of an object or a quality. But the fundamental truth being aimed at is the fact that relative existence teaches us all about itself, that we need only observe it to learn the truth about everything. Buddha speaks of this in the Dhammapada, as well. Life is not just the best teacher, it is the only teacher.

Therefore the sage manages affairs without doing anything, and conveys his instructions without the use of speech. This is an incredible insight, and is beautifully expounded in the Bhagavad Gita under the subject of the gunas, the modes of energy behavior inherent in the creation. (In the following citations, think of "energy patterns" when you read "gunas.")

"The three gunas are the domains of the Vedas. Be free from the triad of the gunas, indifferent to the pairs of opposites, eternally established in reality, free from thoughts of getting and keeping, and established in the Self" (Bhagavad Gita 2:45).

"In all situations actions are performed by the gunas of Prakriti. Those with ego-deluded mind think: 'I am the doer.' But he who knows the truth about the gunas and action thinks: 'The gunas act in the gunas.' Thinking thus, he is not attached" (Bhagavad Gita 3:27-28).

"When the beholder sees no doer other than the gunas, and knows that which is higher than the gunas, he attains to my being. When an embodied being rises above these three gunas, which are the source of the body, freed from birth, death, old age and pain, he attains immortality" (Bhagavad Gita 14:19-20).

2. The Rise of Relative Opposites

The wise realize that they are watching movies: movies that originate in the mind and are combinations of light and sound. The Cosmic Movie originates in the Divine Mind (the Tao) and moves along of itself. Our task is to realize this and learn to the fullest extent through calm observation. In this state of Perfect Silence he acts without acting and speaks without speaking. This is not gobbledegook, but is comprehensible to those who become proficient in meditation.

The great non-dualist philosopher Shankara spoke of it this way in his Hymn to Dakshinamurti (The Divine Teacher): "Strange,… he taught them by keeping silence, and the doubts of the disciples were all cleared up." This has been the experience of many who came burdened with doubts and questions into the presence of the illumined. With a glance those liberated souls dispelled all doubt and lack of understanding.

When I was in India a man told me that a friend of his had several burning questions in his mind. Since he could not find the solutions anywhere or from anyone, he decided to go to the Aurobindo Ashram for Darshan Day when Sri Aurobindo could be seen, but would not speak. He went determined to speak with Aurobindo no matter what he might have to do. He went into a large auditorium with hundreds of other seekers. On a platform at the front there was a large screen. When all were seated and silence prevailed, the screen was moved away revealing Sri Aurobindo sitting there. Beginning at the first row the sage looked into the eyes of everyone present. When he looked into the eyes of my friend's friend, *all his questions were answered simultaneously, in an instant.*

It is not the glib but the (truly) silent who are wise and impart wisdom. It is the Tao alone that teaches through those who have united themselves with It.

One of the major ploys of manipulative religion and esotericism is to insist that there are great secrets, major arcana, that cannot be known without the secret teachings and secret practices given only to the few that make themselves worthy through being completely subjugated to the dispenser(s) of the "hidden wisdom." Secret initiations (a long series of these, preferably) are an especially favored means of keeping the attention and allegiance of the duped.

All things spring up, and there is not one which declines to show itself. Jesus expressed it this way: "Nothing is secret, that shall not be made manifest; neither any thing hid, that shall not be known." (Luke 8:17). It is a matter of evolution. As the consciousness of the individual unfolds, so does the inner and outer universe unfold itself to his inner eye in proportion to his own degree of unfoldment. The cosmos, most particularly the inner world, teaches him as he advances. And all things arise before his awareness in time, "and there is not one which declines to show itself." So there is no need for an external revealer of secrets without whom they would not be known. Everything is self-revealing.

What about teachers, then? They are very important when they are real teachers of truth: when they clearly and directly impart to the student the knowledge of the way to open his own consciousness. For that opening itself then becomes his teacher.

This was demonstrated in the life of my dear friend Swami Rama of Hardwar. At the age of nine he was idly playing in the streets of his birthplace, a tiny village in Kashmir. An elderly yogi came walking down the street, and as he passed by said: "Come with me!" The boy walked along beside him until they had passed a little distance beyond the village. There the yogi stopped and instructed him in a yogic practice, telling him to do it always. Then the yogi walked on and was never seen by him again. The child applied what the yogi had taught him and became a great saint. What is more, he openly taught to everyone the practice his teacher had given him, saying that there was no need for initiation or personal instruction in it. He declined to become a guru in the contemporary sense of becoming the presiding deity of the disciple's life. Rather, he just told what he had been told, and those who applied it also attained higher consciousness. His teacher had known that everything would reveal itself to him in time if he persevered, that he needed nothing more than the simple knowledge he gave him. And Swami Rama proved that to be true.

So let me repeat: a true teacher shows how to be taught by the Tao and Its manifestation as creation. The rest is up the seeker. "All thy children shall be taught of the Lord; and great shall be the peace of thy children"

(Isaiah 54:13). We should read and listen to the words of worthy spiritual teachers, but only those such as I have outlined are worthy.

They grow.... The teachings of the Tao to the questing soul are not external formulations or concepts, neither are they artificial implants. Rather, they are the spontaneous developments of the aspirant's inmost awareness. They are a matter of evolution: *inevitable* evolution. We need not seek here and there, only within. As we grow, so shall we know.

There is no claim made for their ownership. That statement throws a wrench into the workings of most religions and teachers. Every religion claims that it alone knows the truth, even when it is evident that many (and sometimes all) religions say the same thing. For example, Christians try to claim a patent on the Trinity. It may be true that their muddled way of presenting the Trinitarian concept as a mystifying mystery may be unique to them, but every true religion knows about the Trinity and teaches accordingly. It is astounding to see how there are religions claiming that they alone teach the existence of God! When challenged they just shrug off reality by saying that the other religions are teaching a misperception, a superstition, and not the real theism. And of course some even insist that everybody else is worshiping the Devil, not God.

There are many signs of false or foolish teachers, but a fundamental one is the teacher's claim to enlightenment. They say "I am enlightened… I attained my enlightenment…," and so forth. The Kena Upanishad says to such, and to us: "If you think that you have understood Brahman well, you know it but slightly…. To whomsoever it is not known, to him it is known: to whomsoever it is known, he does not know. It is not understood by those who understand it; it is understood by those who do not understand it. When it is known through every state of cognition, it is rightly known, for [by such knowledge] one attains life eternal. Through one's own Self one gains power and through wisdom one gains immortality. If here [a person] knows it, then there is truth, and if here he knows it not, there is great loss. Hence, seeing [or seeking] [the Real] in all beings, wise men become immortal on departing from this world" (Kena Upanishad 2.1, 3-5).

A truly illumined person knows that the Tao alone is the source of enlightenment, that it can never be *my* enlightenment, only *Its/his*. "His shining illumines all this world" (Mundaka Upanishad 2.2.11). So say the truly wise. No one can rightly claim enlightenment for himself. It is the Light of the Tao alone that lightens our darkness. This is not hairsplitting. These self-proclaimed illuminati may not have the cosmic consciousness they claim, but they do approach the level of cosmic egotism.

Another favorite ruse of a false teacher is to claim that he has received a new understanding never before given to anyone else. "Now the world is ready," they crow. And cash in. A variation on this is the claim that they have now been authorized to publicly teach what has been kept in secret by and for the few throughout the ages. "Now humanity has evolved enough," they announce. But truth is never the property of any one individual. And of course there are the "only one world teacher at a time" charlatans who claim to be that only one.

Religions and spiritual institutions like to claim that they alone possess special knowledge, and even label their teachings accordingly. Here in America we have a yoga group that blatantly puts their organization's name on practices that are known universally in India, and require their members to solemnly promise to never reveal them. Even more ridiculous is their claiming the simple equal breathing exercise that is known everywhere: breathe in as you count; hold your breath to an equal count; breath out to the same count. This is found everywhere in books on yoga and breathing, but I actually know of one of their dupes thinking he had to get their formal permission to teach this to someone.

Another shameful deception is the pretence that a teaching will be without power or effect unless it is imparted in the authorized way by the authorized teacher. This is especially done in relation to yoga methods. The truth is this: if a yoga method cannot work by its inherent nature, then it is artificial and cannot lead to higher consciousness or spiritual liberation. It may produce a lot of chills and thrills and wow the crowd, but it will begin and end in this world.

In contrast, a true method of spiritual development will work for anyone who applies it because it is based on the fundamental laws of existence, not on the whim or exclusive franchise of a teacher or group. One group I know of was started by an honest yogi who wrote down in black and white that his methods could be learned from anyone who practiced them. His words are now altered to say the opposite: that only those approved as teachers by the organization can teach the practice. Fortunately the truth is otherwise. (I was present when one of the yogi's senior students was asked by a relative newcomer if he could teach the yoga to others. "Why not?" responded the senior, "you know the methods, don't you?" Nothing more was required.)

I am making such a point of this because one of the Sanskrit terms for spiritual liberation is *Kaivalya*, which means, according to the *Yoga-Vedanta Dictionary*: "the transcendental state of Absolute Independence." Another dictionary defines it as: "spiritual independence." Kaivalya-independence thus is the purpose of true religion and true spiritual teachers. Dependency is never their desire. That is why Swami Vivekananda once asked a disciple: "If you find a better teacher than me, will you leave me and follow him?" When the disciple answered: "Yes, I will." Vivekananda embraced him fervently and said: "Now I know you are truly my disciple!" For a true teacher wants only the freedom of the disciple, and instructs him accordingly.

They go through their processes, and there is no expectation (of a reward for the results). The creation is really an enlightenment machine, however much human beings try to subvert it and make it otherwise. When an aspirant enters into the stream of cosmic evolution everything unfolds and proceeds without any need for interference or direction. He need only keep himself in the stream by his practice. Consequently he does not hold "expectations" in the sense of wanting things to proceed in a particular direction or desiring a particular result, so he keeps himself in readiness for their revelation.

The work is accomplished, and there is no resting in it (as an achievement). Once we have finished the course and completed the race, we leave the racetrack and go home. The purpose of the spiritual race is to transcend it, to pass beyond it. It is like tag: once we touch home base we are free and out of the game. So we do not come to rest at the top of the evolutionary current, we move on out of the stream altogether. Some freed souls do return to lower realms to point the way to freedom for those still moving upwards, but they first step out of the river to "the other shore."

Lao Tzu completes this section with a couplet:
The work is done, but how no one can see;
'Tis this that makes the power not cease to be.

By this he means that the entire work of spiritual liberation is done without the observation of the ego, for that is left far behind alone with the mind and the intellect. Therefore no one sees its progress and completion, though the individual certainly experiences and manifests it. Sri Ramakrishna used to say that a salt doll went to measure the depth of the ocean, but when it entered the ocean it was dissolved, so who was left to tell of its depth? The Tao being "that from which the mind and the senses turn back" according to the Upanishad, It cannot be spoken of, and neither can the ascent to divinity. Like the Tao itself, union with the Tao cannot spoken about. "The Tao that can be trodden is not the enduring and unchanging Tao. The name that can be named is not the enduring and unchanging name."

How is it that Lao Tzu claims: "'Tis this [unseeable character of the liberation process] that makes the power not cease to be"? He is indicating that the moment something comes under the sway of the mind and the intellect it becomes enfeebled and stagnated. Oh, yes, we may play with it and delight in it like an infant with its toes, but the evolutionary flow will be stopped, for we shall have gotten out of the Stream. This again is why "teachers of enlightenment" are just not possible and why authentic spiritual development cannot be institutionalized.

To keep the power going we have to get out of the way–and into The Way.

3. Action Without Deeds

> Exalt not the wise, so that the people shall not scheme and contend; prize not rare objects, so that the people shall not steal; shut out from sight the things of desire, so that the people's hearts shall not be disturbed.
> Therefore in the government of the Sage: he keeps empty their hearts, makes full their bellies, discourages their ambitions, strengthens their frames; so that the people may be innocent of knowledge and desires. And the cunning ones shall not presume to interfere.
> By action without deeds may all live in peace.
> (Tao Teh King 3)

Exalt not the wise, so that the people shall not scheme and contend. "Wise" here means those that are wise in the eyes of those with small understanding. Such people are usually only clever or cunning, not truly intelligent, much less really wise. Many of those that have "great personalities" are really manipulative sociopaths and not particularly bright. (Remember the "class officers" when you were in school?) It is incredible how shrewd mediocrities make their way to the top in so many aspects of life, particularly in religion, politics, and education.

This morning I came across the broadcast of a class in one of America's most prestigious universities. The professor's whole approach was not as serious or challenging as my grade school teachers' had been. It was obvious he expected next to nothing from the students, and his whole manner of speaking implied that they were about six years of age intellectually. It reminded me of preschool Sunday School class. Then I realized that his entire approach was that of Captain Kangaroo! Evidently a generation of educators have modeled themselves on Bob Keeshan. I once worked with a graduate of that university who had learned absolutely nothing about anything, so I was not surprised at what I saw, but still I was appalled.

So if polished mediocrities are not exalted, others like them will not scheme and contend to also be exalted.

Prize not rare objects, so that the people shall not steal. It is strange how people value things that are rare or very expensive, paying no attention at all to their intrinsic value. What people need is a sensible perspective on what is of actual value to them as worthy human beings. During the days of Saint Edward the Confessor in England theft was virtually unknown. Historians assure us that if a traveler's purse dropped on the road it would still be there weeks later. How was this? England at that time was a genuinely religious country and the people valued the eternal over the temporal.

Shut out from sight the things of desire, so that the people's hearts shall not be disturbed. "For a man dwelling on the objects of the senses, attachment to them is born. From attachment desire is born. And from thwarted desire anger is born. From anger arises delusion; from delusion, loss of memory; from loss of memory, destruction of intelligence. From destruction of intelligence one is lost" (Bhagavad Gita 2:62-63). Therefore it is only good sense to avoid all things that can so addict and destroy us. This is way to peace.

Therefore in the government of the Sage: he keeps empty their hearts, makes full their bellies, discourages their ambitions, strengthens their frames; so that the people may be innocent of knowledge and desires. And the cunning ones shall not presume to interfere. As pointed out previously, there is no use in thinking that philosophers can reform government. But each one of us can apply Lao Tzu's principles to ourselves as a micro-kingdom. So here is what we are being advised:

1. Keep our heart empty of all that clutters or corrodes it.

2. Nourish ourselves abundantly on that which is ennobling and satisfy our higher self.
3. Curb our aspirations for that which is worthless, meaningless, and contrary to the revealing of the Tao: our true Self.
4. Establish ourselves in the correct frame of reference or perspective regarding our life and ourselves, as well as others. This includes very defined and positive morality.

If we do this we shall be free of delusions thought to be knowledge and free of desires for that which countermands our true nature: the Tao. Living in such harmony within ourselves we shall have discovered the secret of life and transcended all that is lesser and unworthy of us. Illusions will then no longer cloud or distort our clear sight. As the Gita further says: "However, with attraction and aversion eliminated, even though moving amongst objects of sense, by self-restraint the self-controlled attains tranquility. In tranquility the cessation of all sorrows is produced for him. Truly, for the tranquil-minded the buddhi [intellect] immediately becomes steady" (Bhagavad Gita 2:64-65).

By action without deeds may all live in peace. To understand this I recommend that you read the Bhagavad Gita, for that is one of its main themes. Here is a section from its fourth chapter.

"Actions do not taint me, nor is desire for action's fruit in me. He who thus comprehends me is not bound by actions. Knowing thus, the ancient seekers for liberation performed action. Do you, therefore, perform action as did the ancients in earlier times.

"What is action? What is inaction? Even the poet-sages were bewildered regarding this matter. This action shall I explain to you, which having known you shall be freed from evil. Truly the nature of action, of wrong action and of non-action is to be known. The path of action is difficult to understand. He who perceives inaction in action and action in inaction—such a man is wise among men, steadfast in yoga and doing all action.

"Whose undertakings are devoid of plan and desire for results, whose actions are consumed in the fire of knowledge—him the wise call wise. Having abandoned attachment for action's fruit, always content, not dependent on anything even when acting, he truly does nothing at all. Acting with the body alone, without wish, with thought and lower self restrained, abandoning all acquisitiveness, though acting he incurs no fault. Content with what comes unbidden, beyond the pairs of opposites and free from envy, the same in success or failure, even though acting, he is not bound.

"The karma of one who is free from attachment, whose thought is established in knowledge, undertaking action for sacrifice, is wholly dissolved" (Bhagavad Gita 4:14-23).

4. The Character of the Tao

> The Tao is (like) the emptiness of a vessel; and in our employment of it we must be on our guard against all fulness. How deep and unfathomable it is, as if it were the Honoured Ancestor of all things!
>
> We should blunt our sharp points, and unravel the complications of things; we should attemper our brightness, and bring ourselves into agreement with the obscurity of others. How pure and still the Tao is, as if it would ever so continue!
>
> I do not know whose son it is. It might appear to have been before God.
>
> (Tao Teh King 4)

There is something inexpressibly thrilling about the Eastern expositions of the Absolute Reality. How far these words are from the Western fawning and flattering matter-and-power-oriented effusions of those who seek to placate a testy and haywire deity made in the image of their own flawed egos. Even though no words can really approach the Tao's essence, yet Its glory flows in superabundance into and throughout the worlds of relative existence. Actually those worlds *are* Its superabundance. And when the sages who are united with It speak of Its wonder, those who have evolved to the point of conscious seeking respond with joy and acclamation.

The Tao is (like) the emptiness of a vessel. It is not easy for Western students to understand what is meant in Taoist and Buddhist philosophy by "emptiness." (Especially if they are used to Indian philosophy which refers to the same thing as "fullness.") Just as the No Thing of both Western and Eastern philosophers is in no way "nothing," so also Emptiness does not mean nothingness. It is not a lack of something, but rather The Thing Itself devoid of relative labels.

The little bit we know about the nature of matter can help us comprehend this. "Things" are made of identical components: protons, electrons, and neutrons. Only when these components are set in specific patterns or quantities do they form the elements and their countless combinations. So the Power fundamental to all things is Itself free from "thingness." It is devoid ("empty") of all form or attribute. It is the Primal Being without which none of the superimpositions we experience as objects or qualities could exist (or appear to exist). Unconditioned and Empty are the same thing. The Tao is Unconditioned, Qualitiless and Transcendent. The moment there is even the shadow of the shadow of a quality or relativity we are no longer in touch with (or in) the Tao.

Yet we (and somehow the Tao) have a capacity for conditioning, for quality and thingness. And that capacity is the vessel, the "shell" that can either be empty or with some degree of contents. The Tao embraces this shell, and the shell contains the Tao, but does not confine It. It may be "empty space," but It is *conscious* space (*chidakasha*).

And in our employment of it we must be on our guard against all fulness. There is nothing but the Tao; therefore to "live" and evolve we have to "employ" the Tao in Its conditioned and relative mode. But if the Tao is to free rather than bind us through our "using" of It, we must be on guard against allowing any kind of Its "contents" to touch our inner being. We must preserve our consciousness free from conditioning or "containingness" to any degree. Certainly our body, feelings, senses, intellect, will, and so forth will indeed be "full" and conditioned, composed of myriads of "things." But if we will keep (know) them separate from our true self we will ourselves be within the Tao and *be* the Tao.

How to keep the heart from being defiled by "fulness" is no simple thing. But why should it be, when Infinity is our ultimate goal? The fact that it is realizable should be enough for us and make us ready to tread the path that the Katha Upanishad says is "sharp as the edge of a razor and hard to cross, difficult to tread is that path [so] sages declare" (Katha Upanishad 1.3.14). But again, so what? Is it easy to fly high into the sky? But what else will eagles do?

Lao Tzu is assuring us in these words that we need not fall into the mistaken idea that the only way to manage spiritually is to withdraw from all things and shun all contact with material things, to bury ourselves in inactivity, denying all existence as much as possible. No; rather we should be using our body, mind, intellect, and our life in this world to transcend them. On the battlefield of Kurukshetra, when Arjuna quailed at the sight of the prospective carnage, Krishna told him: "Perform your duty, for action is far better than non-action. Even maintaining your body cannot be done without action" (Bhagavad Gita 3:8). The wise, whether Lao Tzu, Jesus, or Krishna, give us the same message. The rest is up to us.

Meditation is the key here, just as it is in all things pertinent to the spirit and its liberation.

How deep and unfathomable it is, as if it were the Honored Ancestor of all things! The Tao is beyond measure–Its height, Its depth, and Its breadth are impossible to define. It is so far beyond all we know as "existence" that It really does not "exist" in our limited and illusory experience. It is the Source ("Honored Ancestor") and yet It is not. Here again Krishna gives us a hint when he says of the Gunas, the modes of material existence: "Know that sattwic, rajasic and tamasic states of being proceed from me. But I am not in them–they are in me" (Bhagavad Gita 7:12). And regarding the cosmos: "All this world is pervaded by me in my unmanifest aspect. All beings dwell within me, but I do not dwell within them. And yet beings do not dwell within me: behold my Divine Yoga. Sustaining beings and yet not dwelling in them, I myself cause all beings to come into manifestation. As mighty winds move everywhere, yet always dwell in the ether, know that even so do all beings dwell within me" (Bhagavad Gita 9:4-6).

The Tao has "given birth" to all things, yet at no time do those things "touch" the Tao. For "the Tao is like the emptiness of a vessel."

We must bear in mind the relation of the Tao to us, even though we cannot "relate" to the Tao in our present status. As long as we are in the Here we cannot have anything to do with the There. This is confusing, so what shall we do? Lao Tzu continues:

We should blunt our sharp points, and unravel the complications of things; we should attemper our brightness, and bring ourselves into agreement with the obscurity of others. How pure and still the Tao is, as if it would ever so continue! This is not easy to comment on, not because it is hard to understand but because it is most difficult to apply correctly. All we need do is look at the mess and tangle in the thinking and society of the East to see the truth of this. What we see is wisdom gone awry in misapplication. As Vivekananda said, the problem is not the religion but the fact that it has not really (correctly) been practiced. Frankly, not just the East but a great deal of the world is content to passively sit in the dirt and do nothing, avoiding all conflict or ambition that might result in discontent. (Though they have no objection to being virulently jealous of those who get out of the dirt and succeed in material life.) This is a serious charge, but it is a much more serious fact. Vast numbers of people do prefer accepted misery to discontent arising from a determination to better things. As you read what follows, please do not think I am advocating the Oriental distortion of Lao Tzu's principles.

We should blunt our sharp points. By "sharp points" the sage means our simplistic thinking which entails intense either/or insistence and demand. Extreme black/white attitudes are very much sharp points on which we impale others and eventually ourselves. Children are very prone to this; that is why every time their wishes are thwarted, even if only verbally, they cry and go into a kind of emotional fit or seizure. Later they may learn to control the fits and the tears, but the mentality persists. Throughout history, whatever the culture, "youths" have been extraordinarily troublesome to family and society because of their insistence on "truth" and "right."

Since the advent of systematic education in the West, students (usually of university age) have been at the forefront, if not the fomenters, of riots and revolution. That is because they still think in the simplistic manner of the nursery. If anyone expresses an ideal and then fails to embody it perfectly, they begin to scream about deception and hypocrisy. Even though a government may be extremely benevolent and provide much benefit to the citizens, if these young people learn of a single breach or inconsistency in policy by even a single governmental official or agency, then it is time to demonstrate and riot.

As children they could not comprehend the difference between a mistaken statement and a lie, and they still cannot. They would not think of discarding a machine simply because it had a defective part, but they insist that a religion or political policy be totally scrapped if any inconsistency, error or defect be discovered in it. No matter how much their parents have sacrificed and put up with during their upbringing, all it takes is a single denial or demand to make them denounce their parents as "not really caring at all." (Though they will usually be there to collect the next dole from them.)

Most people grow out of this simplistic way of thinking and acting, but many do not. We have all known these types and heard from them about how they "have principles" and "hate hypocrisy" and "mean what they say" and do not "believe in not telling the truth just because of what people will think." They pride themselves on their "honesty" and "truthfulness" and lack of hypocrisy. "People know where I stand," they announce (unnecessarily!), and: "You know me; I believe in speaking my mind." Yes, we all know such people, but none of us knows a single person who likes them for it. "I know people think I talk too much," they growl as they stomp along through life.

Sri Ramakrishna put it in a very homely manner: people with "crazes" do not succeed in spiritual life. There is nothing wrong with having principles, but those who beat the drum and bully others under the guise of having "strong convictions" have much more ego than ideals. We should be firm in our principles, but not be stabbing others with them. There is a difference between expressing ideals and bludgeoning others with them.

Buddha said that "views" can be a terrible defect in a seeker for enlightenment. He did not mean that we should have no opinions, but that we must not bully others with them—nor ourselves, either. We should understand the limitations of our intellect and always be ready to reconsider and even alter our ideas if we find them mistaken or wanting in any way. We should be neither rigidly dogmatic nor wishy-washy. Much of the problem is not in the idea, but in the way we express or try to impose it. Attitude is the problem here, along with egoic attachment to "my convictions." Closed-mindedness is not really firmness in principles any more than vagueness, flabby-mindedness, and lack of principle is open-mindedness. Really, it is our egos that need the blunting.

And unravel the complications of things. Human beings have a natural pendulum action in just about everything. So when we guard against something we have to consider whether we are indulging in its opposite. Simplistic thinking is at one end of the pendulum swing and over-complex thinking is at the other. Many people tangle up their mental feet the moment they look at something. Just as simplistic-minded people blunder on heedless of the consequences, the over-complex dodge and feint and end up in a heap or paralyzed into inaction, overwhelmed by what they think is the complexity of the situation or problem. Of course a lot of people try to avoid responsibility by claiming the situation is too complex. Russians especially like to say: "It is so complicated" when what they mean is: "I don't want to bother," or "I don't want to take responsibility." (They also call someone "a complex personality" when they mean they are nuts or a pain in the neck.) Italians on the other hand like to say: "*Ma, se difficile,*" "But it is difficult." Sometimes it is our laziness and sometimes it is our thinking that is at fault. And sometimes things really are complicated or difficult, but we need to put forth our intelligence and initiative and figure (and work) them out. To a great extent Lao Tzu also means that we need to see through complexities to the simple principles beneath their outward appearance and then act.

Putting the two imperatives together we understand that Lao Tzu is warning us against looking at things either simplistically or in a complicated or complicating manner. Intelligence and insight are the needful.

We should attemper our brightness. Again moderation and circumspection in thought and outlook are being urged upon us by the sage, especially in relation to others. How easy it is for childish people to burst upon the world as "the wise" with "a message for all." There is an old joke about the farmer who claimed he looked up in the sky and saw the gigantic gold letters GPC. Interpreting this as "Go Preach Christ," he became a traveling evangelist. But those who heard him tell of this experience and heard him preach expressed the opinion that the letters really meant "Go Plow Corn." I have met a lot of "New Age Messengers" operating on a similar flimsy basis.

What Lao Tzu is pointing out is our valuation and attitude toward our own understanding of things. Ego often makes us over-value our ideas. And here, too, we can become a nuisance to others when we want to "share the light" that is really no more than our idea about things. Also, I have seen that the truly wise never push their understanding forward and even on occasion silently let ignorance be expressed if they have not been specifically asked about their opinion. "Ephraim is joined to idols, let him alone," (Hosea 4:17) is good advice when dealing with ignoramuses who idolize their own "wisdom."

And bring ourselves into agreement with the obscurity of others. This does not mean that we should adopt a "dull like you" policy in order to get along with people, nor is it a plea for the dumbing down of ourselves and others (this is currently very popular). It means that we must strive to comprehend the view of those we may think have a lesser understanding than ourselves, for we may be the uncomprehending ones and need to learn from them. Again, children are particularly prone to label something or someone not in alignment with their ways as "dumb." We must avoid this. Often we think that those who do not see things our way are not seeing at all. And we are usually wrong. Also it means that we must establish communication with those who do not see as clearly as we do and make our view comprehensible to them. Yes, we may persuade, but should never coerce.

The idea is that we should learn to see with others' eyes and share our vision with them in a unity of spirit that is all too rare in this world. It also means that we should give people the freedom to be "wrong" since we may be the ones that are wrong, and even if we are not, others need to discover the truth for themselves in many instances. The tolerance of the East for divergent opinion is a good example for us as long as it is not a cover for lack of principle or mental vigor. A lot of people say "be tolerant" when they really mean: "Don't have any principles or express them." And as already pointed out, we need to realize that our ideas may not be as "bright" as we think, and those of others may not be as "dull."

How pure and still the Tao is, as if it would ever so continue! This final part of the second section of the fourth chapter of the Tao Teh King is both interesting and at first puzzling because it seems a *non sequitur.* Why does Lao Tzu speak of the purity and stillness of the Tao at this point? Because those who follow the preceding advice will experience these aspects of the Tao.

The Tao is unchanging, so why does the sage then say: "…as if it would ever so continue"? Because the aspirant will certainly enter into a state of mind approximating the purity and stillness of the Tao, but since it is a state of mind, and the mind is ever changing, the experience will not last forever, however much it may seem it will.

One of the most frustrating illusions of the mind is its false assurance to us that at last we are "home free" and there will be no more wandering or change. But there will be. That is the law of relative existence. Only when we step out of the world of body and mind and into the realm of the spirit is there a chance of everlasting peace, and not even then until we are permanently established in spirit consciousness. Until then there is a movement back and forth from silence to the hubbub of conditioned life. Yet for that time Lao Tzu is speaking of we are experiencing just a touch of the Tao. It is real, but not permanent. So he lauds our attainment but cautions us against mistaking its real nature: only a reflection of the Tao proceeding from our nearness and affinity to It. We must strive, then, to enter the Tao and leave all else behind.

Finally, we are told a basic truth that only seems vague:

I do not know whose son it is. It might appear to have been before God. Here we find the concept of the Son of God over five centuries before Jesus was born. For Lao Tzu is certainly saying that the Tao is a Son. We have covered the subject of the Trinity so often in my commentaries that it will be a relief to skip it in this place. Let it suffice to say that the "Son of God" *is* God (Tao) in His immanent, personal aspect, the Way (Tao) to the Transcendent Reality.

Lest we make the mistake of Arius (and others) and think that the Son of God is a being other than God, lesser and only existing in the relative realm of time, the text says: "It might appear to have been before God," before the emanation-manifestation of the Mahat Tattwa or immanent extension of God into creation. And indeed It was before such an extension occurred. For: "In the beginning was the Word" (John 1:1) That is, when a "beginning" began, the Word already was: It is eternal. "And the Word was with God" in a seemingly separate existence, but "the Word *was* God." There was only the One.

How, can the Son of God be *before* God? In the sense that That which we think of as God in the relative communicative sense was preceded by Its own self in Its transcendent reality. Before there was anyone to say "Tao" the Tao already was.

If we follow the counsels of Lao Tzu we shall become like–and then become–the Tao.

5. NATURE

> Heaven and earth do not act from (the impulse of) any wish to be benevolent; they deal with all things as the dogs of grass are dealt with. The sages do not act from (any wish to be) benevolent; they deal with the people as the dogs of grass are dealt with.
>
> May not the space between heaven and earth be compared to a bellows?
>
> 'Tis emptied, yet it loses not its power; 'tis moved again, and sends forth air the more. Much speech to swift exhaustion lead we see; your inner being guard, and keep it free.
>
> (Tao Teh King 5).

This is strong medicine, especially for those of us brought up in the sentimentality of "devotional" religion. It is very hard to shed the golden dreams of spiritual childhood for the glaring and harsh realities of spiritual adulthood. For many people, as Lili Tomlin's character, Trudy, said: "Reality gives you cancer."

In the ninth chapter of the Gita, verse twenty-nine, the Tao through Krishna tells Arjuna: "I am the same to all beings. There is no one who is disliked or dear to me. But they who worship me with devotion are in me, and I am also in them."

The Tao is an absolute unity, an all-embracing unity that includes all beings. Therefore there is no one (and no thing) that the Tao could view as an object separate from It. How could It, being without the conditioned ego which is the source of like and dislike, possibly love or hate anyone? Certainly we, who in our present state of colossal ignorance look at the ways of the Absolute as outside observers and construe them according to our egoic frame of reference, think of It liking or disliking that which pleases or displeases It, but that is pure fantasy. It is not in the nature of the Tao to engage in such reactions, for who will It react to? Seeing the wheels of cosmic law grinding on, raising some and throwing down others, we mistakenly think that God is taking a personal interest and favoring or disfavoring them, rewarding some and punishing others. This is as foolish as thinking that when we eat nourishing food God is pleased with us and blesses us with health, and when we eat poison he becomes angry and kills us. "The Omnipresent takes note of neither demerit nor merit" (Bhagavad Gita 5:15)

It is the machinery of the cosmos that puts down and exalts, but since the Tao is its source and architect, in one sense It does so through the universal law. But that law is not based on whim or opinion, but upon The Way Things Are and is utterly impersonal and impartial.

What other perspective but this is spiritually sensible? In the religions that make God no more than a cosmic dictator there is a lot of talk about pleasing, displeasing, angering, and placating God, but such is nonsense and blasphemy. Certainly we may interpret the phenomena in the cosmos as proceeding from thoughts and ways like ours, but we are very wrong to do so, and such misunderstanding can lead us into grave errors in both thought and deed. Our attempts to make sense of things may only confuse us more if we do not realize the basics of How Things Are.

Children do not like to be spoken to in a straightforward manner about their failings; but we are not children and have no business reverting to childish desires and attitudes when considering spiritual facts. So the Master Lao Tzu is respecting us enough to speak to us as adults who really do want to know What Is Going On.

Heaven and earth do not act from (the impulse of) any wish to be benevolent. The Tao and creation, being essentially one, do not act from an impulse to be "kind" or "nice," but from the pure intention of our ultimate perfection: a perfection that already exists, but which we have lost contact with and fallen into the illusions of imperfection.

"Do not say: 'God gave us this delusion.' You dream you are the doer, you dream that action is done, you dream that action bears fruit. It is your ignorance, it is the world's delusion that gives you these dreams. The Lord is everywhere and always perfect: what does He care for man's sin or the righteousness of man? The Atman is the light: the light is covered by darkness: this darkness is delusion: that is why we dream. When the light of the Atman drives out our darkness that light shines forth from us, a sun in splendor, the revealed Brahman. The devoted dwell with Him, they know Him always there in the heart, where action is not. He is all their aim. Made free by His Knowledge from past uncleanness of deed or of thought, they find the place of freedom, the place of no return" (Bhagavad Gita 5:14-17).

Just as it is an illusion to attribute human attitudes to the Tao, so it is an illusion to attribute either good or evil, sin or righteousness, to our true Self, the Atman. Such attributions can be made to the dream personality we have assumed in our dreaming, but if we would awaken we must first realize that it is all unreal, only a dream. We do not need to "clean up our act;" we need to stop the act. And to do so we must be ruthlessly honest with ourselves. So Lao Tzu proceeds:

They [God and creation] deal with all things as the dogs of grass are dealt with. In ancient China, in the time of Confucius and Lao Tzu, a ritual to produce rain was performed in which grass was shaped into the form of dogs. These grass dogs were then placed in beautiful baskets or boxes and wrapped up in elegantly embroidered cloths. Before presenting the effigies in the rite, the officiants had to fast and purify themselves to be worthy to touch them. During the ritual they were clothed in beautiful brocade, carried solemnly in beautiful containers and handled with reverence–even awe. However, once the ceremony was completed the grass dogs were slung away with no regard whatsoever. The Taoist writer Kwangtze says: "After they have been set forth, however, passersby trample on their heads and backs, and the grass-cutters take and burn them in cooking. That is all they are good for."

The idea here is extremely simple: That which conforms to and is part of the Divine Plan is "real" and meaningful to "heaven" and "earth." That which conflicts, disrupts, or negates the Divine Plan is nothing to heaven and earth: unreal and non-existent. This is why in the Bible we read of God not "hearing" or "seeing" or even *knowing* some people or things. Obviously God cannot be incognizant of any thing, being omniscient. What is meant is that any person or thing that does not contribute actively to the evolution of the cosmos and the beings living within it is for all practical purposes non-existent to both heaven and earth.

"Not every one that saith unto me, Lord, Lord, shall enter into the kingdom of heaven; but he that doeth the will of my Father which is in heaven. Many will say to me in that day, Lord, Lord, have we not prophesied in thy name? and in thy name have cast out devils? and in thy name done many wonderful works? And then will I profess unto them, I never knew you: depart from me, ye that work iniquity" (Matthew 7:21-23).

The Gita indicates that God does not engage in either love or hatred. Yet in Romans 9:13 we find: "As it is written, Jacob have I loved, but Esau have I hated." The thing is, "love" and "hate" are here symbolical of the forces within the evolutionary creation. Those who are moving consciously and without self-hindrance in the stream of upward evolution are fostered by the divine powers of heaven and earth. This is "love" on the part of heaven and earth. Those who are either willfully or ignorantly moving against the stream of upward evolution, sidetracking themselves into cul-de-sacs of egoic involvements of myriad sorts, are utterly disregarded by heaven and earth, literally left to their own devices, immersed in the chaos of the hash they have made of their lives.

The ancient root meaning of the Greek word *miseo*, usually translated "hate" means to thoroughly disregard, to account as nothing and to ignore. Miseo is *indifference*, not animosity. It is this disregard which is the "hate" they incur, not humanlike animosity and enmity.

In the same vein, heaven and earth assist those moving upward, and oppose or resist those who are struggling downward or to the side: who themselves oppose and resist evolution in their own life sphere. That which they have sown, both the wise and the foolish reap. It is a matter of Divine Law, of The Way Things Are, and has nothing to do with an emotional (or even an intellectual) reaction on the part of God. Fools who walk up a downward-moving escalator or down an upward-moving escalator will find themselves impeded. No one is angry with them or hating them, they are simply experiencing the natural reaction of their own foolish action.

The practical meaning of the grass dog simile is this: That which fosters evolution is "favored" by heaven and earth; that which hinders, stops or reverses evolution is trashed by heaven and earth. It has to be faced. This is the basis of the Four Aryan Truths of Buddha: 1) there is suffering; 2) suffering has a cause; 3) suffering can be ended; 4) there is a way to end suffering. There is suffering because we go against the evolutionary grain. Our suffering will be ended when we move with the evolutionary flow. Simple.

There is a Zen story of a roshi who asked a philosophical question of a student. When the student replied, the roshi nodded and said: "Yes." The next day he asked the student the same question. When he gave the same answer as the day before, the roshi shook his head and said: "No." "But you said 'Yes' yesterday," protested the student. "It was 'Yes' yesterday, but 'No' today!" said the roshi. He meant that the previous day's answer was all right because it was in keeping with the student's level of understanding at that time. By the next day, however, his understanding should have changed and grown enough for him to realize that his former opinion was not fully correct. So the answer was "wrong."

When the grass dogs have a legitimate purpose they are treated with honor and respect. In the same way, anything that helps us up the evolutionary ladder is good and fostered by the forces of heaven and earth. But when those things are outgrown and gone beyond to the degree that those things either no longer have a positive effect because they have become unnecessary or actually hold us back through further involvement, they become inconsistent with our continuing development and become garbage. Yes: that which once was noble and worthy because they moved us along the path of expanding consciousness can become ignoble and unworthy if they stop our forward movement.

Saint Paul expresses it very well: When I was a child, I spake as a child, I understood as a child, I thought as a child: but when I became a man, I put away childish things" (I Corinthians 13:11). It is a matter of growth. It is all right for little girls to play with dolls and little boys to play with toy cars, but no sane adult plays with dollies or toy cars. It is good for an infant to crawl, but after a while he must stop crawling and walk. And when he is skilled at walking he needs to learn to run. It is good for an infant to feed from a bottle and eat liquefied food, but in time he must eat mostly solid food. A child should be under the control of his parents, but not forever; he must become independent in deed and thought. School is good, but not if we never graduate. An airplane is wonderful to travel in, but would be a trap if we could never get out. A medication may be good for us to take, but not once we recover.

Throughout life we encounter situations and things that are good for us until we move beyond them. They then are either useless or detrimental. It is good to be a child, but not for all our life. There is a time when belief in Santa Claus may be cute, but not into adolescence and adulthood. The Law is this: Grow, Grow Up and Grow Beyond. "Brethren, be not children in understanding: but in understanding be men" (I Corinthians 14:20).

Although the grass dogs are tossed out and trampled or burned according to Kwangtze, they are not regarded as completely nonexistent. They can actually have a detrimental effect on those who keep them around. After describing their fate as refuse, he continues: "If one should again take them, replace them in the box or basket, wrap them up with embroidered cloths, and then in rambling, or abiding at the spot, should go to sleep under them, if he does not get evil dreams [that is, dreams that presage misfortune], he is sure to be often troubled with nightmare" (illusions of misfortune). Either way, he will be upset and unhappy, even miserable.

The same is true of those who do not move on beyond what at one time may have been essential to their spiritual progress but which now is irrelevant to their present stage. Even the differing concepts of God must be outgrown, as Swami Vivekananda has expounded in some of his discourses. Spiritual practices can also be gone beyond. Attitudes that at one time elevated us can, once their benefits have been fully derived, become hindrances. Just as food that has been fully digested in time becomes expelled from the body, having passed from nourishment to toxicity, so that which has lifted us at one time can pull us down at another. A boat moves us easily over water, but once land has been reached we do not push it over the terrain, laboring to no purpose.

The ways of the divine heaven and earth must be operative in our lives, as well. This is the key to freedom.

In the ocean there are many strata with various species of fish "native" to them. According to the water pressure and level of light, so these strata are marked out in clear zones, and the fish always swim in their appropriate levels. It is the same with our own life; things which are appropriate to some levels are inappropriate in others.

> Build thee more stately mansions, O my soul!
> As the swift seasons roll!
> Leave thy low-vaulted past!
> Let each new temple, nobler than the last,
> Shut thee from heaven with a dome more vast,
> Till thou at length art free,
> Leaving thine outgrown shell by life's unresting sea!

So said Oliver Wendell Holmes regarding reincarnation. But in actuality we live many small lives in our longer life. The more evolved we are, the more "lives" we live. We have to continually build "more stately mansions" and leave the less stately mansions behind until we at length are free, leaving our outgrown shells by life's unresting sea.

In the highly symbolic motion picture, *Labyrinth*, an old woman tries to distract the girl from the search for her baby brother and entrap her by taking her into a room which contains all the things she loved in her childhood. "Ooooh, here's your little teddy! You love your little teddy, don't you?" She chortles as she tries to get the girl to hold on to past "treasures" and forget the infant she is seeking. We, too, seek the lost "inner child" of our own spirit in the labyrinth of this world; and to pause for nostalgic reinvolvement with the things we have outgrown and laid aside is to endanger our quest.

The sages do not act from (any wish to be) benevolent; they deal with the people as the dogs of grass are dealt with. As above, so below: this is the ancient Hermetic Principle that can be applied to all aspects of life. The perspective of the Tao must be our perspective if we would ascend to divine union. Just as there is no hate or love in the Tao, so there is no sentimentality or nostalgia. And there must be none in us, for such is deadly indulgence of ego. In relation to the Tao, others, and ourselves, the Straw Dog Principle must be adhered to. Then we will have a real and enduring relationship with the Tao.

"Among the virtuous, four kinds seek me: the distressed, the seekers of knowledge, the seekers of wealth and the wise. Of them, the wise man, ever united, devoted to the One, is pre-eminent. Exceedingly dear am I to the man of wisdom, and he is dear to me. All these indeed are exalted, but I see the man of wisdom as my very Self. He, with mind steadfast, abides in me, the Supreme Goal. At the end of many births the wise man takes refuge in me. He knows: All is Vasudeva. How very rare is that great soul" (Bhagavad Gita 7:16-19).

May not the space between heaven and earth be compared to a bellows? 'Tis emptied, yet it loses not its power; 'tis moved again, and sends forth air the more. Much speech to swift exhaustion leads, we see; your inner being guard, and keep it free. We have already considered the meaning of Emptiness. Thus all relative existence is Emptiness, which is actually the only Existent. All "things" draw their momentary existence from It. Emptiness is true Fulness (Purna) and the Source of All. It is also known as the Chidakasha, Conscious Space.

Space then, including "the space between heaven and earth," is that from which all things arise and into which they subside. It possesses an infinite capacity for an infinite variety of manifestations. None of which are "things" in themselves, but all of which are The Thing essentially.

Therefore what we mistakenly think is empty space is creative fulness. Lao Tzu asks if we cannot think of it as a bellows. No matter how much streams forth from it, it draws it all back in and projects it, maintaining a perpetual cycle of projection and absorption. In the human being this is especially manifested in the lungs and the breath as the basis of life. Space (akasha) can never be exhausted, for it perpetually renews itself.

This is not true of ordinary human speech, however, which is a projection that does not renew or receive back into itself. The spoken word and the energy, physical and mental, that produced it, are lost to us forever when we speak. Speech, then, is seen to be a depletion. In the most ancient philosophical writings of India, sages are habitually referred to as "munis," those who do not speak, "the silent ones."

In the Bhagavad Gita we find an interesting concept of action that is inaction. "The path of action is difficult to understand" (Bhagavad Gita 4:17), Krishna tells us, then continues: "He who perceives inaction in action and action in inaction–such a man is wise among men, steadfast in yoga and doing all action" (Bhagavad Gita 4:18). The wise know how to act, and yet not be acting.

In the same way the yogi knows how to speak without expending his internal energies. Lao Tzu is exhorting us to this when he concludes: "Your inner being guard, and keep it free." That is, through keeping our awareness centered in our true Self we shall be free from the exhaustion or depletion of our subtle life forces that are usually lost through speaking. For this reason Sanderson Beck renders this phrase: "Much talk brings exhaustion. It is better to keep to the center." And Lin Yutang: "By many words is wit exhausted. Rather, therefore, hold to the core."

6. The Spirit of the Valley

> The valley spirit dies not, aye the same;
> The female mystery thus do we name.
> Its gate, from which at first they issued forth,
> Is called the root from which grew heaven and earth.
> Long and unbroken does its power remain,
> Used gently, and without the touch of pain.
> (Tao Teh King 6)

One of my most cherished memories of India was a day I visited the great Kashmiri yogi, Swami Rama, in his simple ashram on the banks of the Ganges in Hardwar. I had known Swamiji for several years and found that each visit to him opened new and wonderfully clear vistas. This would be no exception. I had brought with me a young Austrian who had taken advantage of his parents' vacation to take a plane to India without their having any idea of where he might be. Actually, he had not much idea either. His reading of purely theoretical books on nothing but the abstractions of Non-dual Vedanta had not prepared him for what he was finding in contemporary, Puranic Hinduism. Seeing his utter bewilderment at all this, I had invited him to go along with me to see Swami Rama, a total contrast to the intellectual backwater he had been struggling to comprehend. (He gave up. A wise decision.)

As always, Swami Rama's presence was a haven of peace and awareness. This was to be our last conversation, though I did not know it. Almost without preamble Swamiji began speaking to me about mantra and its inner aspects. His words were unique and marvelous. After concluding that subject, Swamiji looked at Thomas and asked if he had any particular interest in the field of yoga. To my chagrin, Thomas asked for an explanation of Kundalini. Oh, not again! Both Indians and Westerners were fascinated with Kundalini, as many satsangs had demonstrated to me. But my dismay turned to delight as Swamiji began speaking as no teacher or book ever had. This is not the place for a full recounting of his words, but one thing is relevant to the words of the Tao Teh King cited above.

Swamiji was emphatic that Kundalini, as Mulaprakriti, is not just primal power, but Primal Consciousness. This he said was crucial for the yogi to understand, lest he fall into the absurdity of thinking the Kundalini needed "awakening" and could be directed or "used" in any way. "Imagine thinking that the Creative Consciousness of the Universe needs some yogi to awaken Her!" he exclaimed. "In Her true nature Kundalini is not even energy but the consciousness behind all energy. We need awakening–not Her. She is the one who awakens us, not the other way around." Then he had some pungent but profoundly instructive things to say about the reported experiences of yogis who thought they had awakened their kundalini. Thomas and I were entranced at Swamiji's inspired words, knowing them to be the truth. I have treasured them now for many decades, and they shine as brightly in my mind as ever.

The valley spirit. Strange as it may seem, if we look at two Christian monastic orders we will find the key to these cryptic words.

The first formal or official monastic order in the Christian West was that of Saint Benedict. Although the order had monasteries everywhere in all kinds of places, if possible they built them on the tops of mountains. This was because it expands the mind to look out into boundless space, and attunes the spiritual mind to the Boundless Infinite. Also, this reflected the spiritual psychology of the Benedictine monks, the keynote of which was expansiveness. All the Christians arts were fostered in their monasteries, which were places of beauty and liturgical splendor, both in the externals of worship and in the development of the chant and ritual. All that is splendid and glorious in Western Christendom had its origin in the Benedictine order. The great liturgiologists were Benedictines, the greatest being Saint Gregory the Great who wrote the life of Saint Benedict and was an archetype of Benedictine Christian mysticism. (I recommend *Benedictine Monachism* by Dom Cuthbert Butler for a full exposition of these subjects.)

In contrast, when the Cistercians separated from the Benedictines, they did just the opposite: they made their monasteries in valleys, the narrow and more confined, the better, in order to draw in their minds and center them in the spirit within. Their churches and rites were of utmost simplicity (even barren), but their spiritual lives were not. Rather, they developed a way of ascetic life and mystical practice that enabled them to become completely focused internally, and therefore spiritually.

So what does this tell us about the Valley Spirit? That it has boundaries, it has definition and form. It is circumscribed and thereby has characteristics, qualities, and definition. It is saguna, with form and qualities, rather than nirguna: without any such things. The Benedictines were mystically intent on the obviously Boundless Formless, whereas the Cistercians were intent on the Form that would reveal itself in time as The Boundless. (Since they are both ultimately the same, neither approach is better or more right than the other. It is wise to embrace both.)

So the Valley Spirit is Mahashakti, the Great Power, Mulaprakriti, the Primal Energy that forms all things, the Great Mother. She is all that can be spoken about, all that can be known by sentient beings, and within which they live and evolve. For She is also the Great Womb, as this verse makes clear. She is also Ritam, Divine Order, and therefore all endeavors must be in conformity with her ways, with her laws. Yoga and all mysticism are embodiments of her "ways." That is why mystics of East and West feel such an affinity with the Divine Mother aspect of Reality.

Dies not, aye the same. As the hymn says: "Change and decay all around I see." Birth and death, appearing and disappearing, emerging and withdrawing, forming and breaking apart: all are the Mother's doing. Constant change is the basic trait of her realm, but it is not real, it is the magical power of Maya. Neither birth nor death are real, they are dreams, motion pictures of the mind. Why? Because everything is the Mother, who certainly dies not but remains ever the same. Therefore:

The female mystery thus do we name. The mystery of Maya is the mystery of the Mother. Charles Muller translates it: "the mysterious female." Ramprasad, the renowned Bengali composer, wrote:

Who knows what Mother Kali is?
Even the six systems of philosophy fail to reveal her.
The yogi contemplates her in the two-petalled and the thousand-petalled lotuses.
Mother Kali plays with the swan in the lotus field as a swan.
Kali is the bliss of Brahman, the meaning of Om.
She dwells in every being just as she desires.
Do you know the universe is in the womb of the Mother?
The great womb of time (mahakala) knows the secret of Kali!
Can anyone else know it?
Ramprasad is afloat. People laugh at his attempt to cross the ocean by swimming.
My mind understands but the heart does not;
It is the dwarf's attempt to seize the moon.

Its gate, from which at first they issued forth, is called the root from which grew heaven and earth. Lin Yutang: "The Door of the Mystic Female is the root of Heaven and Earth." The Mother herself is the Door, that which in Sanskrit is called the Brahma Yoni, the Womb of God. All that we see has arisen in the ocean of the Mother who is Mulaprakriti and Mulashakti: Root Matter and Root Power.

A wave is really nothing but a momentary part of the ocean, rising and subsiding. So are all things which "exist." They are only seen for a moment and then they go, never really having been anything but the ever-abiding ocean. The waves are only momentary modifications of the ocean, existing only on the ocean's surface. A little further down in the ocean the waves never exist. Yogananda often spoke of the need to dive into the ocean and know the Reality behind the appearance-waves of relative existence.

Heaven and earth have "grown" from the Mother's Pure Being and shall return there–both "grown" and "return" being mere words covering the truth of the Mother as the Sole Existence. Truly, human beings, however intelligent, cannot think of or speak of the Mother, but perfected yogis can know the Mother.

In India there is a time of the year when children fly kites whose strings have been covered with a mixture of glue and ground glass. They try to use their kite strings to cut the strings of others' kites and see who can cut the most strings without theirs being severed. It is all great fun with a lot of handclapping, laughing, and challenging. Yet it is taken very seriously, too, by the competitors. Regarding this, Ramprasad also wrote:

> In the market place of the world, O dark Mother [Kali], you are flying kites.
> They fly high lifted by the wind of hope and held fast by the string of maya.
> Tied together with bones, flesh and nerves,
> The kites are made by the three gunas themselves.
> You have glued manjapaste (powdered glass) on the strings to make them abrasive.
> One or two among millions of kites are cut free,
> And you, O Mother! clap your hands laughing.
> Prasad says the kites will fly driven by the southern wind,
> And will quickly land on the other side of the ocean of relative existence.

Long and unbroken does its power remain, used gently, and without the touch of pain. The manifestation of name and form does not last forever, but is eventually withdrawn for a period and then projected again in a perpetual cycle. But it does last for a vast period of time.

Here we have the secret of using the Mother's power in our life: it must be used gently, in peace and intelligent reflection, and without the desires that are the inevitable bringers of pain. Our use must also be free from coercion of any kind such as the opinion of others or fear in any form. If we can so live, then we will pass beyond the Mother's realm into the Transcendent Eternal where no illusion or suffering can ever come.

7. Living for Others

Heaven is long-enduring and earth continues long. The reason why heaven and earth are able to endure and continue thus long is because they do not live of, or for, themselves. This is how they are able to continue and endure.

Therefore the sage puts his own person last, and yet it is found in the foremost place; he treats his person as if it were foreign to him, and yet that person is preserved. Is it not because he has no personal and private ends, that therefore such ends are realized?

(Tao Teh King 7)

Heaven is long-enduring and earth continues long. The reason why heaven and earth are able to endure and continue thus long is because they do not live of, or for, themselves. This is how they are able to continue and endure. This seventh verse extols the condition of egolessless. When the ego is operative it is engaged in constant struggle with its environment, inner and outer, and especially with other human beings. The entire lifetime of the ego-directed (and therefore enslaved) individual is a war which expends all its inner and outer resources, ensuring that peace and inner harmony are impossibilities, however "righteous" the ego may pretend that war to be. Only those who live in humility can rest content in the true Self. Here is how the Gita describes such people:

"When he leaves behind all the desires of the mind, contented in the Self by the Self, then he is said to be steady in wisdom. He whose mind is not agitated in misfortunes, freed from desire for pleasures, from whom passion, fear and anger have departed, steady in thought—such a man is said to be a sage. He who is without desire in all situations, encountering this or that, pleasant or unpleasant, not rejoicing or disliking—his wisdom stands firm.... In tranquility the cessation of all sorrows is produced for him. Truly, for the tranquil-minded the buddhi immediately becomes steady.... Like the ocean, which becomes filled yet remains unmoved and stands still as the waters enter it, he whom all desires enter and who remains unmoved attains peace—not so the man who is full of desire. He who abandons all desires attains peace, acts free from longing, indifferent to possessions and free from egotism. This is the divine state. Having attained this, he is not deluded. Fixed in it even at the time of death, he attains Brahmanirvana" (Bhagavad Gita 2:55-57, 65, 70-72).

"He who hates no being, is friendly and compassionate, free from 'mine,' free from 'I,' the same in pain and pleasure, patient, the yogi who is always content, self-controlled and of firm resolve, whose mind and intellect are fixed on me, who is devoted to me—he is dear to me. He who agitates not the world, and whom the world agitates not, who is freed from joy, envy, fear and distress—he is dear to me. He who is indifferent, pure, capable, objective, free from anxiety, abandoning all undertakings, devoted to me—he is dear to me. He rejoices not, he hates not, he grieves not, he desires not, renouncing the agreeable and disagreeable, full of devotion—he is dear to me. The same to enemy and to friend, the same in honor and disgrace, in heat and cold, pleasure and pain, freed from attachment, the same in blame and praise, silent, content with anything whatever, not identifying with any place or abode, steady-minded, full of devotion—this man is dear to me. Those who honor this immortal dharma just described, endued with faith, deeming me the Goal Supreme, devoted—they are exceedingly dear to me" (Bhagavad Gita 12:13-20).

Therefore the sage puts his own person last, and yet it is found in the foremost place; he treats his person as if it were foreign to him, and yet that person is preserved. Is it not because he has no personal and private ends, that therefore such ends are realized? When the ego is pushed to the end of the line, the real Self will be found at its head. That is why Jesus said: "The last shall be first, and the first last" (Matthew 20:16). And: "Whosoever shall seek to save his life shall lose it; and whosoever shall lose his life shall preserve it" (Luke 17:33). When the phenomenal, conditioned personality is seen as really external, and in no way our true Self, it is purified and preserved, becoming a mirror of our inner reality. Those who truly desire nothing find that they attain much. The Yoga Sutras say that when a person is completely indifferent to materiality then all the treasures of the earth are available to him. Also, when the limited ego is set aside, the limitless Self comes into function.

8. WATER

The highest excellence is like (that of) water. The excellence of water appears in its benefiting all things, and in its occupying, without striving (to the contrary), the low place which all men dislike. Hence (its way) is near to (that of) the Tao.

The excellence of a residence is in (the suitability of) the place; that of the mind is in abysmal stillness; that of associations is in their being with the virtuous; that of government is in its securing good order; that of (the conduct of) affairs is in its ability; and that of (the initiation of) any movement is in its timeliness.

And when (one with the highest excellence) does not wrangle (about his low position), no one finds fault with him.

(Tao Teh King 8)

The highest excellence is like (that of) water. The excellence of water appears in its benefiting all things, and in its occupying, without striving (to the contrary), the low place which all men dislike. Hence (its way) is near to (that of) the Tao. Once when someone asked Swami Brahmananda, the great disciple of Sri Ramakrishna, if he would bless him, the swami replied: "We have nothing to give but blessings," referring to the superstitious idea held even today that sadhus have the power to curse as well as bless. The simile of a rose and a piece of sandalwood is often used in relation to truly good people: when crushed they only give forth their sweet fragrance. Without water nothing can live; in the same way the benevolence of the wise extends to every form of being.

Furthermore, the wise occupy the lowliest position as uncomplainingly and as naturally as water flows to the lowest level. Water on the mountaintop and water deep in the earth is still water and possesses the same characteristics. In the same way the sage is unaffected by any external conditions or situations.

Late one afternoon in Delhi I was sitting in a taxi as a friend of mind was buying rice. From a distance I saw a remarkable-appearing sadhu. His entire appearance was that of someone from a century before. Even his eyeglasses were of a style I had only seen in photographs from the previous century. But the outstanding quality of his appearance was his great dignity and tranquility. People flowed all around him, jostling him here and there, but he remained unresponsive, obviously centered within. One man ran into him violently and nearly knocked him over. His reaction was to look at the man with complete calmness and a caring and compassionate look. He had no blame, but understood the inner turmoil that had propelled the man along so heedlessly and so unconsciously that he had made no apology but kept hurtling on. He turned back and resumed his calm pace. Right then my friend returned to the taxi and I asked him to take some money from me and give it to the sadhu. He hurried after him, bowed and touched the sadhu's feet and handed him the money respectfully. The sadhu's demeanor never changed. He turned and looked for a moment as my friend came back to the car and then walked on unaffected by any of it. That day I saw that the ideal of the Gita regarding evenness of mind in the pleasant and the unpleasant, in honor and dishonor, could be realized. As my friend Hari Dutt Vasudeva used to say regarding such people: "That is the glory of India." God is the same, the godly being merely reflections of that Absolute Goodness.

The excellence of a residence is in (the suitability of) the place; that of the mind is in abysmal stillness. It is not the dwelling place of the body, but that of the mind which is of prime importance. And by "dwelling place" we mean the state or level of consciousness, not the type of discursive thoughts. Mere thoughts do not at all indicate where we "live," for they come and go and constantly shift in character. Sri Ramakrishna often mentioned the scriptural scholars that spent hours a day talking about the highest reaches of philosophy, but all the time were intent on the money they were going to be given for their discourse and all the material things that money would buy. "Vultures soar very high in the sky, but their eyes are fixed on rotten carrion on the ground. The book-learned are reputed to be wise, but they are in search of carrion. They are attached to the world of ignorance."

Every religion has its exhortations to keep the mind in heaven or with some sacred figure or deity, but Lao Tzu gives us the ultimate advice: our minds should ever dwell in the silence of transcendental Reality: the Tao. The only way for that to be possible is to often enter that Silence through the portal of profound meditation. It is through meditation alone that our consciousness can be established in the Primal State.

That of associations is in their being with the virtuous. However much we may like someone, if they develop a highly contagious and deadly disease, we stay away from them. Just as association with them would be the height of foolishness, so also is friendship with the unvirtuous, for they, too, carry a deadly disease: vice and the root of vice, ignorance. Association with such people inevitably results in our moral and spiritual contamination.

Yogananda often said: "Company is stronger than will power." That is why in India satsang, the company of worthy spiritual seekers, is considered an essential ingredient of successful spiritual life. It is possible to "catch" virtue as much as it is possible to catch vice. So we should actively seek such association. If we cannot find anyone to establish satsang with, then we should do so through reading books about and by those of higher consciousness. If we can find audio or video recordings of them or their lives, that too is valuable. We should keep their depictions in our homes and where we meditate. In India it is common to see holy imagery in autos, busses, and painted on trucks and taxis (especially three-wheelers). As Jesus said: "Where your treasure is, there will your heart be also" (Matthew 6:21).

That of government is in its securing good order. Lao Tzu did not separate private from public life, and Taoists have always had a goodly bit to say about how society should be ordered. Unhappily, most governments are interested in order only, and not good order. However that may be, it is our duty to secure good order in our minds and lives through regular discipline and spiritual practice.

Any practice that does not produce such order in us is useless. A lot of "yogis" sit and "get high" only to come out of meditation and live very low. One of the most cruel and spiteful people I ever knew would have "ecstatic" meditation every day, being visited by saints, avatars, and gods–or so she said. But when she got up after meditation her family and associates ran for the exits, for she embodied our slang expression "hell on wheels."

I knew a "lady" swami that continually roamed about like a bear with a bur under its tail, though occasionally pausing to write articles and poems about love and devotion for her magazine. It only took a few hours for her to terrorize the entire staff of the Hollywood Roosevelt Hotel. When her long-distance groupies came to escort her to a pre-arranged place for talks and classes, one of the staff at the hotel desk laughed and said: "Are you ever in for a surprise!" He was right, for she came charging into the lobby and into the midst of the groupies and whirled around and shouted at a friend of mine (who would not believe me when I had earlier warned her about "swamiji's" real character): "I WANT A DRINK OF WATER!!!" As the group was leaving the manager quietly told the person who had made the reservation for her that she would not be permitted accommodation in the future. Well, at least she made a mark in the world. But we must be different.

That of (the conduct of) affairs is in its ability. Somehow both East and West have gotten the ridiculous idea that impracticality is a trait of spirituality. It is not. As Sri Ramakrishna said: "If you can weigh salt you can weigh sugar." He was very strict with his disciples about developing good sense and practical and efficient ways. "Be a devotee, but why a fool?" was his comment. We, too, must live effectively on all levels. We should not become sharpsters and wheeler-dealers, but we should be sensible and capable people. This will not be hard if we have an ordered and orderly mind. Meditation is the means for that, too.

And that of (the initiation of) any movement is in its timeliness. Knowing when and how to act is a true virtue of mind, as is the ability to know whether something is even worth doing or not.

And when (one with the highest excellence) does not wrangle, no one finds fault with him. A worthy person is not argumentative, oppressive, or repressive. He lives to himself, setting an example for others but not pestering them. The Gita describes such a one as "he who agitates not the world, and whom the world agitates not" (Bhagavad Gita 12:15). It must be acknowledged, though, that the solitary life is a Taoist ideal, since few are they that follow the example of the wise.

9. The Danger of Overweening Success

> It is better to leave a vessel unfilled, than to attempt to carry it when it is full. If you keep feeling a point that has been sharpened, the point cannot long preserve its sharpness.
> When gold and jade fill the hall, their possessor cannot keep them safe. When wealth and honors lead to arrogancy, this brings its evil on itself. When the work is done, and one's name is becoming distinguished, to withdraw into obscurity is the way of Heaven.
> (Tao Teh King 9)

Although Taoism is often thought of as a mystical system of magic and wonders, with sages flying through the sky and immortals hidden away in secret places, it is actually eminently practical and a philosophy of exquisite simplicity that is yet awesomely profound. But it does have all those other mystical-magical qualities as well in a perfectly consistent manner.

This ninth section of the Tao Teh King deals with the wisdom of "lesser is better" in contrast to our modern "more is better and most is best" unwisdom. The translators of the first part do not agree in their understanding, so we need to look at all views in hope of at least getting the general idea, which I think is rather clear.

9. The Danger of Overweening Success

It is better to leave a vessel unfilled, than to attempt to carry it when it is full. If you keep feeling a point that has been sharpened, the point cannot long preserve its sharpness. This is Legge's translation. Mitchell renders it: "Fill your bowl to the brim and it will spill. Keep sharpening your knife and it will blunt." And Lin Yutang: "Stretch [a bow] to the very full, and you will wish you had stopped in time. Temper a (sword-edge) to its very sharpest, and the edge will not last long."

Flexibility is a cardinal virtue in Taoism, so perhaps Lin Yutang's interpretation is correct. For if a bow is stretched as far as it can go, the archer loses full control and may miss the target, but if there is some leeway (flexibility) he can aim with confidence and accuracy. In the same way, a vessel filled to the maximum can be impossible to move or carry.

The ability to function well (even perfectly) in both the inner and outer worlds is a prime principle of Taoism. It is not enough to speak high-flown philosophy and delight in being able to figure out abstruse (and often obtuse) philosophical points. So whatever the exact translation, the idea is gotten across.

The same principle is embodied in the second half which deals with overdoing something, with being obsessive about obtaining the best or the most. Such an endeavor always results in the best and the most being pushed out of reach by our efforts to reach it. Only those who are relaxed and detached can really live in peace and harmony, and *that* is the true "most" and "best." It is a matter of living, not getting.

When gold and jade fill the hall, their possessor cannot keep them safe. When wealth and honors lead to arrogancy, this brings its evil on itself. When the work is done, and one's name is becoming distinguished, to withdraw into obscurity is the way of Heaven. The meaning here is that too much is too much, and robs us of the very thing we were looking for: security and satisfaction. It is good to know when to stop short of too much.

The belief that very successful and renowned people should withdraw while at the peak of their accomplishments and thereby evade the decline that would inevitably come, is unique to Taoism. Since Taoism was the foundation of Chinese philosophical thought, it pervaded all other philosophies such as Confucianism and Buddhism. As a result people of all persuasions acknowledged this fact, and it was quite the norm for renowned personages to quit all public life and go to out of the way places where they could live a simple life and not be bothered with notoriety. It was considered that the ideal form of withdrawal was to take up the heremitic life and live in solitary tranquility, and in that way continue to benefit society by example. Such hermits were sometimes visited by those who had great power and influence over society, and their advice, given in their "outside" perspective, wrought much good for the entire nation. As a result, even today hermits are looked upon as potential benefactors by the Chinese people.

10. Embracing the One

> When the intelligent and animal souls are held together in one embrace, they can be kept from separating. When one gives undivided attention to the (vital) breath, and brings it to the utmost degree of pliancy, he can become as a (tender) babe. When he has cleansed away the most mysterious sights (of his imagination), he can become without a flaw.
>
> In loving the people and ruling the state, cannot he proceed without any (purpose of) action? In the opening and shutting of his gates of heaven, cannot he do so as a female bird? While his intelligence reaches in every direction, cannot he (appear to) be without knowledge?
>
> (The Tao) produces (all things) and nourishes them; it produces them and does not claim them as its own; it does all, and yet does not boast of it; it presides over all, and yet does not control them. This is what is called 'The mysterious Quality' (of the Tao).
>
> (Tao Teh King 10)

According to scholars, this tenth section is the most difficult to translate of all the Tao Teh King, so we will be feeling our way along, but hopefully we will get some of Lao Tzu's intended teaching.

When the intelligent and animal souls are held together in one embrace, they can be kept from separating. A great deal of the human being's problem is his fragmentation into many parts, or at least having the components of his nature out of synchronization with one another, no longer functioning as a single, whole entity, and even in conflict with one another. That is why we have the expression "personality conflict." In the early days, what we call psychiatrists were called "alienists" because they dealt with those who have become alienated from external reality. But that alienation usually has its roots in internal alienation. This has two forms: alienation from one's own Self (this takes many forms), and the alienation of one's inner factors from one another. The inner gears no longer mesh and may even attack and damage one another or bring one or more gears to a halt.

Lao Tzu is saying that these parts of our makeup can be held together in a complete and harmonious unity that will never revert to the state of separation.

Lin Yutang, however, considers that this sentence is about the individual's capacity to unite himself with the Tao in a permanent manner. Disunity with the Tao is the condition that makes inner, individual disunity possible, so this is relevant, indeed.

Both problems exist, beyond doubt, and they both need to be solved. So now Lao Tzu gives his prescription for our trouble.

When one gives undivided attention to the breath, and brings it to the utmost degree of pliancy, he can become as a babe. Two things need to be done. We must attend to the movements of the breath–inhalation and exhalation–and to the root impulses which produce the inhalation and exhalations. Thus the breath and consciousness become unified and our original, eternal state of union with the Tao is experienced. To explain the way to do this would take up too much space here, so I will just refer you to the book *Soham Yoga: the Yoga of the Self.*

When he has cleansed away the most mysterious sights, he can become without a flaw. Few are those that develop an inward orientation of the mind, and very few of those are able to resist wandering within in the labyrinth of psychic experiences that ultimately prove no more real or worthwhile than idle daydreams. One of the signs of an authentic yoga practice is its cutting off of those psychic distractions right at the beginning of meditation. It is necessary to aim the mind straight at the target and shoot for it with no side excursions. Rare are those who even know how to do this, and rarer still those who crush the ego and do so. Again, see *Soham Yoga: the Yoga of the Self.*

In loving the people and ruling the state, cannot he proceed without any action? Lin Yutang: "In loving the people and governing the kingdom, can you rule without interference?" The Taoists had no use at all for the Confucian approach to government, which was extremely invasive and unrestrainedly heavy-handed. As a result, they usually refused to become government employees of any type. Some, however, felt they should prove the validity of Taoist theories of government by joining and showing the way. Some did succeed. The basic idea of Taoist government was that the officials should be so evidently virtuous and intent on the welfare of people that their example would be followed: that people would do right for its own sake and for their own self-respect and integrity. It often worked, and this challenge of Lao Tzu was vindicated.

In the opening and shutting of his gates of heaven, cannot he do so as a female bird? The translator says that Taoist commentaries on this sentence say that the "gates of heaven" are the two nostrils, and this is in keeping with what has gone before. "Shutting" the gates is making the breath so subtle that it disappears for a while and become totally internal. And this internal breath sustains the body just as well as the outer breath usually does. But this dramatic process is not one that can be done in the usual sense–that is, it is not intentional, but occurs as a side effect of the deep internalization of the awareness. In the East a common simile of this state is the female bird sitting on her eggs. Her attention is completely absorbed on the eggs, not on the things around her. Sri Ramakrishna said that her eyes have a distinctive indrawn expression, and that an adept yogi's eyes look the same.

While his intelligence reaches in every direction, cannot he be without knowledge? Lin Yutang: "In comprehending all knowledge, can you renounce the mind?" There is a knowing that is merely intellectual and therefore theoretical, but there is a knowing that is a matter of direct experience which results in something far beyond intellectuality, so far that it is sometimes called "unknowing." Unknowing is actually intuition which cancels out the need for the lesser knowing of the mind. This is referred to in the Bhagavad Gita (9:1) as "that innermost secret: knowledge which is nearer than knowing, open vision direct and instant,"

Now we come to one of the most wonderful passages in this book, and one that should be carefully pondered especially by those raised in the God Is Watching You And You Had Better Watch Out Or Else religions of the West. The Bhagavad Gita speaks the truth about this superstition, too, but here Lao Tzu has put it so succinctly and yet so completely.

The Tao produces all things and nourishes them; it produces them and does not claim them as its own. This first clause tells us that the Tao is intimately involved with all things, maintaining the existence and the possibility of their evolution. Yet, even though their source, It does not look upon them as Its possessions in the way a human artisan would regard the products of his skill. We do not "belong" to the Tao, we are a part of the Tao. That is a completely different matter altogether. We are not pygmies squatting at the feet of some Big Master, owned by him as his slaves who are dependent on his will for their very life. Few things are more paralyzing and poisonous than this Big Daddy view of God as a Cosmic Tyrant that we had better obey and please or else suffer forever and ever. Just as bad and erroneous is the Big Sugar Daddy idea of God who still has to be obeyed in order to get the sugar. No wonder the West has been so violent, competitive and vengeful throughout its recorded history, ruled by governments that are supreme in authority and in which the individual is so often crushed ruthlessly if not heedlessly. Freedom exists in comparatively few lands, and there it is in constant peril of annihilation. Big Brother is indeed watching in politics, and Big God is watching in religion. Both have little regard for the individual, but delight in a herd mentality they can easily control. The modern outcry for world government and world order comes from hearts and minds intent on domination and suppression of dissent, not peace as they claim. And the sheepwits accept it meekly. As a Greek Orthodox theologian has written, "the 'peace' they want is the feverlessness of a corpse." It is a natural consequence of their religion.

10. Embracing the One

It does all, and yet does not boast of it. Think how full Western scriptures are of gorilla-like chest-beating assertions by God implying that we who would dare question or disobey are as nothing, mere motes floating in a sunbeam. For a perfect example of this, see the thirty-eighth and subsequent chapters of Job which contain megalomaniacal ravings supposedly by God to shut Job up and put him in his place. God supposedly says: "Now prepare yourself like a man; I will question you, and you shall answer Me." Oh my.

Here are just a few of the idiotic questions put to Job:

"Where were you when I laid the foundations of the earth? To what were its foundations fastened? Or who laid its cornerstone?

"Or who shut in the sea with doors?

"Have you commanded the morning and caused the dawn to know its place?

"Have you entered the springs of the sea?

"Have you entered the treasury of snow, or have you seen the treasury of hail, which I have reserved for the time of trouble, for the day of battle and war?

"Has the rain a father?

"From whose womb comes the ice?

"Can you bind the cluster of the Pleiades, Or loose the belt of Orion?

"Or can you guide the Great Bear with its cubs?

"Can you lift up your voice to the clouds?

"Can you send out lightnings, that they may go, and say to you, Here we are?

"Can you hunt the prey for the lion?

"Do you know the time when the wild mountain goats bear young?

"Can you mark when the deer gives birth?

"Who set the wild donkey free?

"Will the wild ox be willing to serve you?

"The wings of the ostrich wave proudly, but are her wings and pinions like the kindly stork's?

"Have you given the horse strength?

"Shall the one who contends with the Almighty correct Him?

"Have you an arm like God?

"Can you draw out Leviathan with a hook? Can you put a reed through his nose?"

Who would find this convincing and humbling or intellectually devastating? Yet: "Job answered the Lord and said: Behold, I am vile; What shall I answer You? I lay my hand over my mouth.... Therefore I abhor myself, And repent in dust and ashes." For a satirical treatment of this divine psychosis of both God and Job, see *The Adventures of the Black Girl in her Search for God*, by George Bernard Shaw.

It presides over all, and yet does not control them. This is a major point. Naturally the omniscient and omnipresent Tao is aware of all things and holds all things within Its consciousness, otherwise they would cease to be. But, having manifested them within a framework of natural law, the Tao needs do nothing more. Human beings, on the other hand, can indeed control both themselves and their environment as an exercise in the evolution of consciousness. It is all in our hands, including the consequences we call karma. This is what free will is all about: an inescapable faculty that God never interferes with. No, neither Mommy-God nor Daddy-God will kiss it and make it well. That is what we are intended to do for ourselves.

This is what is called 'The mysterious Quality' of the Tao. However, it is only mysterious to limited human consciousness, for it is the only possible Order (Ritam) of things.

In conclusion we need to realize that in our personal life sphere we must eventually be exactly like the Tao, for that, too, is *our* Mysterious Quality.

11. The Utility of Not-Being

The thirty spokes unite in the one nave; but it is on the empty space (for the axle), that the use of the wheel depends.

Clay is fashioned into vessels; but it is on their empty hollowness, that their use depends.

The door and windows are cut out (from the walls) to form an apartment; but it is on the empty space (within), that its use depends.

Therefore, what has a (positive) existence serves for profitable adaptation, and what has not that for (actual) usefulness.

(Tao Teh King 11)

Mitchell's translation is a bit more clear:

"We join spokes together in a wheel, but it is the center hole that makes the wagon move.

"We shape clay into a pot, but it is the emptiness inside that holds whatever we want.

"We hammer wood for a house, but it is the inner space that makes it livable.

"We work with being, but non-being is what we use."

The idea here is that we simply see things wrongly. We think that "solid matter" is real, and that absence of matter is "nothing." But in actuality there is no such thing as solid matter except to the sense of touch. There is far more space in an object than there are atomic particles. So "things" are mostly empty space. If the space was removed, the particles would collapse into a dense blob and we would have another form of nothing.

So emptiness gives shape to everything, and that is why the ancient yogis of India realized that there is a fifth element: Space (Akasha). Akasha, or Ether, is like the canvas on which a picture is painted by spreading pigments over it. It is unseen, but without it the picture could not even exist. The yogis went even further in their investigations and found that Space is not just an element, but is properly called Chidakasha: Conscious Space or the Space of Consciousness. Consciousness is the fundamental reality upon which the illusion of thingness rests. In India they use the simile of a pond covered with algae. All the observer sees is the algae, but if it is moved aside the water is revealed and the algae is seen as only incidental. In the same way Maya, the Appearance of Illusion, is only a veneer behind which is Eternal Reality: the Tao.

Emptiness is seen in this verse as Potential, as observable being. The many forms will eventually disappear, but the frame or background on which they were resting remains forever. That is the Tao.

So all things depend on the Tao, and to be united with the Tao in our consciousness is to be limitless in our potential and in our actualization of the potential.

12. The Senses

> Color's five hues from th' eyes their sight will take;
> Music's five notes the ears as deaf can make;
> The flavors five deprive the mouth of taste;
> The chariot course, and the wild hunting waste
> Make mad the mind; and objects rare and strange,
> Sought for, men's conduct will to evil change.
> Therefore the sage seeks to satisfy (the craving of) the belly, and not the (insatiable longing of the) eyes. He puts from him the latter, and prefers to seek the former.
> (Tao Teh King 12)

Lin Yutang has it somewhat easier to comprehend:

"The five colors blind the eyes of man;
"The five musical notes deafen the ears of man;
"The five flavors dull the taste of man;
"Horse-racing, hunting and chasing madden the minds of man;
"Rare, valuable goods keep their owners awake at night.
"Therefore the Sage:
"Provides for the belly and not the eye.
"Hence, he rejects the one and accepts the other."

In the last verse we saw that Emptiness is the only real Substance, even though we see it differently through mental and sensory illusion.

Now Lao Tzu assures us that the objects of the senses actually paralyze the senses and prevent us from really seeing, hearing, tasting, etc. In the same way the objects of the mind keep us from knowing the mind and submerge it beneath experiences that in essence are dangerous lies. In other words, they make us crazy.

What is the solution? It is not to just say: "It is all illusion!" and go mentally comatose. Rather, Lao Tzu tells us to pick out the strands of the web that are connected at least obliquely to some level of reality and through them begin to work our way out of the web of delusion. He chooses hunger as something to pay attention to because if we do not eat we will die. People can live without one or more of the senses, but not without the body on which the senses depend. This is the basis of authentic asceticism which is not denial or rejection, but a cultivation of what is real by turning from the unreal.

13. Praise and Blame

Favor and disgrace would seem equally to be feared; honor and great calamity, to be regarded as personal conditions (of the same kind).

What is meant by speaking thus of favor and disgrace? Disgrace is being in a low position (after the enjoyment of favor). The getting that (favor) leads to the apprehension (of losing it), and the losing it leads to the fear of (still greater calamity): this is what is meant by saying that favor and disgrace would seem equally to be feared.

And what is meant by saying that honor and great calamity are to be (similarly) regarded as personal conditions? What makes me liable to great calamity is my having the body (which I call myself); if I had not the body, what great calamity could come to me?

Therefore he who would administer the kingdom, honoring it as he honors his own person, may be employed to govern it, and he who would administer it with the love which he bears to his own person may be entrusted with it.

(Tao Teh King 13)

Favor and disgrace would seem equally to be feared; honor and great calamity, to be regarded as personal conditions (of the same kind). This is going to be explained later, but here at the beginning we have the assurance that such things as favor and disgrace, gain and loss, etc., are simply so from the way that we view them. Of themselves they are nothing, but our valuation of them gives them a character. Many people have found that calamities were good for them and that successes were burdens and miseries. It is all according to our personal view of them, a view that can change with time. This is a valuable piece of knowledge because it can help us to be even-minded in times of intense change.

What is meant by speaking thus of favor and disgrace? Disgrace is being in a low position (after the enjoyment of favor). The getting that (favor) leads to the apprehension (of losing it), and the losing it leads to the fear of (still greater calamity): this is what is meant by saying that favor and disgrace would seem equally to be feared. This is quite reasonable. When we are high on the ladder we fear a fall, and when we are low on the ladder we scramble to climb higher. Both are a torment to us. Realizing this, if we develop indifference to them and put our attention on inner cultivation, we will not suffer.

And what is meant by saying that honor and great calamity are to be (similarly) regarded as personal conditions? What makes me liable to great calamity is my having the body (which I call myself); if I had not the body, what great calamity could come to me? Relative existence is a great calamity if we do not know how to deal with it, how to make it an instrument for wisdom and peace. But once we do know how to use it meaningfully, then the disaster becomes great good fortune.

Therefore he who would administer the kingdom, honoring it as he honors his own person, may be employed to govern it, and he who would administer it with the love which he bears to his own person may be entrusted with it. If only we could find such people in government! For now we will be wiser to turn our attention to our own life and make sure that we live it with honor and integrity, placing the highest value on this chance for higher consciousness and the freedom it brings.

14. Prehistoric Origins

We look at it, and we do not see it, and we name it 'the Equable.' We listen to it, and we do not hear it, and we name it 'the Inaudible.' We try to grasp it, and do not get hold of it, and we name it 'the Subtle.' With these three qualities, it cannot be made the subject of description; and hence we blend them together and obtain The One.

Its upper part is not bright, and its lower part is not obscure. Ceaseless in its action, it yet cannot be named, and then it again returns and becomes nothing. This is called the Form of the Formless, and the Semblance of the Invisible; this is called the Fleeting and Indeterminable.

We meet it and do not see its Front; we follow it, and do not see its Back. When we can lay hold of the Tao of old to direct the things of the present day, and are able to know it as it was of old in the beginning, this is called (unwinding) the clue of Tao.

(Tao Teh King 14)

This section really reveals how incredibly, inconceivably vast is the distance (gulf, actually) between Eastern and Western religion. It is simply not true that it is a tiny step from East to West. Reading a paperback book, going to a yoga class, seeing a super-guru when he passes through town on his annual world tour, or liking what is seen of the Dalai Lama on a TV spot (usually brief), does not make anyone able to leap the gulf and really become a practicer of Dharma. A person has to be able to *think* East, not just *talk* East. The very observable fact that Western "Buddhists" and "Hindus" almost never follow the moral precepts of those religions is proof that, to paraphrase the Bible, they do not have the mind of Buddha or the mind of Krishna (Vyasa). For if they did, they would comprehend the wisdom of those precepts and naturally follow them as necessary principles of life.

I am not saying that everyone born in the East really is Eastern, or that everyone born in the West is Western. Actually, we are not speaking of geographical East and West, for after all, America is the far East to people living in China and Japan. What we are dealing with is a matter of brain dominance: of left-brain dominance versus right-brain dominance. And I mean *dominance*, not just a hint. Drug-use can warp a person's brain enough to make him open to the paradoxes of Eastern religious thought, but that is neither understanding them nor evidence of the complete psychology necessary to be of the East.

This is not just my idea about the matter. During my first visit to India I was fortunate enough to meet with Swami Maheshananda Giri, who for many years had held the chair of Sanskrit and Indology at Harvard. For decades he had encountered many Western students of Eastern religion, men and women of highly developed intellects, certainly not superficial in their interest. But when I asked him if he had met a single Westerner who truly understood Eastern religion, his answer was "No. Nor have I met a single Easterner who really understood Western religion. To understand Eastern religion a person would have to tear down every bit of their Western background and build up a new frame of reference to really comprehend Hinduism or any other Oriental philosophy. And it is the same with Easterners if they would understand Western religion." I agreed with him, but in later years I came to understand that something more besides is really needed: not an intellectual catharsis, but a shifting from left-brain to right-brain dominance. And that is accomplished by diligent practice of authentic yoga meditation.

I have seen people that could be called typical Westerners become typical Orientals after taking up yoga practice. I am not speaking culturally, but psychologically. I well remember the day Sri Kaka Sahib Kellelkar, one of Gandhi's closest associates, said to another one of Gandhiji's disciples regarding myself and some of our ashramites: "I have travelled throughout the world and met people from every land, yet today for the first time I have seen people who truly have a kinship with us." Many times very strict Hindus have said to me: "You are not an American, you are one of us." Now so many years later, there are some real American Hindus, I am glad to say, and in India there are very authentic sadhus that were born in the West. They crossed over the gulf or were born already there inwardly. That is why Mahendranath Gupta, the author of the *Gospel of Sri Ramakrishna*, once said: "Undoubtedly there are good people in every land, but they are aliens in those lands and their faces are toward India."

Lin Yutang's translation of this section is a bit better: "Looked at, but cannot be seen—That is called the Invisible (*yi*). Listened to, but cannot be heard—That is called the Inaudible (*hsi*). Grasped at, but cannot be touched—That is called the Intangible (*wei*). These three elude our inquiries and hence blend and become One."

The Absolute Reality, the Tao, can be looked at but not seen, listened to but not heard, and touched but not felt. Only those who have seen, heard, and touched the Tao know that It cannot be seen, heard, or touched. This is not some Zen-like string of contradictions, but carefully considered fact. And this is the authentic position of Eastern Christianity: only when you have seen God will you know that God cannot be seen.

Two eyes, two ears, and two hands cannot perceive or contact the Tao, for they are external and dual, but the single eye, ear, and hand of our internal being can see, hear, and touch that to which the outer faculties are blind, deaf and numb.

When these three experiences elude the dual mind, persistent inner search results in the single perception of the Single (and Sole) Reality. This only makes sense to the yogi.

Its upper part is not bright, and its lower part is not obscure. Ceaseless in its action, it yet cannot be named, and then it again returns and becomes nothing. This is called the Form of the Formless, and the Semblance of the

Invisible; this is called the Fleeting and Indeterminable. Lin Yutang: "Not by its rising, is there light, nor by its sinking, is there darkness. Unceasing, continuous, It cannot be defined, and reverts again to the realm of nothingness." The yogi knows the unknowable; knows It as everything, yet knows that in essence It is the No Thing.

We meet it and do not see its Front; we follow it, and do not see its Back. When we can lay hold of the Tao of old to direct the things of the present day, and are able to know it as it was of old in the beginning, this is called (unwinding) the clue of Tao. Lin Yutang: "That is why it is called the Form of the Formless, the Image of Nothingness. That is why it is called the Elusive: Meet it and you do not see its face; follow it and you do not see its back." "Front," "back," and "sides" do not apply to the Tao. Yet, since the Tao does assume form we sometimes get a fleeting perception of it in an expressible form, but It is gone before we even begin to speak of it. Yet we did perceive It, so we know It exists, but Its almost instant disappearance tells us that It really is formless and No Thing. After a few encounters of this kind we begin to realize that the same is true of us. We are as indefinable as the Tao, because we are the Tao.

15. THE WISE ONES OF OLD

The skilful masters (of the Tao) in old times, with a subtle and exquisite penetration, comprehended its mysteries, and were deep (also) so as to elude men's knowledge. As they were thus beyond men's knowledge, I will make an effort to describe of what sort they appeared to be.

Shrinking looked they like those who wade through a stream in winter; irresolute like those who are afraid of all around them; grave like a guest (in awe of his host); evanescent like ice that is melting away; unpretentious like wood that has not been fashioned into anything; vacant like a valley, and dull like muddy water.

Who can (make) the muddy water (clear)? Let it be still, and it will gradually become clear. Who can secure the condition of rest? Let movement go on, and the condition of rest will gradually arise.

They who preserve this method of the Tao do not wish to be full (of themselves). It is through their not being full of themselves that they can afford to seem worn and not appear new and complete.

(Tao Teh King 15)

The skillful masters (of the Tao) in old times, with a subtle and exquisite penetration, comprehended its mysteries, and were deep (also) so as to elude men's knowledge. As they were thus beyond men's knowledge, I will make an effort to describe of what sort they appeared to be. The Tao is incomprehensible, even though It is in all things, and human beings can perfectly embody It. The problem is, those who do embody It are then as incomprehensible as the Tao. "The wind bloweth where it listeth, and thou hearest the sound thereof, but canst not tell whence it cometh, and whither it goeth: so is every one that is born of the Spirit" (John 3:8).

Yet we need to have some idea of the ways of such masters so we will know if we meet them. For meeting them opens vast opportunities for advancement in wisdom and practical development. Because of this Lao Tzu wishes to give us some idea of them. We should notice that Lao Tzu is not the originator of what we call Taoism, for he speaks here of ancient masters. The Tao Itself is Taoism. The philosophy and practice we call Taoism is the way to the eternal Tao/Taoism. This, too, should be understood.

Shrinking looked they like those who wade through a stream in winter. Lin Yutang: "Cautious, like crossing a wintry stream." The sages were never brash and overconfident. They had never heard the Western adage: "Fools rush in where angels fear to tread," but they certainly acted according to it like angels. This sentence does not mean that the sages were fearful, for fearlessness is a main ingredient of spiritual life, but they were extremely careful in their words and acts. I found this to be true in India. The worthy teachers would not teach unless asked to, and even then they proceeded very leisurely and subtly. The fools, of course, would latch on to me and dump their unwisdom on me. They were walking mines of spiritual misinformation. Sages are like ripe oranges: you have to squeeze them to get the juice, and how much juice you get depends on how well and how persistently you squeeze.

Also the masters live carefully, thinking out things well ahead, truly ordering their lives and controlling the situations in which they place themselves. Because intelligence always prevailed, to the unwise they appeared unsure. So Lao Tzu continues:

Irresolute like those who are afraid of all around them. Lin Yutang: "Irresolute, like one fearing danger all around." Again, they do not fear, but they are well aware of how dangerous and unsure is this world.

Masters know that a single misstep can result in long-term disaster, and think and act accordingly. Buddha vigorously warned against heedlessness, and Lao Tzu is describing the opposite of that failing. Through the years one thing that has most amazed me about people who are supposedly seeking God is their complete lack of the realization that a spiritual seeker is in constant danger from influences in the world around him, and that he needs to protect himself from them and preserve and increase the strength of his aspiration. Instead they dawdle around, put themselves in questionable situations, do not take advantage of favorable situations, do very little to inform or prepare themselves for a real spiritual life and pay no attention to what is happening to them. I have met people that had spiritually come to a halt decades before and yet did not know it. They were dead and unburied. Minimalism does not work in spiritual life.

Grave like a guest. In most cultures there is a strong awareness of the obligations of a host, but in China they knew that the guest also had serious obligations. Courtesy was a prime factor in Chinese society, and people were deeply aware that it was worse to fail as a guest than as a host. That is why Lao Tzu speaks of a worthy guest as an example of the gravity which characterized the wise of earlier times. They possessed a deep regard for those with whom they interacted and showed it by their conduct at all times. The social conscience of a master is concerned with those he meets daily, not with some abstraction used for political manipulation of society in general. It was his obligation to be the best possible kind of person. That was his debt to society. It was deeply personal and not at all theoretical. This, too, I saw in all the holy people I met. Their sensitivity and care for everyone impressed me greatly. They had realized that a person must first be a perfect human being before they can advance to a higher level of evolution.

Evanescent like ice that is melting away. Lin Yutang: "Self-effacing, like ice beginning to melt." "Written in stone" was not an ideal for the ancient masters. They valued flexibility and unpretentiousness. They did not define themselves, but remained fluid and open to positive change. They never pushed their ideals on others or even spoke them unless asked. They were the kind of people Jesus had in mind when he spoke of the meek that inherit the earth (Matthew 5:5). Freed from the compulsion of form, they would never impose form in the sense of egoic definition on others. As we have seen and will see, they had very definite ideas about government, but realizing that human society was not capable of following them, they simply withdrew, content to fulfill their ideals in their own life at peace and harmony. This is why Taoist hermitages would be hidden away in very inaccessible places, for they did not want to intrude on anyone. Yet, their hospitality was renowned, and they received guests with a warmth and solicitude not found anywhere else. They were true "humanists" in all things.

Unpretentious like wood that has not been fashioned into anything. Lin Yutang: "Genuine, like a piece of undressed wood." In English we have the expression: "Plain as an old shoe," and its variation: "Comfortable as an old shoe." Both were applicable to the Taoist masters. They were plain and straightforward, yet with a courtesy that was thoroughly comfortable. They were what they were: they spent a lifetime uncovering what they really were and establishing themselves in it. They never "made anything" of themselves, and lived free of the compulsion to be anything in the eyes of others. Artificiality was childish in their opinion. As a result they had perfect mastery of everything, within and without. Not wanting to strut or display themselves on earth, they literally walked in the sky and controlled nature from deep within where they were one with all. They did not live in the Tao, the Tao lived in them. This was a blessedness unthought of by the busy and notable of the world. Yet, when those harried denizens of an ever-fermenting society sought them out, they gently did their best to reveal the way of wisdom to them. The Taoist hermits were a great force in Chinese culture, though they never sought to be so.

Vacant like a valley. Lin Yutang: "Open-minded, like a valley." The sages were always ready to see, to learn, to change. This is almost impossible for most everyone, adults especially, because they have defined themselves and loaded themselves with mental furniture in accordance with their definition. Consequently they are both blind and resistant to anything different, anything that does not fit into or accord with their definition. Their response to anything different tends to fall into three categories: complete unawareness, rejection or hostility.

No matter what passes through a valley, it remains a valley. Even if fires destroy all vegetation, still it is no less a valley. If a river flows through it or if it dries up, the valley remains. Seeming to be empty, virtually nothing since it is empty space, the valley is yet more permanent than anything that comes into it. This is a marvelous ideal for all. It is unfortunate that these magnificent ideals are little noticed, because people become totally occupied with the exotica of Taoism and not its eternal foundations of wisdom.

Dull like muddy water. The old Taoists greatly admired water, as did Saint Francis, for its power to be ever yielding and accommodating without at any time violating or altering its nature in any way. Eventually water wore away obstacles in it path by just flowing and being itself. No effort was need at all. So water was a symbol of placid stability for them, of rightness and effortless order and integrity.

"Dull like muddy water" indicates that the wise are willing to seem valueless, for who wants muddy water? They do not mind being disregarded by others. Again we have their love for being unremarkable outwardly. However, Lin Yutang renders this: "Mixing freely, like murky water" meaning that water is not rejective, but receives into itself, mingles within itself, whatever it encounters. This is even more profound. Here, too, we see the lack of definition. Water does not say: "I am not earth or opaque material, so I want nothing to do with it. I refuse to let it touch or infuse me." No, it is totally accepting, yet water will return eventually to its pure nature. Lao Tzu continues with awesomely profound words so simple, yet so large in scope that it is a marvel.

Who can (make) the muddy water (clear)? Let it be still, and it will gradually become clear. Just be still and the silt of mind and heart will settle out and all will be clear and pure. But the water does not agitate itself to do so, otherwise the muddiness will remain. Stillness clarifies the mind: not an empty mind, but a still mind. They are not the same. Meditation is the way of stillness.

Who can secure the condition of rest? Let movement go on, and the condition of rest will gradually arise. This is clarified by two verses from the Gita: "Not by abstaining from actions does a man attain the state beyond action, and not by mental renunciation alone does he approach to perfection. Truly, no one for even a moment exists without doing action. Each person is compelled to perform action, even against his will, by the gunas born of prakriti" (Bhagavad Gita 3:4-5).

External actions must go on–there is no choice–while complete inactivity, "the condition of rest," is established within. This is all a matter of extremely subtle and competent practice, and when I say "competent" I mean that both the methodology and the practicer must be competent.

They who preserve this method of the Tao do not wish to be full (of themselves). It is through their not being full of themselves that they can afford to seem worn and not appear new and complete. Of course, by "themselves" is meant ego and imposition of finite individuality on everything, making that the standard by which the universe is evaluated in all its parts. Those who follow the Tao do not hold any formalized self-concept, nor do they strive after one. Genuine Taoists do not think of themselves, nor do they think of the Tao. They merge with It. They embody it.

Lao Tzu understood human folly, especially the utterly baseless idolizing and idealizing of "new" and "contemporary" and "modern." So they resigned themselves to being sneered at as old and irrelevant, outdated and outworn. It did not upset them because they had a wonderful secret: They knew they were eternal and therefore ever new, relevant, and total. In other words: the Tao.

16. Knowing the Eternal Law

The (state of) vacancy should be brought to the utmost degree, and that of stillness guarded with unwearying vigour. All things alike go through their processes of activity, and (then) we see them return (to their original state). When things (in the vegetable world) have displayed their luxuriant growth, we see each of them return to its root. This returning to their root is what we call the state of stillness; and that stillness may be called a reporting that they have fulfilled their appointed end.

The report of that fulfillment is the regular, unchanging rule. To know that unchanging rule is to be intelligent; not to know it leads to wild movements and evil issues. The knowledge of that unchanging rule produces a (grand) capacity and forbearance, and that capacity and forbearance lead to a community (of feeling with all things). From this community of feeling comes a kingliness of character; and he who is king-like goes on to be heaven-like. In that likeness to heaven he possesses the Tao. Possessed of the Tao, he endures long; and to the end of his bodily life, is exempt from all danger of decay.

(Tao Teh King 16)

The translation of Lin Yutang is much clearer, I think; here it is: "Attain the utmost in Passivity, hold firm to the basis of Quietude. The myriad things take shape and rise to activity, but I watch them fall back to their repose. Like vegetation that luxuriantly grows but returns to the root (soil) from which it springs. To return to the root is Repose; it is called going back to one's Destiny.

"Going back to one's Destiny is to find the Eternal Law. To know the Eternal Law is Enlightenment. And not to know the Eternal Law is to court disaster. He who knows the Eternal Law is tolerant; being tolerant, he is impartial; being impartial, he is kingly; being kingly, he is in accord with Nature; being in accord with Nature, he is in accord with Tao; being in accord with Tao, he is eternal, and his whole life is preserved from harm."

Attain the utmost in Passivity, hold firm to the basis of Quietude. The ideal of the Tao Teh King, the Bhagavad Gita and the teachings of Buddha are the same: we must transfer our awareness into the Stillpoint, the Silence that is the unmoving Consciousness which is our true Being. At the same time we must move through the world skillfully, so living as to end the compulsion to further rebirth. Meditation enables us to "attain the utmost in Passivity." That is, it enables us to live centered in the unmoving Silence while being fully and effectively active. Through long practice of meditation we become able to "hold firm to the basis of Quietude" at all times.

The myriad things take shape and rise to activity, but I watch them fall back to their repose. Like vegetation that luxuriantly grows but returns to the root (soil) from which it springs.

Here we have another unanimity. All things arise into manifestation from the "primal soup" that consists of numberless elements that themselves are composites. Since coming implies going, and getting implies losing (for there is an inexorable impulse to ever return to the original state), it is inevitable that all things will return to non-manifestation, which Lao Tzu sees not as death or destruction, but a return to repose, to peace and freedom from the tension or stress inherent in all forms. There is a Root to all things: the Tao which is both Origin and Completion.

To return to the root is Repose; it is called going back to one's Destiny. Total union/identity with the Tao is the only real destiny anything or anyone has. There is no real distinction between sentient and insentient being: all is Tao. And about That nothing can be said.

Going back to one's Destiny is to find the Eternal Law. This is a perfect definition of Dharma: the return to the One. Anything that aids in this return is dharmic, and that which hinders the return is adharmic. This is the only basis upon which we should determine what is right or wrong, good or evil. Return is "the Eternal Law."

To know the Eternal Law is Enlightenment. "Of the born, death is certain; of the dead, birth is certain" (Bhagavad Gita 2:27). Those who are born are without exception destined to die, so in a sense they are "dead" the moment they are born. In the same way, those that tread the way of the Eternal Law which ends in enlightenment are already enlightened by the fact of their pilgrimage. For this reason, those who walk the Way deserve our utmost respect, and those who persevere unto the end deserve our reverence and imitation.

And not to know the Eternal Law is to court disaster. That is so obvious it needs no comment.

He who knows the Eternal Law is tolerant; being tolerant, he is impartial; being impartial, he is kingly; being kingly, he is in accord with Nature; being in accord with Nature, he is in accord with Tao; being in accord with Tao, he is eternal, and his whole life is preserved from harm. Those who walk the Way advance in unfoldment of character step by step as outlined here until they are the Tao alone.

17. Rulers

> Of the best rulers the people (only) know that they exist; the next best they love and praise; the next they fear; and the next they revile.
>
> When they do not command the people's faith, some will lose faith in them, and then they resort to oaths!
>
> But (of the best) when their task is accomplished, their work done, the people all remark, 'We have done it ourselves.'
> (Tao Teh King 17)

Of the best rulers the people (only) know that they exist; the next best they love and praise; the next they fear; and the next they revile. It is interesting that Taoism was traditionally very outspoken about society, and especially about government. At the same time Taoism advocated being distanced from the regular run of things and was insistent that no coercion in any form was to be applied to other people. So Taoism was a fundamentally live-and-let-live philosophy that felt an obligation to present wisdom to all and then stand back and see what happened. This is of course characteristic of the major Eastern religions (Taoism, Hinduism, Jainism and Buddhism), at least ideally. It is no surprise that human beings in the grip of ego have always gone contrary to this principle, but anyone who reads the scriptures and the teachings of true sages can see that coercion and even persuasion is a violation of their essential nature. For true religion frees a person, it does not bind or obligate him in in any way. In no other way can hypocrisy and corruption be avoided.

17. RULERS

Now I have my own story. If the best rulers are only known to exist, and nothing more, what about rulers that no one knows even exist? That is the way it was in my one-mile-square hometown of four hundred and fifty residents in the nineteen forties. We had no mail delivery, everything came to our tiny post office on the town square. Any outsider wanting to find a house or business had to ask and be directed to it. So imagine our amazement when my uncle George came home one evening and asked: "Did you know all our streets have names?" Our town was over one hundred years old, yet my family who had lived there for three generations had never heard of any street names. It seems that my uncle had found an old map at the town hall which gave the street names.

After everyone had expressed surprise, he topped himself by asking: "Did you know we have a mayor?" Again, this was astonishing. *No one* had ever heard of a mayor or any form of town government whatever. And when he told us the mayor's name we were really flummoxed because it the name of a rich drunk that no one even gave a second thought. (I had been told when very small that I must never go into his large impressive house because his family were the wrong kind of people–typical F. Scott Fitzgerald type of moral degenerates, not appreciated in a community like ours in which "poor but honest" topped the list.)

Anyhow, it turned out that the town was "governed" by a town board who had some time in the past decided to call its chairman the mayor. What town board? No one knew of them because they had been appointed long ago and given the power to appoint replacements when one of them died or resigned. That was even more shocking. But since the board did not seem to do anything, we shrugged it off and went on as before. (Actually they did a few things, but very slowly and made it seem that it was county regulation.)

Nearly forty years went by. When I was visited by a cousin and his wife I learned that the old town hall was falling to bits. It contained the library and a huge auditorium where school plays and suchlike were performed, so my cousin's wife was especially concerned about its imminent demolition and was trying to persuade the locals to raise money on their own to preserve it. Some hope! A few months later my father and mother came for their annual visit and in conversation my father revealed that in the flurry and fury of Save the Town Hall my cousin and his wife had discovered that the sleepy little town actually had over two hundred thousand dollars in the bank gathering interest: enough to repair several town halls. Another aspect of the invisible board's inactivity. So the hall was saved and today a photograph of it is displayed on the town's minimal website. (Another board project I suppose.) By the way, the town now has street signs.

The government that governs least is not the best, it is the government that is unknown and does virtually nothing. What my story demonstrates is the wisdom of the Taoist position. Invisible government is best. Next best is government that governs so minimally and wisely that all love and praise it. Not at all good is government that rules by fear, and the worst is reviled by those with good sense.

Since we do not run government as individuals, what is the message of the Tao Teh King to us? It shows us how benevolent detachment while doing our personal best within society is the way of wisdom.

When they do not command the people's faith, some will lose faith in them, and then they resort to oaths! Moral coercion precedes active physical coercion, so beware. Also they vehemently praise and congratulate themselves and hold themselves up to the people as the pinnacle of virtue and wisdom, implying that those who oppose them are stupid and without right moral sense. In this, government is following the lead of religion much of the time, for religions do just the same. The further a religion drifts from being based on the individual's free choice, the worse it gets until it, too, is a monstrosity everyone with good sense prays will go away.

But (of the best) when their task is accomplished, their work done, the people all remark, 'We have done it ourselves.' And so they truly will have done, as a free society acting willingly on right principles. It is the same with religion. Each person attains moral perfection and enlightenment on their own. The religion pointed the way, but they lived out what they learned and proved its value by reaching the Eternal even while living in time.

18. THE DECLINE OF TAO

When the Great Tao (Way or Method) ceased to be observed, benevolence and righteousness came into vogue. (Then) appeared wisdom and shrewdness, and there ensued great hypocrisy.

When harmony no longer prevailed throughout the six kinships, filial sons found their manifestation; when the states and clans fell into disorder, loyal ministers appeared.

(Tao Teh King 18)

Lin Yutang is a bit more on target: "On the decline of the great Tao, the doctrine of 'humanity' and 'justice' arose. When knowledge and cleverness appeared, great hypocrisy followed in its wake.

"When the six relationships no longer lived at peace, there was (praise of) 'kind parents' and 'filial sons.' When a country fell into chaos and misrule, there was (praise of) 'loyal ministers.'"

On the decline of the great Tao,... The Taoists felt that "in the beginning" the Tao was known and therefore followed. Yet in time people began to lose their grip on the Tao. As a result it was not the Tao that faded away or declined, but the people themselves faded away and declined. So when we have the phrase "on the decline of the great Tao," it means when the awareness of the Tao declined in people's minds.

...the doctrine of "humanity" and "justice" arose. When people lost their innate awareness of the Tao, and therefore of their true selves, they

began to violate their true nature which was the Tao. Instead of natural and true virtue in thought, word, and deed, they began to behave in disorderly and destructive ways. In order to stop this aberration and chaos at least externally, various codes for human behavior were formulated. Some were merely presented for consideration, and others were imposed through social and civil law. Infraction of these laws resulted in either loss of reputation, the "losing face" so abhorrent to the Chinese, and risk of social ostracism or even punishment by the civil authorities.

Taoists considered the Confucian definitions and prescription for right behavior to be trivial and hypocritical, especially when they became so rigid and heavy-handed that authentic humanity and justice became extinct to a troubling degree. The individual became less and less as "society" and "order" gained in importance and overt dominance.

The Tao has "declined" throughout the world, and as a result nearly all people believe that by acting a certain way we can make ourselves into what we really only appear to be. It is believed that people who act "nice" really are nice, that those engaged in "helping" others are kind, caring and compassionate. And so it goes in many directions. But any intelligent and insightful person, though in a minority, is aware that this is a superficial and simplistic way of seeing things that is really self-deception. We all know "godly" people who are hellish, and "caring" people that are nothing but manipulative sociopaths, and "helping" people that are exploitive opportunists.

Remember the hateful teachers, especially in grade school, that constantly bellowed: "If I did not like children I would not have become a teacher!"? And: "I am not a policeman!" I'll say they weren't! They were commandants of a gulag, tyrants with unquestionable authority, social fascists of the worst sort.

Isn't it interesting that at this point in time the label of hypocrite is only applied to religious people? Everyone else is to be accepted at face value and not questioned. Otherwise we will be "negative" and "obstructive." Heaven only knows what would be thought of Taoists today if they did not have the (wrong) reputation for being advocates of supersex and therefore "one of us" in society's eyes.

18. The Decline of Tao

When knowledge and cleverness appeared, great hypocrisy followed in its wake. When intelligence and integrity waned, education and craftiness took over. P. J. O'Rourke has written an excellent essay, "A Plague of 'A' Students" that is gospel truth. As I once read, schools are places where pebbles are polished and diamonds made dull. If we observe children we can see their natural creativity and spontaneity being eroded year by year by public schools. It is a revelation to meet and converse with a home-schooled child.

As Byrn translates this: "When intellectualism arises, hypocrisy is close behind." Fakery on all levels becomes rife, even though often unintentional.

When the six relationships no longer lived at peace, there was (praise of) "kind parents" and "filial sons." When real families declined in numbers, "ideal" families that were artificial and hypocritical appeared. Parents were praised for being humane, or appearing to be, and children were praised for being "good" and "respectful." Love being the basis of family life, there is no need for such labels when there is genuine love between parents and children. As Blackney translated this: "The six relations were no more at peace, So codes were made to regulate our homes." Byrn renders it: "When there is strife in the family unit, people talk about 'brotherly love'."

In ancient China the rules of subservience developed from the Six Kinships of Confucius. Under its order of loyalties, the older is always master of the younger, man is master of woman, the lord is master of the subject, the father is master of the son, the husband is master of the wife, and the brother is master of the sister. This a very poor model for a real family.

"When a country fell into chaos and misrule, there was (praise of) "loyal ministers." Blackney: "The fatherland grew dark, confused by strife: Official loyalty became the style." Byrn: "When the country falls into chaos, politicians talk about 'patriotism'." Things have not changed much, have they? All of these troubles come from losing touch with the Tao, which is one's own primal Self. Consequently no one can be what they really are, and artificial standards arise and compound the present problems and create many more. There is only one solution: return to the Reality of the Tao.

19. Realize the Simple Self

Banish "wisdom," discard "knowledge," and the people shall profit a hundredfold. Banish "humanity," discard "justice," and the people shall recover love of their kin. Banish cunning, discard "utility," and the thieves and brigands shall disappear. As these three touch the externals and are inadequate, the people have need of what they can depend upon:
Reveal thy simple self,
Embrace thy original nature,
Check thy selfishness,
Curtail thy desires.
(Tao Teh King 19).

The Taoists were very outspoken in their opinion of Confucius and Confucianism as nothing more than busybodies that had ruined society by advocating veneer rather than solid substance. Jesus spoke of this as "the righteousness of the scribes and Pharisees" (Matthew 5:20). Neither he nor the Taoists were listened to very much. He withdrew to India and the Taoists to solitary places in the countryside. It is wisdom to know when nobody really wants to hear or think about what you have to say, and greater wisdom when you consequently go away and keep silent.

So why did Lao Tzu say what he did in the Tao Teh King? Because he was literally leaving society forever, and when the gatekeeper asked him to write down his insights he did so, not with any intention that people would heed and reform society, but so the few that really had ears to hear and a brain to comprehend would reform themselves and be at peace. For this reason we must not think of Taoism as a rival of Confucianism, having the wish to reform others. Taoism is a marvelously solitary and independent approach to cultivation of inner worth.

Once a man came to Swami Keshabananda (written about in *Autobiography of a Yogi*) and begged him to cure his son who was dying. The great yogi told him: "I will tell you how to cure your son yourself, but you will not do it and he will die." And so it was. In the same way Lao Tzu is explaining how society can be corrected, knowing full well that it will never be done. But wise and blessed is he who applies Lao Tzu's words to himself and his own mode of life. So let us consider them in that context, for we are each one of us little "kingdoms" that need correction.

Banish 'wisdom,' discard 'knowledge,' and the people shall profit a hundredfold. Lao Tzu is speaking of intellectual, spoon-fed "wisdom" and "knowledge" both social and religious that have been put into our heads from various sources that have in no way proved the validity of that which they have imposed on us. It is very difficult for us to sweep away all the things we have been told from childhood, because it means rejection of the authority or trustworthiness of those that crammed them into our heads. Moreover, it is much easier for the mentally and morally lazy to accept the clichés society and religion run on, and thus avoid any conflict or the pain of straining the brain to figure out what is really wisdom and knowledge. But those who do toss aside mere words and seek experience of reality shall "profit a hundredfold."

Banish 'humanity,' discard 'justice,' and the people shall recover love of their kin. Again, Lao Tzu is speaking of artificial rules of thought and behavior that are not rooted in sincere good will but in a desire to be thought humane and just. A great deal of inhumanity and injustice are perpetrated under the accepted clichés of society and religion, all "for the greater good" they say.

Banish cunning, discard 'utility,' and the thieves and brigands shall disappear. "People are so skillful in their ignorance," Yogananda used to say. People can be very creative in justifying their foolishness and in reasoning themselves out of good sense. They are equally skilled in demonstrating how "practical" and "beneficial" their desires and whims are. "It is all for the best" rarely is even good, much less best. This is used in conforming to wrong on many levels, especially social, rather than rejecting the false and holding to the real and consequently getting censured and even in trouble with "them." It is sad but true that we are usually ourselves the thieves and brigands that plunder our spiritual treasure of divine potential.

As these three touch the externals and are inadequate, the people have need of what they can depend upon. These three rules, though of great value, yet lack the supreme value because they deal with our response to external factors, leaving aside internal matters. Thus they are inadequate, because we must build our life structure on bedrock reality to be secure and at peace. So Lao Tzu gives us four rules to ensure this.

Reveal thy simple self. We must put ourselves in touch with our essential being, really come to know our Self by removing the veils that hide it. The Self being interior in nature, this requires an interior life: in other words, meditation. And our meditation practice should be putting us in touch with the Self immediately, not in some far away time. It will not give us instant and total enlightenment, but it should certainly begin the process right away. We should come out of our first meditation having touched at least the periphery of our Self, and things should increase from there. We must not stop until the Self is fully revealed (realized). (I suggest you read *Soham Yoga, the Yoga of the Self* for information on meditation that does what I have just described.)

Embrace thy original nature. We must not just experience the Self, we must "embrace" it by making it manifest in our entire life, by establishing ourselves in Self-knowledge outside meditation as well as in meditation. We must live out what we perceive inwardly, and if our inner experience is real, it will be natural and easy.

Check thy selfishness. Do not pay attention to the ego; just forget it. Drop it and all egotism will vanish in the newly-revealed Self. Be intent on that eternal reality and the ego and its delusive realm will simply vanish.

Curtail thy desires. Again, do this by being satisfied and fulfilled in the Self. Desire the Self: that will end all desires.

20. The World and I

Banish learning, and vexations end. Between "Ah!" and "Ough!" how much difference is there? Between "good" and "evil" how much difference is there? That which men fear is indeed to be feared; but, alas, distant yet is the dawn (of awakening)!

The people of the world are merry-making, as if partaking of the sacrificial feasts, as if mounting the terrace in spring; I alone am mild, like one unemployed, like a new-born babe that cannot yet smile, unattached, like one without a home.

The people of the world have enough and to spare, but I am like one left out, my heart must be that of a fool, being muddled, nebulous!

The vulgar are knowing, luminous; I alone am dull, confused. The vulgar are clever, self-assured; I alone, depressed. Patient as the sea, adrift, seemingly aimless.

The people of the world all have a purpose; I alone appear stubborn and uncouth.

I alone differ from the other people, and value drawing sustenance from the Mother.

(Tao Teh King 20)

Banish learning, and vexations end. "Learning" means the mistaken idea that reading a book and mindlessly repeating back its contents is wisdom, that intelligence can be gained in a classroom. Intelligence and insight are the needed elements for wisdom.

Between "Ah!" and "Ough!" How much difference is there? Various translations give different sounds, all meaning a kind of response or reaction, but without meaning to us in the modern West. My speculation is that "Ah!" is an expression of liking or appreciation, and "Ough!" is one of dislike or disgust: "Ugh!" or "Uck!" Since the same object can elicit approval or rejection from people, there is no absolute to their reaction which is, therefore, fundamentally meaningless. So the "difference" is substantially nil. Lao Tzu is saying that the reactions or judgments of people really mean very little if anything at all.

Between "good" and "evil" how much difference is there? He is not speaking here of actual good and evil, but of the labels which inherently mean very little, since different people will react differently to the same thing. Some people think narrow-mindedness is good and openness is bad, while others think just the opposite. Lao Tzu is especially urging us to ignore the labels of society in general and not be influenced by them. We should come to our own conclusions and keep them to ourselves, not imposing them on others, though we should express them if asked to.

That which men fear is indeed to be feared. Many translators agree, however other translations are like this one by Wu: "Must I fear what others fear? What abysmal nonsense this is!" Both make sense.

Intellectual labels are one thing, but practical experience is another, and fear is based on experience or observation. People fear erupting volcanoes if they are nearby, and so should any sensible person. Yet we should be cautious regarding that which so many people fear and hope to avoid. It is silly to fear something just because others do so. For centuries in the West it was believed that tomatoes were deadly poison, and I was brought up on the belief that one half of a buckeye (the seed of the Ohio buckeye tree) is poison and the other is not, and only a squirrel could tell the difference. Worse, I grew up in the era when no one would put a burn under cold water or apply ice. The dogma was that to do so would "drive in the fire" and make it worse. So as we suffered we put butter or Unguentine on it, which did absolutely nothing. Nowadays

20. The World and I

we know that the severity of a burn can be dramatically lessened by the application of cold in some form. We also continually put Mercurochrome on cuts and scrapes, which is utterly useless. The only thing it did was turn our skin red. So it is sometimes wise to fear what others do, and sometimes it is completely foolish. There is no substitute for experience and intelligence.

But, alas, distant yet is the dawn (of awakening)! For those caught up in the gears of society and public opinion, even the beginning of awakening is far in the future. Only those who quietly and unobtrusively live according to their independent understanding can hope to eventually pass into higher knowing. That is why the Gita says: "He who agitates not the world, and whom the world agitates not, who is freed from joy, envy, fear and distress–he is dear to me" (Bhagavad Gita 12:15). Saint Paul said: "The world is crucified unto me, and I unto the world" (Galatians 6:14).

The people of the world are merry-making, as if partaking of the sacrificial feasts, as if mounting the terrace in spring; I alone am mild, like one unemployed, like a new-born babe that cannot yet smile, unattached, like one without a home. Happy are those than can live out of step with the herd that runs on to nothing at all. As Jesus said: "But whereunto shall I liken this generation? It is like unto children sitting in the markets, and calling unto their fellows, and saying, We have piped unto you, and ye have not danced; we have mourned unto you, and ye have not lamented" (Matthew 11:16-17). Blessed are they that can be called "odd" or "unsociable" and be contented when "they think it strange that ye run not with them to the same excess of riot, speaking evil of you" (I Peter 4:4). "Peer pressure" means nothing to the worthwhile, but everything to many others.

So Lao Tzu says that in the midst of the mindless merrymaking of the heedless the wise is calm and disengaged from the fuss going on all around him, and likens the sage to a new-born babe that never reacts to its environment because it simply does not perceive it. The sage ignores the world and the world certainly ignores the sage as long as he does not spoil their "fun" by being obviously out of their track. Lao Tzu had the right idea: he went far away and was at peace, "unattached, like one without a home," for we can have no home but the Tao.

Now Lao Tzu is going to be sarcastic yet right on target as to how the foolish view the wise.

The people of the world have enough and to spare, but I am like one left out, my heart must be that of a fool, being muddled, nebulous! How enamored "the people of the world" are of their abundance of worthless nonsense. The wise, however, choose to be "left out," "losers" in the sight of the world, foolish, unaware and "without direction"–"underachievers" for sure! What a blessed state.

The vulgar are knowing, luminous; I alone am dull, confused. The vulgar are clever, self-assured; I alone, depressed. Patient as the sea, adrift, seemingly aimless. How proud are the small and the petty as they strut around, masters of all they survey, "in the know" and "bright as a button" in contrast to the dull, boring, and "confused" man of wisdom. The "unique" run-of-the mill people see themselves as clever and confident. The sage is considered isolated for he is not "a good mixer." How miserable the world considers him to be. "We've got to bring him out of himself," they assure one another if he is unlucky enough to be noticed by them. His patient contentment is considered a lack of "get up and go" since he is not a "go getter," "self-starter," or a "doer," adrift and seemingly aimless.

The people of the world all have a purpose; I alone appear stubborn and uncouth. I alone differ from the other people, and value drawing sustenance from the Mother. Yes, there is no doubt about it: the sage is a party pooper, refusing to have fun and therefore very unmannerly, out of step and obsessed with a lot of daft ideas about metaphysics and God knows what else. How impossible it is for the world to know that the unsociable kook and wierdo they so indignantly despise is living abundantly in and by the Mother Tao, knowing a fulfillment they do not even dream about, and to which they cannot even aspire in their pedestrian minds. How shocked they would be to find that the sage really does live in Dream Castles and feasts daily on Pie In The Sky. A happy man indeed.

21. Manifestations of Tao

> The marks of great Character follow alone from the Tao.
> The thing that is called Tao is elusive, evasive. Evasive, elusive, yet latent in it are forms. Elusive, evasive, yet latent in it are objects. Dark and dim, yet latent in it is the life-force. The life-force being very true, latent in it are evidences.
> From the days of old till now its Named (manifested forms) have never ceased, by which we may view the Father of All Things. How do I know the shape of the Father of All Things? Through these (manifested forms)!
> (Tao Teh King 21)

The marks of great character follow alone from the Tao. This is an essential piece of wisdom. Only when the Infinite is revealed in and through the finite, only when the cosmic is shown as the true essence of the individual life, is there any greatness of character. Tao being the Source, the more our consciousness is being merged in that Consciousness the more the traits of the immanent Tao manifest in us as the eternal seeds they are, and the further we move along the path of transcendence whose goal is That which is completely without character or attribute (guna) of any kind.

Only those who increasingly dwell in the Tao possess "great character." Any other traits are evanescent mirages, being fundamentally unreal. Therefore only those who know and reveal the Tao are worthy of our respect. All others are phantoms.

The thing that is called Tao is elusive, evasive. The East has always known that the Real is also the Unknowable, the Unseeable, the Inconceivable. But such insight is possible only to those who have known, seen and accurately perceived It as truly unknowable, unseeable, and inconceivable. This makes no sense to the left-brain intellect of the West, but is perfectly good sense to the right-brain intellects of the East.

The Absolute Reality that is Tao eludes the grasp of thought and conception, but to the purified consciousness that fact itself is a revealing mystical experience, a knowing beyond the mind: the intuition of the spirit.

Evasive, elusive, yet latent in it are forms. Elusive, evasive, yet latent in it are objects. Dark and dim, yet latent in it is the life-force. The life-force being very true, latent in it are evidences. It is usually thought in non-dual philosophy that the Absolute Non-dual Being is the antithesis of all relativity, that the relative and the Absolute are incompatible, that when one prevails the other is banished. But Lao Tzu is telling us that forms, in the sense of subtle archetypes, are an inherent part of the Tao, as are their manifested objects which we perceive; that unless the Tao existed they would not exist even as mirages. Further, the Tao enlivens all that exists in relative mode. Their existence is not false or illusory, but those that do not see the one Tao in all have the error and illusion in their own minds. Of course, duality never really exists, it is a matter of the One appearing as Many. It all comes down to perception.

From the days of old till now its named (manifested forms) have never ceased, by which we may view the Father of All Things. How do I know the shape of the Father of All Things? Through these (manifested forms)! So relative existence is not a veil hiding the Tao from us, but is a revealing of the Tao to us. The problem lies in our not seeing this to be true. Again, it is all in the seeing. As Swami Sri Yukteswar said regarding astrology: "If ignoramuses misread the heavens, and see there a scrawl instead of a script, that is to be expected in this imperfect world. One should not dismiss the wisdom with the 'wise.'" The same is true in relation to the entire creation. The Tao is is present right in front of us at all times.

22. Futility of Contention

To yield is to be preserved whole. To be bent is to become straight. To be hollow is to be filled. To be tattered is to be renewed. To be in want is to possess. To have plenty is to be confused.

Therefore the Sage embraces the One, and becomes the model of the world. He does not reveal himself, and is therefore luminous. He does not justify himself, and is therefore far-famed. He does not boast of himself, and therefore people give him credit. He does not pride himself, and is therefore the chief among men.

Is it not indeed true, as the ancients say, "To yield is to be preserved whole?" Thus he is preserved and the world does him homage.

(Tao Teh King 22)

The Tao is the Source of All and the Indweller of All, yet It does not assert Itself, at least not in the manner of human beings. Seeking to be like the Tao we can recover our identity as the Tao in essence. Consequently Lao Tzu is giving us several points of likeness to the Tao that we should cultivate.

To yield is to be preserved whole. First we must understand that Lao Tzu is not telling us to become mental and moral jellyfish, always giving in to everything and never at any time standing firm on anything: that is the way of the morally lazy. Considering the pungent things Lao Tzu has to say about aspects of personal and social life, it is obvious he took a very firm stand on many things, and expressed his opinion. What he is inculcating here is both flexibility and simply stepping away from the tar baby of situations in which we would be caught and shaped by involving or committing ourselves. Almost the only activism advocated by Lao Tzu is personal discipline.

So what is he advising us? He is telling us to never get involved in a manner which will seize our mind and narrow it, which is the great danger of all advocacy and resistance, especially in social matters. To be fervent in a "cause" can be very harmful because it usually involves obsession, indignation, the spending of large amounts of time, interference, the adoption of a "pro" or "con" self-identity and a narrowing of interest and awareness. I have known people who were really a one-note personality, continually thinking and speaking of a single thing: their advocacy or their opposition.

One of the worst aspects of this is a supposedly moral insistence that a person "stand up and be counted" or "speak out whenever necessary." This can entail being a real nuisance. I think we all know people who consider it an obligation for them to express an opinion on everything no matter how small, often arguing on and on, if they are to be really honest. I knew a woman who felt it an obligation to rebuke anyone who said or did anything she considered mistaken or wrong, and I do mean *anything*. Contempt, bullying and often cruelty spiced her "honesty." She often boasted about her practice of writing what she called "get straight letters" to those who transgressed her principles. All she really did was vent her resentments and prejudices.

Lao Tzu is certainly advocating the ability to know when to speak and when not to speak, when to act and when not to act. And when we do speak and act we must know how to be quit of the matter and not hang on to it like a dog worrying a rag. There are times when we should express our convictions, but then end it right there and put it out of our mind and get on with our life. We often hear about being possessed by possessions. The remedy is not to have nothing, but to be able to own things and not be owned by them. It is the same way with

22. Futility of Contention

our words and actions. We need to know how to let go, not to keep on. The ability to let go is a necessary factor for inward peace. Actually, Lao Tzu is recommending the attitude expressed in the Gita where we are told to act as we should and then let the results be what they are: to let go, move on and put our energies where they should be.

If we follow the sage's counsel, we will "be preserved whole," not shattered or reshaped in the image of any object or situation. Simply facing facts and accepting them for what they are is part of this wisdom. Ultimately Lao Tzu is urging us to a kind of benevolent and wise indifference, the ability to let things be and go on our way. Is it any surprise that the Taoists tended to the heremitic life? Even when living in a large city, Taoists lived in a very self-contained manner, with a light touch all around.

To be bent is to become straight. If we can be flexible, we will have the ability to be "straight" within ourselves, not shaped or twisted by outer influences. Even if something pushes at us, we will be able to retain our footing. Years ago we had salt and pepper shakers that were round, but could not be knocked over because there was a heavy metal weight in their base. Children (me included) loved knocking or pushing them down over and over, watching them immediately come right back to upright, and not rocking around, either. They were a perfect symbol of mental equilibrium, though we did not realize it. It is the same with the wise, and the same with the Tao. In its manifestation the Tao undergoes an infinite variety of changes, yet remains unchanging. All around us is the Tao, and no matter how much we assault It and seek to destroy It, it yields and bends and thus remains Itself in total integrity.

To be hollow is to be filled. Byrn: "If you want to become full, first let yourself become empty." Chan: "To be empty is to be full." Both of these differing translations give a valid aspect to this principle. Only an empty vessel can be filled. A vessel with rocks in it will not be able to receive and hold the intended amount of water. In the same way, a life cluttered with extraneous things will not be the truly full life it was intended to be. Those who mentally "possess" nothing can possess everything, for they are open to all things. To not keep any ego-centered identity enables us to be everything. To "know" nothing is the way to know everything. Basically we must be ever open and ready for what comes to hand. This is the way to live in totality. When our hands are holding on to something they cannot grasp anything else, so to live with open hands is to accept and receive all. This is to be understood in an intelligent (not in a simplistic or minimal) manner. Life offers infinite possibilities to the "empty" sage.

To be tattered is to be renewed. In childhood I knew quite a few elderly people who had lived through very hard times economically, so they had a fear of things wearing out and becoming useless. Their response to this was not use anything they bought. It was really absurd. In *Mill On The Floss* there is a character who keeps all her newly-bought clothing in drawers with paper between them. Only after a long while can she bring herself to wear them, and by that time they are completely out of style and she looks ridiculous. I knew people like that, even some that hardly drove their auto lest it wear out or break, so they rarely went anywhere. One of my great-aunts was really obsessive about anything she got. She would not even allow her grandchildren to play with the toys she bought them. But life is not like that: it is self-renewing. So the more we live the more life will come to us. The fuller we live life the more it expands and increases. This is one of the reasons Taoists lived to be so old and retained their youthfulness. One of my dearest friends, "Grandma Sullivan," used to climb around on her roof, repairing it herself, mowed her own extensive yard, made her own repairs to her house, and was thoroughly independent. She had been that way when young and kept it up, living to be nearly a century old without lessening any activity. She was "tattered" but renewed. Using life keeps it new.

Another aspect is in this translation by Byrn: "If you want to become new, first let yourself become old." We must grow, develop, and be adults. Those who cling to childhood just become childish, those who do not want to grow up frustrate the purpose of life. Those who let themselves become "seasoned citizens" continue to grow and be new in mind and heart. Further, those who live worthily and wisely attain a good rebirth when the present life ends. Many are those that return to birth with a continuing consciousness from the previous life, retaining the wisdom gained there, and so able to build on it in the new life, ever moving forward.

To be in want is to possess. To have plenty is to be confused. Better is the translation by Chan: "To have little is to possess. To have plenty is to be perplexed." This has two meanings. One is that only when we have a few simple necessities can we really own them in the sense of profitably using them to our benefit without anxiety, for they will be easy to replace if need be. But when we own a lot of things we are worried and unsure as how to retain or maintain them. They cause us anxiety just by being in our lives and minds, cluttering them up in many ways. The other meaning is that those who own little can "own" all things by appreciating them and yet not having to possess or "relate" to them in any way. He who owns nothing can yet own all: so Lao Tzu tells us.

Therefore the Sage embraces the One, and becomes the model of the world. Byrn: "For this reason the Master embraces the Tao, as an example for the world to follow." This is quite clear and needs no comment, but I would like to point out that Lao Tzu tells us the Tao-embracing sage is an example for us to follow, not just admire and consider beyond our scope to imitate. "That is for saints" is not the view of the Taoist, for we are all part of the Tao and so no ideal, however exalted, is beyond our capacity to fulfill.

He does not reveal himself, and is therefore luminous. Feng and English: "Not putting on a display, They shine forth." Obviously they do not "shine forth" to the eyes of the ordinary person, but to those whose "Tao eyes" are open to at least some degree. I have known saints in East and West who were disregarded or sneered at by the ignorant (even if religious), but revered by those who themselves had some degree of spiritual progress. All of them simply lived the holy life and minded their own business, often hiding or downplaying their virtues and accomplishments. Nor could they be drawn out by those who wanted to enter into controversy with them or test them in any way.

One of my friends was a yoga-siddha, possessing astonishing psychic powers, and head of his own ashram in western India. I loved him for his good qualities, but he was amazingly rude and contemptuous to people who did not have similar psychic experiences and powers. One of my painful memories is his treatment of a wonderful one-hundred-eight-year-old sadhu who lived next to me in the Sapta Rishi Ashram outside the holy city of Hardwar (not any more: the city has extended and engulfed the ashram property). Having learned about his advanced age, he asked me to arrange a meeting with the swami, whose name really was "Swami Om Namah Shivaya." My heart and stomach sank. I knew he would have no use for the wonderfully humble and simple little sadhu. And I was right. After a few minutes he stood up and walked out without even a farewell to the swami. So next day when he went to Sivanandashram in Rishikesh I refused to accompany him, dreading the outcome. That night he told me that he had gotten a private interview with Sivananda and had trotted out all his psychic experiences/phenomena. Sivananda listened attentively and then quietly said: "I would not know about these things. I have never had any psychic experiences." And that was right: he had only *spiritual* experiences. "But I still respect him," was Dattabal's comment, "because he is a great karma yogi." Many people met Sivananda and thought he was an ignoramus and a fool because he was so unassuming and egoless. Yet many others saw his greatness and loved him as the colossal Master he was. Having myself been fooled by great yogis who could perfectly hide their inner status, I cannot boast of my great insight, but I can express gratitude for their eventually revealing themselves to me. Lao Tzu would understand.

He does not justify himself, and is therefore far-famed.

A man once came storming into Alfred Deller's dressing-room after a concert. "Mister Deller, I just want to know that I hate your voice!" he shouted. Deller calmly replied: "Well, that is between you and your psychiatrist." It is the same with the really wise: they live their life and what others think of them is their own problem. As Sri Ramakrishna said, when the elephant walks down the street the little dogs bark, but the elephant just keeps on walking. One mark of fake teachers and institutions is their constant anxiety about how they appear to prospective followers and the public in general. But the real ones have their consciousness focussed on the Transcendent and are satisfied with that. When people tried to get Sri Ramakrishna to define his spiritual status he would say: "I am the dust of your feet" and then bow down to them.

One time someone phoned the church where FDR usually attended to ask if the President would be there the next Sunday. The pastor had answered the phone, and he replied: "We are not sure, but we are confident that God will be here." It is all according to one's priorities.

The wise do not expound themselves and project an image of wisdom and worthiness. They know that what they really are is the only thing that matters, and that most people are clueless regarding themselves, what to say of others. So they do not worry. Many great ones have fled from place to place to get away from clamoring adorers who understood nothing of their purpose.

He does not boast of himself, and therefore people give him credit. Feng and English: "Not boasting, They receive recognition." So it is.

He does not pride himself, and is therefore the chief among men. What is more humble than the Tao? It is and does all things, yet never announces Itself, never gives commands or revelations, but awaits for awakening intelligences to figure out Its existence. It has no interest in right views or wrong views: in fact it has no interest in anything, not even Itself. This is humility that only the Supreme Reality can have. So it is with those that know the Tao and themselves as part of the Tao. They are not only "the chief among men," they are the only men among "men."

Is it not indeed true, as the ancients say, 'To yield is to be preserved whole?' Thus he is preserved and the world does him homage. So now we are back at the beginning, and a good beginning it is, indeed. For such a one the whole world is his domain. Humanity may ignore him, but Reality does not. He is in the Tao and the Tao is in him.

23. Identification with Tao

Nature says few words: Hence it is that a squall lasts not a whole morning. A rainstorm continues not a whole day. Where do they come from? From Nature. Even Nature does not last long (in its utterances), how much less should human beings?

Therefore it is that: He who follows the Tao is identified with the Tao. He who follows Character (*Teh*) is identified with Character. He who abandons (Tao) is identified with abandonment (of Tao). He who is identified with Tao–Tao is also glad to welcome him. He who is identified with character–Character is also glad to welcome him. He who is identified with abandonment–Abandonment is also glad to welcome him.

He who has not enough faith will not be able to command faith from others.

(Tao Teh King 23)

Nature says few words: hence it is that a squall lasts not a whole morning. A rainstorm continues not a whole day. Where do they come from? From Nature. Even Nature does not last long (in its utterances), how much less should human beings? Byrn: "Nature uses few words: when the gale blows, it will not last long; when it rains hard, it lasts but a little while; what causes these to happen? Heaven and Earth. Why do we humans go on endlessly about little when nature does much in a little time?" This is really quite clear. We should give only the amount of attention

23. Identification with Tao

to a subject that it really needs and then let it go. The same is true of action. Our actions should be very economic and efficient. We should do a thing with the minimum expenditure of energy, involvement and attention. This does not mean we live absent-mindedly, carelessly, slovenly and miserly with time and energy, but that we should do all things as simply and effectively as we can. That itself will conserve energy. Another reason for doing this is to keep ourselves from obsessing on things and getting stuck up in them, having them revolve around and around in our mind to no end but frustration and pain.

Basically, we should live with a light touch, which does involve both simplicity and frugality. The idea of someone living in splendor and luxury while indifferent to it is absurd. Who retains what they are indifferent to? A king may have a palace, but if he is a wise king he will live simply and never lavishly.

One of the most splendid places in the world is the Vatican. Its contents are beyond price, and certainly beyond any other place in the world. There are entire countries whose assets cannot equal the Vatican's. Yet the Pope lives in incredible simplicity. Pope Pius XII's bedroom was tiny with little more than his cast-iron bedstead. All worthy Popes have lived with great frugality, however the unworthy may have indulged themselves.

Paramhansa Yogananda lived in two little rooms with a little kitchen across the hall. In one of his talks he speaks of having only a little box with a slot in the top for money. He never counted it, but it always contained enough. His mind was in God, so the universe was his. The same was true of Swami Sivananda, who lived in total simplicity.

My sannyasa guru, Swami Vidyananda Giri, lived in a small, barren room containing a plain wooden bed, a tiny wood table and two wooden chairs. He possessed two changes of clothes, one chaddar (shawl) and one pair of canvas shoes. He was providing education (mostly free of charge) for nearly one thousand rural students, many of whom were residents. Yet, when visiting government officers asked him how much money he was given a month by the spiritual organization he was affiliated with, he laughed and truthfully told them: twenty rupees a month (at that time exactly two American dollars).

They were not just surprised, they were shocked. How, then, they asked did he manage? "God provides just enough," he replied. They were so impressed that even though the war with China was going on and most government aid to schools had been cut or stopped, on their recommendation he was given five hundred thousand rupees! God does provide. That is the real lesson. If we make the Tao our support, our very existence, we will live lightly and happily.

Therefore it is that: He who follows the Tao is identified with the Tao. He who follows Character (Teh) is identified with Character. He who abandons (Tao) is identified with abandonment (of Tao). He who is identified with Tao–Tao is also glad to welcome him. He who is identified with character–character is also glad to welcome him. He who is identified with abandonment–abandonment is also glad to welcome him. He who has not enough faith will not be able to command faith from others. Byrn: "If you open yourself to the Tao, you and Tao become one. If you open yourself to Virtue, then you can become virtuous. If you open yourself to loss, then you will become lost. If you open yourself to the Tao, the Tao will eagerly welcome you. If you open yourself to virtue, virtue will become a part of you. If you open yourself to loss, the lost are glad to see you. When you do not trust people, people will become untrustworthy." Sri Ramakrishna used to say: "Mind is everything," and so it is. Everything about us in this realm of relative existence is a manifestation of our mind, which includes will. If our mind is changed, really changed, those things change, too. Over and over throughout history unfit people have been given everything they needed only to wreck everything and put themselves right back in the mud wallow. This is why Gandhi advocated teaching beggars to work for a living rather than just giving money that would be spent in a day, returning them to their former state. In this way many were rescued from poverty.

Lao Tzu tells us that what we choose to identify with will be just what we will become in this world. Whatever we choose, that will be awaiting us, for the world is but a mirror for our divine, creative will. Our entire surroundings are revelations of our mind. So if we choose the Tao, we will be revealed as the Tao.

24. THE DREGS AND TUMORS OF VIRTUE

> He who stands on tiptoe does not stand (firm); he who strains his strides does not walk (well); he who reveals himself is not luminous; he who justifies himself is not far-famed; he who boasts of himself is not given credit; he who prides himself is not chief among men. These in the eyes of Tao are called "the dregs and tumors of Virtue," which are things of disgust. Therefore the man of Tao spurns them.
>
> (Tao Teh King 24)

The Feng and English translation is a bit more on target: "He who stands on tiptoe is not steady. He who strides cannot maintain the pace. He who makes a show is not enlightened. He who is self-righteous is not respected. He who boasts achieves nothing. He who brags will not endure. According to followers of the Tao, 'These are extra food and unnecessary luggage.' They do not bring happiness. Therefore followers of the Tao avoid them."

He who stands on tiptoe is not steady. Those who try to overreach themselves and try to appear to others as much more than they really are, are always uncertain, in flux and unbalanced. In time they fall over, such is the folly of the ego. But those who stand firmly on the ground with feet secure, will be certain, steady and balanced, able to cope with any forces that might seek to push them over. Honesty with themselves and others is an essential character of the wise. Truth in living is as important as truth in speech.

He who strides cannot maintain the pace. Here again we have the folly of those that overextend themselves in the hope of gaining the admiration of others for qualities they do not really have. Such persons may maintain a good appearance for a short while but soon they stumble and fall, making their real status clear to all.

He who makes a show is not enlightened. Legge: "He who displays himself does not shine." In Greek there is a term: *agia phania*, "holy show." In religion this takes many forms of outer display, and the same is true of "show" in any area of life. The very fact that a person must make a show of something is an indication of his lacking it. For a show is an appearance only, not a reality. Many people are busy starring in the theater of life, but not really living at all since they are so absorbed in being a lie.

He who is self-righteous is not respected. Legge: "He who asserts his own views is not distinguished." Those who let the world know how good or intelligent, or capable, or whatever they are, are not such at all. Those who display themselves or seek to force themselves and their ways and ideas on others are only mirages, not real people. They are themselves lies.

He who boasts achieves nothing. Legge: "He who vaunts himself does not find his merit acknowledged." I think we all know braggarts who exemplify the old adage: "The empty wagon rattles the most." Nothing ever comes of them since all their energy is spent in claiming to be something rather than really being it. Their boasting is a dead-end. Such people end up with nothing but themselves: a pitiful reward, indeed.

He who brags will not endure. Legge: "He who is self-conceited has no superiority allowed to him." Arrogance, pride and boasting are sure pathways to loss and ruin. I knew a very wise old man who, when he saw such persons, would laugh and say: "They are headed for the ashheap, and it won't be long now." Many years of intelligent observation had given him that insight, and now over fifty years after his sharing that with me, I can say it is my observation, too. "Pride goeth before destruction, and an haughty spirit before a fall" (Proverbs 16:18), is as true as the day it was first spoken.

24. The Dregs and Tumors of Virtue

According to followers of the Tao, "These are extra food and unnecessary luggage." They do not bring happiness. Therefore followers of the Tao avoid them. Legge: "Such conditions, viewed from the standpoint of the Tao, are like remnants of food, or a tumor on the body, which all dislike. Hence those who pursue (the course) of the Tao do not adopt and allow them." Let us turn from all these follies and seek the Tao in all things and in ourselves.

25. The Four Eternal Models

Before the Heaven and Earth existed there was something nebulous:

Silent, isolated, standing alone, changing not, eternally revolving without fail, worthy to be the Mother of All Things.

I do not know its name and address it as Tao. If forced to give it a name, I shall call it "Great." Being great implies reaching out in space, reaching out in space implies far-reaching, far-reaching implies reversion to the original point.

Therefore: Tao is Great, the Heaven is great, the Earth is great, the King is also great. There are the Great Four in the universe, and the King is one of them.

Man models himself after the Earth; the Earth models itself after Heaven; the Heaven models itself after Tao; Tao models itself after nature.

(Tao Teh King 25)

Before the Heaven and Earth existed there was something nebulous: silent, isolated, standing alone, changing not, eternally revolving without fail, worthy to be the Mother of All Things. This is the potential for manifestation known in Sanskrit as Mulashakti or Mulaprakriti: Primal Power that breathes without breath and moves without motion, not to be confused with the manifestation we call Shakti or Prakriti. It is more allied to Pradhana, the primordial "substance" that evolves into Divine Energy, producing the evolving cosmos and the evolving vehicles within the cosmos in which the individual consciousnesses are embodied. It is this understanding that divides the Oriental religions from those of the West.

The West sees relative existence as a kind of mechanistic toy, totally unlike the Toymaker who uses it for his amusement, destroying it when it displeases him and venting his anger and frustration on it when it does not go according to his intentions. Human beings are caught in the middle of this, subject to materiality yet desperately needing to placate the Toymaker and win his favor so he will eventually take them out of the present toy and put them into a better one for their own enjoyment. What happens then is anyone's guess.

The East sees our present status as living entities within a living "womb" whose purpose is to lead us into higher and higher "births" which enable us to become increasingly more conscious until we realize our eternal and infinite potential, recognizing ourselves as waves or points in an infinite expanse of Life and Consciousness which is our own essential being. At the full opening of our consciousness we realize that we are ourselves the source and empowerer of this entire process of perfection, that perfection has always been ours in potential, that nothing has ever begun or ended for us, only manifested within our own consciousness linked to Infinite Consciousness.

I do not know its name and address it as Tao. If forced to give it a name, I shall call it "Great." The Tao is not great in the sense of being big or powerful, but in the sense of being Everything and Nothing at the same time, embracing both form and formlessness, being and non-being, life and death, knowing and unknowing, while transcending them all and remaining what It has always been.

Being great implies reaching out in space, reaching out in space implies far-reaching, far-reaching implies reversion to the original point. It has long been said that if we go far enough in a straight line we will eventually come back to the original point. That is the way of the Tao. Its very greatness means that eventually It returns to Its original unmanifested potential state. In the beginning is the ending. A yogi needs to keep this in mind when considering the nature of his practice and its ultimate purpose.

Therefore: Tao is Great, the Heaven is great, the Earth is great, the King is also great. There are the Great Four in the universe, and the King is one of them. Heaven and Earth are the manifested duality of the power, taking on the forms of endless dwandwas or "pairs of opposites." (I will let you formulate your own list.) "The King" here represents any human power which affects us, and that includes our own power. At the time of Lao Tzu the Emperor was an absolute force that had unlimited power over all within the boundaries of his empire. The King can also represent the forces of nature, as we will see from the next verse.

Man models himself after the Earth; the Earth models itself after Heaven; the Heaven models itself after Tao; Tao models itself after nature. Naturally man conforms to the material world around him and therefore mistakenly identifies with it. The "earth" is material creation which ever expands and strives to transcend itself in order to return to the measureless "heaven" of creative intelligence from which it expanded and became separate. Heaven is the direct "offspring" of Tao and consequently seeks to reunite to the Tao as the earth seeks to reunite with heaven. The Tao, in contrast with those that seek to be like the higher, seeks to conform to the lower, to Mother Nature spoken of in the opening verse. That is, the Tao reaches out to the further reaches of manifestation, secure in the sureness of eventually returning to Its own starting point. Someone has said that waves are the laughter of the ocean, and all its extensions are the joyful play of the Tao. In India this is known as the Nitya and the Lila, the Absolute and Its momentary play at being the ever-changing many while yet remaining at rest in Its own unchanging nature.

26. Heaviness and Lightness

> The Solid is the root of the light; the Quiescent is the master of the hasty. Therefore the Sage travels all day yet never leaves his provision-cart. In the midst of honor and glory, he lives leisurely, undisturbed. How can the ruler of a great country make light of his body in the empire (by rushing about)? In light frivolity, the Center is lost; in hasty action, self-mastery is lost.
>
> (Tao Teh King 26)

Human beings habitually live backwards like Merlin. That is, they confuse cause with effect, and continually mistake the order in which things arise. They also confuse things with one another. For thoroughly negative people, peace is war and war is peace, virtue is vice and vice is virtue. So Lao Tzu is going to dispel some of our misperceptions.

The universe is composed of two basic processes: involution and evolution. They are mirror images of one another, exact opposites. For example, the involution process involves moving from formlessness into form, but evolution involves moving from form into formlessness. In this section of the Tao Teh King Lao Tzu is speaking of evolution.

The Solid is the root of the light. Legge: "Gravity is the root of lightness." We must first be perfectly "grounded," defined and stabilized, before we can consciously, intelligently and purposefully begin to refine, expand, and ultimately resolve back into all-pervasive formlessness, into pure consciousness.

The Quiescent is the master of the hasty. Legge: "Stillness, the ruler of movement." We cannot act meaningfully until we can be perfectly still within action, identifying with the core of silent, unmoving consciousness that is at the heart of everything.

Therefore the Sage travels all day yet never leaves his provision-cart. Legge: "Therefore a wise prince, marching the whole day, does not go far from his baggage wagons." We must never leave the center of our existence, spirit-consciousness, however far we "travel" in our lifespan. For that is the essence of our life, our very existence. To forget our selves in wandering through earthly life is to invite frustration, misery, decay, and death.

In the midst of honor and glory, he lives leisurely, undisturbed. Legge: "Although he may have brilliant prospects to look at, he quietly remains (in his proper place), indifferent to them." Unpleasant things at least have the advantage of causing us to withdraw into ourselves in defense and retain our independence and integrity. But pleasant things may draw us outward into identification with them and forgetfulness of our true nature as the Tao. We may literally lose ourselves in them. Great and wise, then, is the one who can live in the midst of glamor and glory, untouched and undisturbed by it.

How can the ruler of a great country make light of his body in the empire (by rushing about)? Legge: "How should the lord of a myriad chariots carry himself lightly before the kingdom?" Our life sphere is our "kingdom," but we must not trivialize ourselves by becoming so absorbed in the kingdom that we forget our kingship and forsake our throne. The sage is the absolute opposite of the shallow and trivial people who rush around "living life" to their own detriment.

In light frivolity, the Center is lost. Legge: "If he does act lightly, he has lost his root (of gravity)." This is a truth that should occupy our concern. Although there are many ills in the world today, perhaps cheapness, shallowness, insubstantiality and triviality are the worst of all. Our "consumer society" is the fruition of such deadly roots.

In hasty action, self-mastery is lost. Legge: "If he proceed to active movement, he will lose his throne." Once again we encounter the necessity to act from the still point within so that only the body acts while the mind and spirit remain in perfect stillness. In this way all things can be accomplished within the ever-moving, ever-quiescent Tao.

27. On Stealing the Light

A good runner leaves no track. A good speech leaves no flaws for attack. A good reckoner makes use of no counters.

A well-shut door makes use of no bolts, and yet cannot be opened. A well-tied knot makes use of no rope, and yet cannot be untied.

Therefore the Sage is good at helping men; for that reason there is no rejected (useless) person. He is good at saving things; for that reason there is nothing rejected. This is called stealing the Light.

Therefore the good man is the Teacher of the bad. And the bad man is the lesson of the good.

He who neither values his teacher nor loves the lesson is one gone far astray, though he be learned. Such is the subtle secret.

(Tao Teh King 27)

None of these statements are meant to be taken literally. Lao Tzu is speaking of living life skillfully, to use the parlance of Buddha.

A good runner leaves no track. Along with those absurd Young People The World Is Now In Your Hands graduation speeches, modern youth are bombarded with the insistence that they should "leave their mark" in the world, that they should leave the world a different place from the way they entered it. "Making a difference" is a kind of idol reared in today's society.

27. On Stealing the Light

To pass through the world so subtly and lightly as to leave not a trace is a high ideal, but it can be accomplished by those who live illumined by the Inner Light. The sage does not live in the world, nor does the world live in him. Neither bothers or influences the other, but each goes their own way in peace. The Bhagavad Gita describes such a one as "he who agitates not the world, and whom the world agitates not" (12:15).

Although the sage will have no effect on the world and those immersed in the world, he may have a profound effect on those like himself. There are many accounts given of great masters simply walking by someone and that person following and seeking contact with them, as in the case of Jesus and Saint Matthew (Matthew 9:9). Saint John wrote of the experience of himself and his brother James. Seeing Jesus walk by, they followed after him. "Then Jesus turned, and saw them following, and saith unto them, What seek ye? They said unto him, Rabbi, (which is to say, being interpreted, Master,) where dwellest thou? He saith unto them, Come and see. They came and saw where he dwelt, and abode with him that day" (John 1:38-39). As bees come to the flower, so ripened souls come into the orbit of great souls and are helped by coming into contact with them. But the seeking is all on the side of the "bees," the flower simply remains what it is. In India I right away discovered that the wise would not speak a word of wisdom unless asked, but the ignorant would take every opportunity to sermonize whomever they could corner.

The sage does not make a difference in those who seek him out. Rather, the seekers make a difference in themselves (just as he did previously) by learning from him and applying it in their lives. All real change comes from within at the will of the individual. The wise know this to be unfailingly true. So "a good runner leaves no track." He ignores the world and the world ignores him: an ideal arrangement.

A good speech leaves no flaws for attack. Legge: "The skillful speaker says nothing that can be found fault with or blamed." The only way this can be true is if the sage only speaks to the worthy. If the world hears his words it goes into a tailspin and tries to silence him. So Lao Tzu is speaking of the teachings of a master-soul to qualified hearers. Such a one teaches perfectly, for he not only coveys his ideas in a manner that informs and removes all doubts even before they can arise, he also teaches fully, leaving not a word unsaid. In this way the student has complete understanding of all he hears. The Chandogya Upanishad tells us about a seeker named Satyakama and his teacher Gautama. At one point the text says: "To him, he then declared it [the truth of the Self]. In it nothing whatsoever was left out, yea, nothing was left out" (Chandogya Upanishad 4:9.3). So it is. The sage leaves nothing out, nor does he waste the student's time with irrelevant and trivial words.

A good reckoner makes use of no counters. Legge: "The skillful reckoner uses no tallies." Wu: "Good calculation makes no use of counting-slips." Since the abacus was invented much later than Lao Tzu, this does not refer to it, but considering the practical genius of the Chinese people, it is certainly likely that some kind of calculation device was in use at his time, though Wu thinks it means some kind of written notation or "scratch sheets." Whichever it might be, the idea is that the good mathematician does all calculation in his head with no external assist or expression whatever. This is symbolic of the totally inward life and perception of the sage. He needs no external source to draw from nor an external means of expression, but retains everything in his skillful intellect (buddhi). Such a one does not look outside to find truth, but looks inward. In this way he comes to know all things, while those of externalized consciousness stumble around either seeing nothing or perceiving only partially. The complete picture is to be "seen" only within. All solutions to all problems are internally discovered, as well as the understanding as to what is a problem and what is not, what should be considered and what should be ignored.

Again, as in the first sentence, we are being given a picture of a thoroughly self-contained and independent individual. The sage is at no time "a member of society," but lives in solitude wherever he may be, even in a crowded place. Saint Silouan of Mount Athos once commented that many people go into desert places and take the whole world with them, but Saint John of Kronstadt, though surrounded day and night by many people, was always alone in his inmost self.

A well-shut door makes use of no bolts, and yet cannot be opened. Legge: "The skillful closer needs no bolts or bars, while to open what he has shut will be impossible." Wu: "Good shutting makes no use of bolt and bar, And yet nobody can undo it." As just mentioned, the sage is a solitary being. His "door" is well shut and cannot be opened. In relation to society this is especially true. As Emily Dickinson wrote:

The soul selects her own society,
Then shuts the door;
On her divine majority
Obtrude no more.

Unmoved, she notes the chariot's pausing
At her low gate;
Unmoved, an emperor is kneeling
Upon her mat.

I've known her from an ample nation
Choose one;
Then close the valves of her attention
Like stone.

This also means that when a sage shuts the door on ignorance and evil they are excluded forever, that he totally expunges all misperception and wrong thinking from his mind. Rebirth is also a closed door to him as are all forms of weakness and failing. Living in an iron fortress he is safe, secure, and at peace. Yet he need not hide away from anything, for he knows how to exclude externals without necessarily secluding himself. That is why Lao Tzu continues:

A well-tied knot makes use of no rope, and yet cannot be untied. Legge: "The skillful binder uses no strings or knots, while to unloose what he has bound will be impossible." Wu: "Good tying makes no use of rope and knot, And yet nobody can untie it." Having determined in his mind what is to be shut out from his consciousness, he accomplishes this exclusion by an act of will, a sankalpa, which is a life-changing exercise of will or determination. A sage never wishes, he wills. And what he wills in that moment comes to be. The wise make no use of externals to accomplish what they will. Thus it cannot be reversed or dissolved.

This has a very practical application. Lao Tzu further says:

Therefore the Sage is good at helping men; for that reason there is no rejected (useless) person. Because the sage is totally self-contained, neither needing nor wanting anything from others, he is of great benefit to the true, worthy seeker, for he leaves him alone in freedom. If the seeker ignores what he is taught or if he follows it, it is all the same to the sage, for he knows that everyone is moving at the right pace in exactly the right place on the path to liberation. As Krishna says: "One acts according to one's own prakriti–even the wise man does so. Beings follow their own prakriti; what will restraint accomplish?" (Bhagavad Gita 3:33). Even if it were possible to influence another, such a thing would be a terrible transgression, an act of spiritual sociopathy. Religion attempts to do it all the time, and only ends up with discontented hypocrites.

If the seeker is moving toward freedom, he must be given freedom at every step along the way. That does not mean that the teacher does not warn against missteps, but his warning is only for the student's information. The choice must be his alone. Trying to motivate the student is deadly, for the only right motivation comes from within, not from without. Attempting to influence the student by speaking of reward and punishment, even of "right" and "wrong," "do" or "don't," is unknown to the real sage. Enslavement in any form is despicable to an honest person, and certainly to a wise one. Buddha said that a true teacher is like a finger pointing to the moon in silence. There is no attempt to persuade anyone to look at the moon, only a simple indication. The intelligent look up and see, and the ignorant just keep plodding on looking down. A good and true teacher is a teacher of men, not a trainer of animals.

The sage rejects no one, for he knows the eternal potential of each person. Nevertheless, his illumined vibration ensures that the unfit pass on and do not become groupies or fixtures in his orbit. That is why multitudes crowd around false teachers, while only a comparative handful remain near a great master. Sri Gajanana Maharaj of Nashik was one of the most remarkable yogis of the first half of the twentieth century, yet he was almost totally unknown in Nashik, and a few years before his leaving this world it was estimated that he had less than fifty students. The same was true of Paramhansa Yogananda's guru, Swami Sriyukteswar Giri.

In the twelfth chapter of his autobiography Yogananda says this: "…Master was not popular with superficial students. The wise, always few in number, deeply revered him. I daresay Sri Yukteswar would have been the most sought-after guru in India had his words not been so candid and so censorious.…Students came, and generally went. Those who craved a path of oily sympathy and comfortable recognitions did not find it at the hermitage. Master offered shelter and shepherding for the aeons, but many disciples miserly demanded ego-balm as well. They departed, preferring life's countless humiliations before any humility. Master's blazing rays, the open penetrating sunshine of his wisdom, were too powerful for their spiritual sickness. They sought some lesser teacher who, shading them with flattery, permitted the fitful sleep of ignorance."

At the time Yogananda was speaking eternal wisdom on Sundays in Hollywood to gatherings of only sixty or so people, in Long Beach a fundamentalist preacher was speaking to audiences of three to four thousand, and sometimes to six thousand.

A great master like Swami Sivananda can be a clarion call to the worthy. He was merciful, kind, and loving, but he was also so awake in God that his mere presence awakened others. His faith in their divine potential communicated itself to them and they accomplished great things inwardly in the spirit and outwardly in the world where their living example inspired others. At the same time the unworthy considered him unworthy of their attention and busied themselves with lesser teachers who would welcome and flatter them.

He is good at saving things; for that reason there is nothing rejected. Through the ages it has been seen that contact with the holy can enable divine potential to manifest in those who come into their orbit, and Lao Tzu makes an interesting statement regarding the matter:

This is called stealing the Light. That is, the sage can bring forth the Light of the Tao in a true seeker's consciousness as skillfully as a thief can penetrate into a house and remove all the valuables there. A sage is like a very good safecracker. His senses of inner hearing and touch are so subtle that he can figure out the combination that will open the inmost consciousness of those around him and set them free–*if they apply it themselves.* There is no doubt that the presence of the illumined can affect and even change those who meet him, but that only lasts a short time. If they use that blessing to uplift themselves by following the master's teachings, then it will not drain away but will be compounded by the evocation of their own spiritual treasury. Otherwise the benefit will be lost completely. It is a total waste of time to approach the wise if we do not intend to become wise ourselves.

An example comes to mind from my own experience. One time a saint recommended that I see a certain popular movie. Knowing that it was all about brutality and violence, I was determined not to see it, even though I respected the saint. And there we have the first lesson: admiring and respecting a sage means absolutely nothing if we do not listen to him. Anyway, after some time a friend came to visit me and was very eager to see that motion picture, so reluctantly I went with him to see it, and it changed my life, literally. During the picture I experienced profound and detailed past life recall which made clear where I was at that point in my development and the way in which I should proceed for further progress. The second lesson is obvious: pay attention to the words of the wise and wisdom will open to us. I must admit to several times ignoring the counsel of holy ones, but in time I would follow their words and be astounded at the results. So I learned to look, listen and do.

Therefore the good man is the Teacher of the bad. Since all are part of the Tao, all are essentially good, "bad" being only an illusory veneer. However, human beings are caught in the web of bad dreams and need to extricate themselves. But how will they do it? Through the teaching of the truly good, whether they learn from them directly, face-to-face, or whether they learn through written records of their teaching. True masters never die, their bodies only disappear from our sight. Having become infinite, they are always just as present in the world as they were when "alive."

There is more to this, though. When a person resolves to attain higher consciousness and follows it up with practical application, especially in the form of meditation and other spiritual disciplines, he imperceptibly begins to transfer his consciousness, his real existence, into higher dimensions. Although he appears to still be "in the world" he increasingly becomes a resident of higher worlds, of higher levels of consciousness. In time he hardly lives in this material world at all, but mostly lives in those rarefied worlds which only the yogi can ascend to. Liberated masters are never really born into this world, even though a body vehicle appears for their habitation, nor do they ever die. That is why the great master, Yogananda, said at one of his birthday celebrations: "Yogananda was never born, nor will he ever die." When Panchanon Bhattacharya, a disciple of Yogiraj Shyama Charan Lahiri (Lahiri Mahasaya), was grieving over his master's death, the guru suddenly materialized before him and said: "Why are you sorrowing? You do not live in this world. You live with me!"

And the bad man is the lesson of the good. Wise are those who observe others and learn from both their wise and unwise ways. The good learn from the bad how not to live, just as they learn how to live from the example of the good.

He who neither values his teacher nor loves the lesson is one gone far astray, though he be learned. There is a great deal of wisdom in what we consider children's rhymes and fairy stories. Many of them contain profound wisdom, especially the stories that often have practical esoteric teaching. Although the teacher rejects none and freely shares his knowledge, that does not prevent unqualified people and even outright fools from approaching him. I always think of such people as Simple Simons, for the little comic poem portrays them quite well.

> Simple Simon met a pieman,
>   Going to the fair.

Said Simple Simon to the pieman,
    "Let me taste your ware."

Said the pieman unto Simon,
    "Show me first your penny."
Said Simple Simon to the pieman,
    "Indeed I have not any."

Simply being interested in higher consciousness means very little if the seeker does not have the requisite inner development and will power to understand the principles of spiritual life and to persevere in the practice of spiritual disciplines. People of this type always say things such as: "I am sincerely interested," "I realize it is time for me to get serious," and "I am willing to do whatever is needed." These noble statements are mere sham intended to impress the prospective teacher and get him to overlook their obvious lack of qualification for even the rudiments of spiritual life. The fact is, they do not have the "penny" necessary to "purchase" (comprehend and value) authentic wisdom, much less apply it. So in time they get bored or disillusioned, blame the teacher and the teaching for the lack that is really in themselves, and wander on to the next diversion. But if the teacher is as unworthy as are they, they stay around for life, secure and safe from making any real change in their life or awareness.

What do they lack? The rest of the poem tells it all:

Simple Simon went a-fishing,
    For to catch a whale;
But all the water he had got
    Was in his mother's pail.

Without increasing his understanding by study and listening and certainly without purifying his mind and heart by discipline, the Simple Simon thinks to catch the whale of boundless divine consciousness in the tiny pail of his mind which he has not enlarged since childhood.

27. On Stealing the Light

Often such types chortle over "childlike saints" and the need to "become as little children" to excuse their mental and spiritual infantilism. And they love the silly little ditty about "It's a gift to be simple." It is their habit to say at every opportunity: "It's really all so simple." I knew a person like this, and after the umpteenth time of hearing how simple it all was, I said: "Yes. It is so 'simple' it doesn't even work!" And of course that is the intention.

> Simple Simon went to look,
>   If plums grew on a thistle;
> He pricked his fingers very much,
>   Which made poor Simon whistle.

A favorite Simple Simon ploy is to ask stupid questions or make stupid statements *ad infinitum* as an intellectual smokescreen to veil their utter emptiness of mind and soul. One of their favorite activities is looking for the right thing in the wrong place so they will be guaranteed not to find it. They especially love foolish and shallow teachers to whom they "resonate" readily. Sometimes they rhapsodize about such teachers to let a real teacher know that if he does not do what they like or want he may "lose" them (a blessing he would welcome gladly).

Simple Simons "whistle" a lot about how disappointed and even "hurt" they are, but they never see that it is the result of their own foolish deeds.

> He went for water in a sieve,
>   But soon it all fell through;
> And now poor Simple Simon
>   Bids you all adieu.

Since they have a mind and heart like a sieve, shot full of holes by worldly ways and wrong thinking, whatever "water" the teacher gives them falls to the ground almost immediately. Simple Simons are continually having to be told the same things over and over. Constantly they come up with problems that are no problems, troubles that are no troubles, and baseless arguments and excuses in relation to what they have been taught. The teacher may waste his time explaining and "helping" them to "understand," and as they leave they turn and smile broadly and say: "I'm so glad we had this talk. I really needed to hear these things." And one or two days later they are right back at Square One. They also at some time will demand of the teacher: "Why can't you accept me as I am?"

Now a teacher may not reject anyone in the sense of not seeing that person's divine Self, but that does not mean he wastes his time with Simple Simons. Quite some time ago the BBC made a funny series called *Hallelujah!* about a Salvation Army officer (played by Thora Hurd). In one episode a sleazy family showed up and began demanding all sorts of "help" and attention. At one point they even claimed the doctor had prescribed gin for "Dad" as a medicine, and expected the Salvation Army to supply it to him. One weekend they went away for a vacation (it is amazing how professionally "poor" people suddenly find the money to do what they want) and when they came back "mum" showed up for some more handouts. But she was told that the officers had decided they should panhandle elsewhere. Like all such frauds, the woman whined: "I thought you were *Christians*!" To which she got the reply: "Christians, yes. But damn fools, NO." So authentic teachers often get rid of fake seekers by stating the simple truth to them. I particularly enjoyed watching Swami Sivananda do this. He was kind and even used humor, but he got the point across. Some really got the idea and straightened up and others left in a huff. But truth prevailed, always.

Anyhow, laying aside ego-based "compassion," it is always wonderful to hear the words: "And now poor [put-upon and mistreated] Simple Simon bids you all adieu," that are music to the ears of the teacher. Indeed, there is joy in heaven over a sinner that reforms himself (Luke 15:7), but there is a great sigh of relief over an incorrigible sinner that departs, having "gone far astray" in his heart long before. Again, truth prevails.

Such is the subtle secret.

Wu: "This is an essential tenet of the Tao." We must learn to discern the true and the false in the people around us and respond accordingly, for good sense in relation to ourselves and others is definitely an aspect of the Tao.

28. Keeping to the Female

He who is aware of the Male but keeps to the Female becomes the ravine of the world. Being the ravine of the world, he has the original character (*teh*) which is not cut up. And returns again to the (innocence of the) babe.

He who is conscious of the white (bright) but keeps to the black (dark) becomes the model for the world. Being the model for the world, he has the eternal power which never errs, and returns again to the Primordial Nothingness.

He who is familiar with honor and glory but keeps to obscurity becomes the valley of the world. Being the valley of the world, he has an eternal power which always suffices, and returns again to the natural integrity of uncarved wood.

Break up this uncarved wood and it is shaped into a vessel. In the hands of the Sage they become the officials and magistrates. Therefore the great ruler does not cut up.

(Tao Teh King 28)

Existence has two (seeming) aspects, the transcendent and the immanent, the Absolute and the Relative. One is an absolute Unity and the other is an absolute Duality, even though they are both the one Tao. The Tao is one, yet It is also dual as is illustrated in the yin-yang symbol. In the Tao Teh King this duality is spoken of in more than one place as "male" and "female." In Indian cosmology the passive transcendent principle is considered male and the active creative power which manifests as the

28. Keeping to the Female

entire field of relative existence in considered to be feminine (though this was not always so, as the symbol of Nataraja indicates). In Taoism the opposite is postulated: the passive is feminine and the active is masculine. We must keep this in mind whenever the Tao Teh King speaks of male and female.

He who is aware of the Male but keeps to the Female becomes the ravine of the world. There is no reason to tune out material existence. Certainly the artificial world of human making is mostly deadly or useless, but the natural world around us is both beneficial and necessary. The yogi is keenly aware of the natural world, but does not identify with it or allow any of its phenomena to dislodge his consciousness from being centered in the spirit-self.

Those who never lose their awareness of spirit have no danger of being ensnared by matter, but I am speaking of a state of consciousness, not an intellectual outlook or attitude. Many are those who claim to be "above it all" or "understanding" materiality while being hopelessly enmeshed in and addicted to it. There is no way to spiritualize delusion, but many dishonest ways to justify it. One time while I was eating in Yogananda's marvelous vegetarian restaurant on Sunset Boulevard some carnivore related to me that when Edgar Cayce was questioned about eating a pork chop he said: "If I can't raise the vibration of this pork chop, what good am I?" I saw no reason to point out that Edgar Cayce had proved to be of very little worth, spiritually speaking, and that only a very foolish person would try to raise the vibration of a dead pig, much less waste energy doing so even if it were possible. And anyway, why EAT it? A number of people have bragged to me about their "holy" drug use and sacred sexual indulgence, but their state of mind and life proved them either liars or dupes. So "keeping to the Female" involves very real detachment and non-involvement with the world of deluded humans.

Lao Tzu informs us that those who move through the world while remaining centered in spirit-awareness will be like a ravine into which water flows: all the good and valuable elements of the world will flow to such a one naturally. He will live life to the fullest, and his time on this earth will not be a misery or a weary awaiting of death so he can escape it, though this is the attitude of negative religion. Rather, his life will be full and a means of his development, inner and outer. There is no richer or more satisfying life than that of the yogi, as the Bhagavad Gita describes so beautifully. Here is the result of "keeping to the Female":

"Yoga-yoked, with the lower self purified, with the lower self subdued, whose senses are conquered, whose Self has become the Self of all beings–he is not tainted even when acting.

"'I do not do anything;' thus thinks the steadfast knower of truth while seeing, hearing, touching, smelling, eating, walking, sleeping, breathing, speaking, releasing, and holding, opening and closing his eyes–convinced that it is the senses that move among the sense-objects.

"Offering actions to Brahman, having abandoned attachment, he acts untainted by evil as a lotus leaf is not wetted by water. Karma yogis perform action only with the body, mind, intellect, or the senses, forsaking attachment, performing action for self-purification.

"He who is steadfast, having abandoned action's fruit, attains lasting peace. He who is not steadfast, attached to action based on desire, is bound. Renouncing all actions with the mind, the embodied one sits happily as the ruler of the city of nine gates, not acting at all, nor causing action.

"Those whose minds are absorbed in That, whose Selves are fixed on That, whose foundation is That, who hold That as the highest object, whose evils have been shaken off by knowledge, attain the ending of rebirth" (Bhagavad Gita 5:7-13, 17).

Being the ravine of the world, he has the original character (teh) which is not cut up. Identifying with the Eternal Witness, the Tao, the sage returns to and lives in perfect and undisturbed Unity. Fragmentation is the root evil of the deluded and bewildered who stumble through life after life in this world. Only when the mind and heart are unified along with the body can peace and wisdom be attained. To live in and as The One is the secret of freedom.

And returns again to the babe. Taoist texts speak of the spiritual embryo: the arising in the consciousness of the original state of Tao. We must all return to that primal state. Jesus was referring to that when he prayed: "O Father, glorify thou me with thine own self with the glory which I had with thee before the world was" (John 17:5). We must be clothed again in the Tao, the Tao must become our body and soul. Nothing but the Tao can remain in our consciousness, for the Tao IS consciousness. We must "know" the Tao and "unknow" everything else. The Tao is the Divine Darkness which is the only true Light. All viable mystical traditions tell us this and urge us onward to its realization.

He who is conscious of the white (bright) but keeps to the black (dark) becomes the model for the world. Those who can be aware of and deal successfully with the world and yet never lose awareness of their true nature are a model for all sentient life. Why?

Being the model for the world, he has the eternal power which never errs, and returns again to the Primordial Nothingness. Conserving his inner powers by refusing to expend them in externals, especially in emotions and desires, he is enabled to return to that Unity which existed before Diversity and to which all must return, for that is the sole Goal of evolving life.

He who is familiar with honor and glory but keeps to obscurity becomes the valley of the world. Being the valley of the world, he has an eternal power which always suffices, and returns again to the natural integrity of uncarved wood. This is a reaffirmation of the first two verses. Those who prefer to be unknown to a world which clamors for notoriety (usually undeserved) become reservoirs of creative power which develops into recreative power which of its own turns back to the Primal Integrity and rejoices in the peace and stillness of eternal Formlessness that is hidden by form.

Break up this uncarved wood and it is shaped into a vessel. In the hands of the Sage they become the officials and magistrates. Therefore the great ruler does not cut up. To make something we must destroy the unity and integrity of the material(s) from which it is to be made. That is why the Zen Master Seung Sung advocated the simple maxim: "Make Nothing." It is the same with people: they can be "made" into many things, but in the "making" they cease to be what they really are. The great authorities, the masters of wisdom such as Lao Tzu, show us how to be what we are, for we can really be nothing else. As long as we try to be something we are not, only great confusion, pain, and evil can result. A yogi I once travelled with in the West was approached by a child on a ferry boat. Seeing his Indian sadhu clothing as well as his long hair and beard, she asked him: "What are you supposed to be?" He smiled radiantly and answered: "Oh, just What I'm supposed to be!"

The truly wise do not disturb the original integrity of people or things. In this way the Tao alone prevails.

29. Warning Against Interference

There are those who will conquer the world and make of it (what they conceive or desire). I see that they will not succeed. (For) the world is God's own Vessel. It cannot be made (by human interference). He who makes it spoils it. He who holds it loses it.

For: Some things go forward, some things follow behind; some blow hot, and some blow cold; some are strong, and some are weak; some may break, and some may fall.

Hence the Sage eschews excess, eschews extravagance, eschews pride.

(Tao Teh King 29)

In *The Great Divorce* C. S. Lewis writes of a woman who cannot stand to not be running other people's lives. "Give me someone to 'do' something with," is her constant demand. She cannot exist on her own, but must live through others. A great many people do this, not least those addicted to "spectator sports" as well as adulation of heroes and "stars" in many areas of life: usually all useless and mostly destructive in the long run. Terrible suffering is produced by the insistence of governments and families that their members must be ordered about and changed in various ways "for their own good." I would like to offer you some advice: Whenever anyone says to you: "I only want you to be happy…,"

RUN. For they really only want to be happy themselves by controlling and reshaping you to their ideas. Few things are more vicious.

My mother used to laugh and say: "There is not a thing in the world my father doesn't think he can't improve." Actually, he was right, for my grandfather was a great creative genius who could accomplish just about anything in the external world, especially in improving gadgets and machines. Still, the addiction to tinkering with the people and things around us can be a grave defect, as Lao Tzu now explains.

There are those who will conquer the world and make of it (what they conceive or desire). I see that they will not succeed. Wu: "Does anyone want to take the world and do what he wants with it? I do not see how he can succeed." Swami Vivekananda has expounded this far better than I ever could. Ego is at the root of the problem of "world changers," and he explained their folly in this way in his book *Karma Yoga*.

"There was a poor man who wanted some money; and somehow he had heard that if he could get hold of a ghost, he might command him to bring money or anything else he liked; so he was very anxious to get hold of a ghost. He went about searching for a man who would give him a ghost, and at last he found a sage with great powers, and besought his help. The sage asked him what he would do with a ghost. 'I want a ghost to work for me; teach me how to get hold of one, sir; I desire it very much,' replied the man. But the sage said, 'Don't disturb yourself, go home.' The next day the man went again to the sage and began to weep and pray, 'Give me a ghost; I must have a ghost, sir, to help me.' At last the sage was disgusted, and said, 'Take this charm, repeat this magic word, and a ghost will come, and whatever you say to him he will do. But beware; they are terrible beings, and must be kept continually busy. If you fail to give him work, he will take your life.' The man replied, 'That is easy; I can give him work for all his life.' Then he went to a forest, and after long repetition of the magic word, a huge ghost appeared before him, and said, 'I am a ghost. I have been conquered by your magic; but you must keep me constantly employed. The moment you fail to give me work I will kill you.' The man said, 'Build me a palace,' and the ghost said, 'It is done; the palace is built.'

'Bring me money,' said the man. 'Here is your money,' said the ghost. 'Cut this forest down, and build a city in its place.' 'That is done,' said the ghost, 'anything more?' Now the man began to be frightened and thought he could give him nothing more to do; he did everything in a trice. The ghost said, 'Give me something to do or I will eat you up.' The poor man could find no further occupation for him, and was frightened. So he ran and ran and at last reached the sage, and said, 'Oh, sir, protect my life!' The sage asked him what the matter was, and the man replied, 'I have nothing to give the ghost to do. Everything I tell him to do he does in a moment, and he threatens to eat me up if I do not give him work.' Just then the ghost arrived, saying, 'I'll eat you up,' and he would have swallowed the man. The man began to shake, and begged the sage to save his life. The sage said, 'I will find you a way out. Look at that dog with a curly tail. Draw your sword quickly and cut the tail off and give it to the ghost to straighten out.' The man cut off the dog's tail and gave it to the ghost, saying, 'Straighten that out for me.' The ghost took it and slowly and carefully straightened it out, but as soon as he let it go, it instantly curled up again. Once more he laboriously straightened it out, only to find it again curled up as soon as he attempted to let go of it. Again he patiently straightened it out, but as soon as he let it go, it curled up again. So he went on for days and days, until he was exhausted and said, 'I was never in such trouble before in my life. I am an old veteran ghost, but never before was I in such trouble.' 'I will make a compromise with you;' he said to the man, 'you let me off and I will let you keep all I have given you and will promise not to harm you.' The man was much pleased, and accepted the offer gladly.

"This world is like a dog's curly tail, and people have been striving to straighten it out for hundreds of years; but when they let it go, it has curled up again. How could it be otherwise? One must first know how to work without attachment, then one will not be a fanatic. When we know that this world is like a dog's curly tail and will never get straightened, we shall not become fanatics. If there were no fanaticism in the world, it would make much more progress than it does now. It is a mistake to think that fanaticism can make for the progress of mankind. On the contrary, it is a retarding element creating hatred and anger, and causing people to fight each other, and making them unsympathetic. We think that whatever we do or possess is the best in the world, and what we do not do or possess is of no value. So, always remember the instance of the curly tail of the dog whenever you have a tendency to become a fanatic. You need not worry or make yourself sleepless about the world; it will go on without you. When you have avoided fanaticism, then alone will you work well. It is the level-headed man, the calm man, of good judgment and cool nerves, of great sympathy and love, who does good work and so does good to himself. The fanatic is foolish and has no sympathy; he can never straighten the world, nor himself become pure and perfect."

(For) the world is God's own Vessel. It cannot be made (by human interference). He who makes it spoils it. He who holds it loses it. Wu: "The world is a sacred vessel, which must not be tampered with or grabbed after. To tamper with it is to spoil it, and to grasp it is to lose it." The paragraph that comes right after the words of Vivekananda cited above will complete this picture. "To recapitulate the chief points in today's lecture: First, we have to bear in mind that we are all debtors to the world and the world does not owe us anything. It is a great privilege for all of us to be allowed to do anything for the world. In helping the world we really help ourselves. The second point is that there is a God in this universe. It is not true that this universe is drifting and stands in need of help from you and me. God is ever present therein, He is undying and eternally active and infinitely watchful. When the whole universe sleeps, He sleeps not; He is working incessantly; all the changes and manifestations of the world are His. Thirdly, we ought not to hate anyone. This world will always continue to be a mixture of good and evil. Our duty is to sympathize with the weak and to love even the wrongdoer. The world is a grand moral gymnasium wherein we have all to take exercise so as to become stronger and stronger spiritually. Fourthly, we ought not to be fanatics of any kind, because fanaticism is opposed to love. You hear fanatics glibly saying, 'I do not hate the sinner. I hate the sin,' but I am prepared to go any distance to see the face of that man who can really make a distinction between the sin and the sinner. It is easy to say

so. If we can distinguish well between quality and substance, we may become perfect men. It is not easy to do this. And further, the calmer we are and the less disturbed our nerves, the more shall we love and the better will our work be."

It is essential that we come to perceive truly that the world is the ever-perfect Tao.

For: Some things go forward, some things follow behind; some blow hot, and some blow cold; some are strong, and some are weak; some may break, and some may fall. Wu: "In fact, for all things there is a time for going ahead, and a time for following behind; A time for slow-breathing and a time for fast-breathing; A time to grow in strength and a time to decay; A time to be up and a time to be down." Everything in the world changes, and a skillfully living person knows when to change his response to them in accordance with their altered character. First he must be able to perceive the change and perhaps even to anticipate the change and prepare himself for the altered circumstances. It is only natural to wish stability in our life and mind, but we must be sure that what we mistake for stability is not really stagnation. Most people have stale personalities because their lives are stale. Instead of growing and changing they have been running in the same tracks for their entire life. We all know of people who dress, speak, and act like they did when they were in high school, the "best years of their lives" to those who have remained stunted in their minds and hearts. Such people always respond just as they have always responded. They make no differentiation between past or present, so when the future arrives they are the same old "psychological antiques" to use Yogananda's expression. He said that they are so boring that when they die the angels say: "Oh, let's send this one back quickly."

Besides the teaching of this verse, it also demonstrates an important truth: the Essenes within Judaism studied the scriptures of other religions, for which they were officially condemned by the other Jews. (See *The Christ of India*.) In the book of Ecclesiastes, attributed to Solomon, we find the following:

"To every thing there is a season, and a time to every purpose under the heaven:

"A time to be born, and a time to die; a time to plant, and a time to pluck up that which is planted;

"A time to kill, and a time to heal; a time to break down, and a time to build up;

"A time to weep, and a time to laugh; a time to mourn, and a time to dance;

"A time to cast away stones, and a time to gather stones together; a time to embrace, and a time to refrain from embracing;

"A time to get, and a time to lose; a time to keep, and a time to cast away;

"A time to rend, and a time to sew; a time to keep silence, and a time to speak;

"A time to love, and a time to hate; a time of war, and a time of peace." (Ecclesiastes 3:1-8).

This is not coincidence, but a restating of what the author had read for himself in the Tao Teh King. The *Aquarian Gospel* also reveals that the Essenes were very conversant with the Taoist philosophy, and that Jesus had Taoist disciples that came to learn from him after his return to Israel from India.

Hence the Sage eschews excess, eschews extravagance, eschews pride. Wu: "Therefore, the Sage avoids all extremes, excesses and extravagances." Knowing that whatever his present situation, it will eventually change, and so will everything including the people around him, the wise man does not allow himself to overreact to anything, but to avoid extremes, excesses, and extravagances at all times, including his own internal conditions. Especially he keeps his mind and heart unclouded by intense emotional or intellectual reactions, and consequently also acts at all times in a temperate and deliberate manner. In this way he perfectly expresses the Tao.

30. Warning Against the Use of Force

He who by Tao purposes to help the ruler of men will oppose all conquest by force of arms. For such things are wont to rebound. Where armies are, thorns and brambles grow. The raising of a great host is followed by a year of dearth.

Therefore a good general effects his purpose and stops. He dares not rely upon the strength of arms; effects his purpose and does not glory in it; effects his purpose and does not boast of it; effects his purpose and does not take pride in it; effects his purpose as a regrettable necessity; effects his purpose but does not love violence.

(For) things age after reaching their prime. That (violence) would be against the Tao. And he who is against the Tao perishes young.

(Tao Teh King 30)

He who by Tao purposes to help the ruler of men will oppose all conquest by force of arms. For such things are wont to rebound. Byrn: "Those who lead people by following the Tao do not use weapons to enforce their will. Using force always leads to unseen troubles." Mabry: "A leader who is advised to rely on the Tao does not enforce his will upon the world by military means. For such things are likely to rebound." This verse applies to both nations and individuals. Military action should be avoided as much as is possible and practical because violence always causes a negative rebound, as will be explained in the second verse. Actually, government should avoid any type of coercion, for those who bring pressure on others and force them to go against their principles or will, in time will find the same thing happening to them. Those who use reason and benevolence will find the same virtues being directed at them. This also applies to individuals: kindness and reason bolstered by good example are the only way we should affect others–if possible. Of course this has to be qualified because just as there are incorrigible governments there are also incorrigible people who cannot be dealt with as rational. The basic attitude should be that following the Tao will in time bring about all that is good. Refugees from the Soviet Union told me of amazing instances of people who boldly lived in a manner that often brought imprisonment and execution of others by the Communist regime, yet those individuals would not even be reprimanded by the government, but continued to openly follow their principles and defy the evil power. Questioning about them revealed that they were perfectly honest and consistent in all things, having a completely peaceful and kindly attitude toward those that could have jailed or killed them. Patanjali said that when a person is perfect in ahimsa (non-violence) violence cannot arise in their presence. Buddha proved this more than once.

Where armies are, thorns and brambles grow. The raising of a great host is followed by a year of dearth. Byrn: "In the places where armies march, thorns and briars bloom and grow. After armies take to war, bad years must always follow." Armies of aggression bring terrible misery in their wake. It is as if the earth is cursed by the touch of their feet, and the civilians become overwhelmed with darkness of mind and heart. Liberating armies do just the opposite, fortunately. Although in a war there may be a good or "right" side, nevertheless war itself always has terrible consequences, even if evil forces were eliminated by it. For example, immediately after World War I the terrible influenza plague swept through the world and killed more people than the war had killed. Close examination shows that the countries that are forced into war in order to fight evil are without exception experiencing moral and civil degeneration afterward. After every war there is a marked lowering of the quality of civilized and moral life.

A multitude of "natural disasters" accrue to a world that tolerates and even encourages violence. Consider the last twenty-five years of the twentieth century. A heavy toll of civilian life was taken by various natural disasters in so many ways as the karmic reaction to the many small wars that raged constantly around the world.

Right now there are more people in slavery than at any time in the past. Even more surprising, although governments and media suppress knowledge of it, piracy is thriving throughout the world as well. Institutions of evil that we smugly assure ourselves have been long eliminated in our "more advanced times" are actually on the increase. And look at the proliferation of bizarre and unheard-of diseases that are bringing horror to the world daily. There is a law that demands equalization and it must be satisfied.

Yogananda has said it perfectly, as usual: "The year 1945 has also ushered in a new age–the era of revolutionary atomic energies. All thoughtful minds turn as never before to the urgent problems of peace and brotherhood, lest the continued use of physical force banish all men along with the problems.

"Though the human race and its works disappear tracelessly by time or bomb, the sun does not falter in its course; the stars keep their invariable vigil. Cosmic law cannot be stayed or changed, and man would do well to put himself in harmony with it. If the cosmos is against might, if the sun wars not with the planets but retires at dueful time to give the stars their little sway, what avails our mailed fist? Shall any peace indeed come out of it? Not cruelty but good will arms the universal sinews; a humanity at peace will know the endless fruits of victory, sweeter to the taste than any nurtured on the soil of blood."

Therefore a good general effects his purpose and stops. He dares not rely upon the strength of arms. Mabry: "A good leader accomplishes only what he has set out to do And is careful not to overestimate his ability." Wu: "What you want is to protect efficiently your own state, but not to aim at self-aggrandizement." This, too, applies to individuals and nations. Only what is truly needed should be done or aspired to. Ego must not fool us into doing more. The Bhagavad Gita describes those of demonic character as saying: "Today this has been acquired by me. This I shall also obtain. This is mine, and this gain also shall be mine. That enemy has been slain by me, and I shall slay others, too, for I am the Lord, I am the enjoyer, I am successful, powerful and happy" (Bhagavad Gita 16:13-14). This is the direct route to destruction of ourselves and others. Wise are those who know their limitations and also know when to rein in their capacities and not go further even if they are able to do so. It is important to live with the lightest possible touch in all things. Moderation and frugality in themselves are not the purpose; rather we are to learn to engage in external involvements as little as possible. In this way peace and contentment will be ours. The bulk of our attention and time should be on cultivation of the Tao.

[He] effects his purpose and does not glory in it; effects his purpose and does not boast of it; effects his purpose and does not take pride in it; effects his purpose as a regrettable necessity; effects his purpose but does not love violence. Byrn: "When victory is won over the enemy through war it is not a thing of great pride. When the battle is over, arrogance is the new enemy. War can result when no other alternative is given, so the one who overcomes an enemy should not dominate them." Wu: "After you have attained your purpose, You must not parade your success, You must not boast of your ability, You must not feel proud, You must rather regret that you had not been able to prevent the war. You must never think of conquering others by force." The nobility of this passage is so evident that there is no need to comment on it. I would like to point out that in my visits to India I have met many rajahs and maharajas and saw in them exactly what a warrior (kshatriya) should be: compassionate and interested only in the welfare of those under their care, detesting all violence and conflict, yet able to intelligently engage in it for the good of others without any enmity toward those they must oppose and conquer. They were all of outstanding courage and strength of character, yet gentle though firm and dedicated. Every one of them practiced meditation and were markedly religious. One, the Raja of Solan, whom we called Yogi

30. Warning Against the Use of Force

Bhai (Brother Yogi), was of outstanding spiritual attainment, simplicity and humility.

(For) things age after reaching their prime. That (violence) would be against the Tao. And he who is against the Tao perishes young. Byrn: "The strong always weaken with time. This is not the way of the Tao. That which is not of the Tao will soon end." Mabry: "Things that grow strong soon grow weak. This is not the Way of the Tao. Not following the Tao leads to an early end." Wu: "For to be over-developed is to hasten decay, and this is against Tao, And what is against Tao will soon cease to be." Duality is not just a law of relative manifestation, it is a law governing the externals of life. Ma Anandamayi used to say: "Getting implies losing." Everything gained must eventually be lost, otherwise we could never return to our original status and be liberated. Happily, this applies to bad as well as good, so nothing can hold to us nor can we hold to it. That is blessed freedom, frustrating to the ego but a balm to the Self. So we must realize that all our gains will in time pass away and that all the "good" we accomplish will fade away after a while. And this is as it should be, otherwise the Tao would not be unconditioned and perfect. We are the Tao, and to seek to be otherwise is to willfully suffer and fail. Consequently we should be ever detached from everything but the Tao, which we should seek and find to discover we have always been inseparable from It.

31. Weapons of Evil

Of all things, soldiers are instruments of evil, hated by men. Therefore the religious man (possessed of Tao) avoids them. The gentleman favors the left in civilian life, but on military occasions favors the right.

Soldiers are weapons of evil. They are not the weapons of the gentleman. When the use of soldiers cannot be helped, the best policy is calm restraint.

Even in victory, there is no beauty, and who calls it beautiful is one who delights in slaughter. He who delights in slaughter will not succeed in his ambition to rule the world.

The things of good omen favor the left. The things of ill omen favor the right. The lieutenant-general stands on the left, the general stands on the right. That is to say, it is celebrated as a Funeral Rite.

The slaying of multitudes should be mourned with sorrow. A victory should be celebrated with the Funeral Rite.

(Tao Teh King 31)

I have mentioned this previously, but I want to make a point of the fact that armies of liberation are not quite as awful as Lao Tzu says. But in his time such things did not exist: all armies were armies of conquest and greed that relied on violence and cruelty to win. Nevertheless there is a down side to all war as was made clear in the previous section.

31. Weapons of Evil

Of all things, soldiers are instruments of evil, hated by men. Therefore the religious man (possessed of Tao) avoids them. The gentleman favors the left in civilian life, but on military occasions favors the right. The wise avoid all forms of secular power because it eventually comes into conflict with wisdom since all things secular stem from the ego and before them all principles and convictions melt away as the foolish make all kinds of excuses and rationalizations for that. During times of peace the wise advocate calm, passivity, and non-interference, preferring to live in peace and non-involvement. But when it is necessary, he advocates strength in opposition and even aggressive conflict for the protection of that which is good and which will ensure the return to tranquility. In other words, he is never a "peace at any price" person, knowing well that some prices are much too high to pay. Regarding the venerable Swami Sri Yukteswar, his guru, Yogananda related: "My guru personally attended to the details connected with the management of his property. Unscrupulous persons on various occasions attempted to secure possession of Master's ancestral land. With determination and even by instigating lawsuits, Sri Yukteswar outwitted every opponent. He underwent these painful experiences from a desire never to be a begging guru, or a burden on his disciples."

Although the wise do not initiate conflict they must be adamant in resolving it in such a way that it will not rise again from the same roots. It is this outlook which has given rise to the martial arts of the East in which a person engages in intense conflict while remaining still in mind and heart.

This section also applies to the individual's inner life. He should refuse in his private life to engage in outer disturbances, and should ruthlessly eliminate from his inner self all forms of violence and selfish aggression. Even when he must act in opposition to wrong, he never lets that be a justification for ill will toward another. He puts forth intelligent, dispassionate effort to bring about the cessation of evil, but never utilizes the passions such as "righteous indignation," "holy anger" and other such evils masquerading as good and necessary.

Soldiers are weapons of evil. They are not the weapons of the gentleman. When the use of soldiers cannot be helped, the best policy is calm restraint.

Wise government engages in conflict governed by calmness and restraint. If this had been observed in World War I there would never have been a Nazi Germany in reaction to the unreasonable vengefulness of the Versailles Treaty, and therefore no World War II.

On a personal level, the wise never employ negative means, and even in using right means they are always calm and restrained.

Even in victory, there is no beauty, and who calls it beautiful is one who delights in slaughter. He who delights in slaughter will not succeed in his ambition to rule the world. To consider victory won by injury, destruction and death as a beautiful thing betrays the craven heart of the violent and sadistic. Those who love slaughter will never ultimately rule, for their own evil will destroy them in time.

The wise individual detests harming another and never considers any advantage won by crushing another to be truly good and desirable. Those who are ruled by malice and vengefulness will never remain for long in the ascendency. They will be their own downfall.

The things of good omen favor the left. The things of ill omen favor the right. The lieutenant-general stands on the left, the general stands on the right. That is to say, it is celebrated as a Funeral Rite. Those things that arise from calm observation and non-involvement or objective, careful, and passionless involvement in action always move toward the good. But jumping in and thrashing around with ego and emotion running at top level will end in distress and eventual ill. The lieutenant-general represents calm objectivity and quiet living, while the general represents charging ahead and "getting things done" with expenditure of life force and mental strength. It is a kind of funeral rite before the fact.

The slaying of multitudes should be mourned with sorrow. A victory should be celebrated with the Funeral Rite. This is the perspective of those who possess rare wisdom and humility. Such behavior is actually recorded in the annals of ancient India, especially in the Mahabharata, where the victory of the Pandavas was observed by them through undergoing intense spiritual discipline for purification of heart and with much grief at the loss of life on both sides.

In the same way the individual should be saddened at any "winning" which has involved the physical or mental injury of others, and should be accompanied with the endeavor to compensate for the unavoidable situation. This is why the Gita says that we should not rejoice at either victory or defeat.

32. Tao is Like the Sea

Tao is absolute and has no name.
Though the uncarved wood is small, it cannot be employed (used as vessel) by anyone.
If kings and barons can keep (this unspoiled nature), the whole world shall yield them lordship of their own accord.
The Heaven and Earth join, and the sweet rain falls, beyond the command of men, yet evenly upon all.
Then human civilization arose and there were names. Since there were names, it were well one knew where to stop. He who knows where to stop may be exempt from danger.
Tao in the world may be compared to rivers that run into the sea.
(Tao Teh King 32)

Tao is absolute and has no name. We hear about things that are "too big to be ignored," meaning they are too vital or even crucial to our welfare or so obvious that they cannot be overlooked. But the Tao is not "big" or "small" and is not "looked at" or "overlooked." Therefore the unenlightened mind has no perception of It whatsoever, and therefore no response of any kind. The mind simply cannot deal with the Tao, and in the first verse of the Tao Teh King we were told that it could not be named, much less spoken about. This approach to Reality is common to the religions of the East.

32. Tao is Like the Sea

Though the uncarved wood is small, it cannot be employed (used as vessel) by anyone. In order to be usable by human beings, wood must be shaped into a form conforming to their intentions, but the Tao is never shaped into any mode of being or function, for It cannot be "used." The Tao is eternally What It Is. Not only is the Tao inexpressible, It is untouchable. No one can relate to the Tao. They either know themselves as the Tao or they do not. As Yogananda often said, God cannot be intellectually known, but God can be known by direct experience beyond the intellect. This is because the Tao is the Truth of our being, "open vision direct and instant" (Bhagavad Gita 9:1). Knowing (Gnosis) is our nature, for we are consciousness itself. We must come to realize this for ourself. "Therefore, become a yogi" (Bhagavad Gita 6:46).

If kings and barons can keep (this unspoiled nature), the whole world shall yield them lordship of their own accord. I once read in a book (so many years ago I have no memory of its name) a fictional dialogue between Tiberius Caesar and a high Roman official who remarked that the Christian ideal of love and overcoming evil with good was impossible. "How do you know?" asked Tiberius, "No one has ever tried it." To do so would take a faith and daring that could only be supernatural. In the same way, it is doubtful that government officials would dare to put to the test Lao Tzu's assertion that if they live as manifestations of the Tao they will be acknowledged as such and listened to by all people. Considering the careers of all great master teachers of humanity, we can see why politicians would have "reasonable doubt." Yet we find this in the Gospel: "And while he yet spake, lo, Judas, one of the twelve, came, and with him a great multitude with swords and staves, from the chief priests and elders of the people.… And, behold, one of them which were with Jesus stretched out his hand, and drew his sword, and struck a servant of the high priest's, and smote off his ear. Then said Jesus unto him, Put up again thy sword into his place: for all they that take the sword shall perish with the sword. Thinkest thou that I cannot now pray to my Father, and he shall presently give me more than twelve legions of angels? But how then shall the scriptures be fulfilled, that thus it must be?" (Matthew 26:47, 51-54). So the difficulties of the great teachers of humanity are part of the natural order of things: of the Tao.

Yet we who are of lesser social order can often find Lao Tzu's principle to be true. Many spiritual aspirants find that strangers are friendly to them and that they are given help by others on occasion without having to ask for it. I have known holy people who were spontaneously loved wherever they went, but I suspect that was because they did not have "bad people karma" and so never encountered them. Nevertheless, we must endeavor to live in the Tao literally.

The Heaven and Earth join, and the sweet rain falls, beyond the command of men, yet evenly upon all. Since ego grips human beings, it is no surprise that religions claim to be the special and chosen (even the *only*) people of God. But the Tao is not an egotist and looks upon all people as integral parts of Its own Being. And in the Gita: "I am the same to all beings. There is no one who is disliked or dear to me" (Bhagavad Gita 9:29) in the sense of rejecting or favoring anyone. "The Omnipresent takes note of neither demerit nor merit" (Bhagavad Gita 5:15).

Therefore when heaven, earth, the human and the divine, are united in harmony, good will toward all prevails. Those who would be one with the Tao must cultivate this equal-vision and have benevolence toward all sentient beings.

Then human civilization arose and there were names. Since there were names, it were well one knew where to stop. He who knows where to stop may be exempt from danger. When human beings live together, obviously there must be rules all agree to, and as long as this association is simple and small, a grass-roots matter, things work very well and the integrity of the individual is not violated but preserved. But when the association grows and the inevitable conflicts appear, then "civilization" with accent on "civil authority" begins to develop with classifications and institutions meant to preserve the original harmony but not the the original freedom of the individual. For example, in the administration of FDR we had the rise of a multiplicity of governmental departments adorned with strings of capital letters representing their titles. Put all together they meant regulation of rights and freedom that really entailed the loss of rights and freedoms. From that point on government *to* the people began to steadily replace government *by* the people. The wisdom to stop was certainly not exercised, here or in other countries. Only some of the "third world" nations today are free of such false development and advantages that have put citizens in civil strait jackets from which there seems little hope of escape.

As said before, each of us is a kingdom-nation unto ourselves. Therefore we, too, need to know "where to stop" and not clutter up and clog the flow of our lives. The Tao is simple, and an uncomplicated life is an advantageous setting for the pursuit of the Tao. Danger comes from going too far in the elaborations of the ego, including the spiritual ego. That brings great danger; but knowing when and where to stop can exempt us from further danger. And tracing our way back by eliminating the ego's tangles can free us from all possible dangers. Simplicity and Unity are inseparable.

Tao in the world may be compared to rivers that run into the sea. Byrn: "All things end in the Tao just as the small streams and the largest rivers flow through valleys to the sea." Wu: "The Tao is to the world what a great river or an ocean is to the streams and brooks." Mabry: "All the World is to the Tao as rivers flowing home to the sea." Blackney: "In this world, compare those of the Way to torrents that flow into river and sea."

Each of the foregoing translations has a special nuance of its own. The essence is that we are all flowing toward the Tao. This is our inviolable nature and therefore our inevitable and unavoidable destiny. To delay the flow is to continue in birth, death, suffering, and frustrated hope. But to accelerate the flow through the right ordering of our lives and the cultivation of interior evolution is the way to end all that. As Yogananda said: "Spirit to Spirit goes...."

"Purified by knowledge-based tapasya, many have attained my state of being" (Bhagavad Gita 4:10).

33. Knowing Oneself

> He who knows others is learned; he who knows himself is wise.
> He who conquers others has power of muscles; he who conquers himself is strong.
> He who is contented is rich.
> He who is determined has strength of will.
> He who does not lose his center endures.
> He who dies yet (his power) remains has long life.
> (Tao Teh King 33)

Byrn's translation is so superior that I will comment on that:

"Those who know others are intelligent; those who know themselves are truly wise.

"Those who master others are strong; those who master themselves have true power.

"Those who know they have enough are truly wealthy. Those who persist will reach their goal. Those who keep their course have a strong will.

"Those who embrace death will not perish, but have life everlasting."

Those who know others are intelligent; those who know themselves are truly wise. We are not meant to walk through this world with blinders on or our eyes closed. That is the ideal of those who do not understand that the world is not a creation, a lifeless thing, but rather is a revelation of God, a manifestation of Divine Consciousness. We do not need to

33. Knowing Oneself

just get away from here, we have come here to learn, and those who hide under their desks or keep their eyes closed and their ears stopped up will never learn, but will have to return over and over and over until they open their eyes and ears, apply their minds and hearts and learn the lessons. Then they need never return; and if they do, it will be to teach others.

Trees, rivers and mountains are often wondrous to behold, but as the ghost of Jacob Marley told Scrooge: "Mankind was my business." The intelligent person really learns to see people clearly and to understand them. Often we see in people what we are blind to in ourselves. You would think that first we would know ourself and then we would know others, but the world often (if not usually) works backwards because of its flawed character. So we have to know others first and then can come to understand ourself. That is silly, I know, but that is what ignorance is all about: folly.

The first step, then, is to really gain knowledge of people, to observe and come to understand. That is easy to say, but a herculean task to manage. We must learn to be an intelligent and perceptive witness and analyst of others. Having cultivated this habit of objective observation, when we turn inward we will be able to see and understand what we find there. For example, people often dislike and reject in others whatever they will not face in themselves. People with a propensity for some negative or foolish behavior will bitterly, even violently, denounce such behavior in others, in that way hiding the truth about themselves from themselves and pointing others' attention away from themselves.

Often we hear the baseless and ego-serving cliché that if we do not love ourselves first we cannot love others, but it is just the opposite: when we can accept and be sympathetic and friendly towards others we can be the same to ourselves. This I have seen. I have never known anyone in love with themselves that had the capacity to love others, because ego is a rapacious, insatiable demon. Those who love themselves sacrifice others to their ego, whereas those who love others sacrifice themselves for others. This also I can assure you: love entails and often necessitates sacrifice. So we either sacrifice others or we sacrifice ourselves. The latter is the way of God, who has projected himself and entered into this world to undergo the experiences of all sentient beings as he guides their evolution. This is why several times in the Bhagavad Gita it is stated that God is dwelling in the hearts of all beings. Therefore the twentieth-century mystic, Bishop James Ingall Wedgwood, wrote in his original, esoteric revision of the Mass: "Uniting in this solemn Sacrifice with Thy holy Church throughout all the ages, we lift our hearts in adoration to Thee, O God the Son, consubstantial, co-eternal with the Father, who, abiding unchangeable within Thyself, didst nevertheless in the mystery of Thy boundless love and Thine eternal Sacrifice breathe forth Thine own divine life into Thy universe, and thus didst offer Thyself as the Lamb slain from the foundation of the world, dying in very truth that we might live."

It is imperative that those seeking higher consciousness be perceptive, because no matter how many guides and helpers we may have along the way, still the final authority is our own judgement based on our own understanding. That is why when an American once told Swami Sivananda that he had come to India to find a guru, Sivananda immediately replied: "You are the guru." First we learn from others and then we learn from ourselves. Nevertheless, Lao Tzu makes a distinction in those two modes of learning, saying that those who know others are intelligent, but those who know themselves are wise. So knowing others is meant to be a stepping-stone to self-knowledge, for as Chan translates it: "He who knows others is wise; he who knows himself is enlightened."

Those who master others are strong; those who master themselves have true power. It is evident that although we may start with others, we must end up with ourselves. Power can be a great evil or a great good, depending on whether it comes from ego or true knowledge. It is also true that power over others distorts and corrupts those who wield it, but those who have power over themselves will find themselves restored to their primal clarity and purity. That is why in India a respected spiritual figure is addressed as Maharaj, "great king." As Lao Tzu says: self-mastery is true power, for it alone can last forever.

33. Knowing Oneself

Those who know they have enough are truly wealthy. There is an Italian folk-tale, "The Happy Man's Shirt," that so perfectly illustrates this that I must include it here.

A king had an only son that he thought the world of. But this prince was always unhappy. He would spend days on end at his window staring into space.

"What on earth do you lack?" asked the king. "What's wrong with you?"

"I don't even know myself, Father."

"Are you in love? If there's a particular girl you fancy, tell me, and I'll arrange for you to marry her, no matter whether she's the daughter of the most powerful king on earth of the poorest peasant girl alive!"

"No, Father, I'm not in love."

The king issued a decree, and from every corner of the earth came the most learned philosophers, doctors, and professors. The king showed them the prince and asked for their advice. The wise men withdrew to think, then returned to the king. "Majesty, we have given the matter close thought and we have studied the stars. Here's what you must do. Look for a happy man who's happy through and through, and exchange your son's shirt for his."

That same day the king sent ambassadors to all parts of the world in search of the happy man.

A priest was taken to the king. "Are you happy? asked the king.

"Yes, indeed, Majesty."

"Find. How would you like to be my bishop?"

"Oh, Majesty, if only it were so!"

"Away with you! Get out of my sight! I'm seeking a man who's happy just as he is, not one who's trying to better his lot."

This the search resumed, and before long the king was told about a neighboring king, who everybody said was a truly happy man. He had a wife as good as she was beautiful and a whole slew of children. He had conquered all his enemies, and his country was at peace. Again hopeful, the king immediately sent ambassadors to him to ask for his shirt.

The neighboring king received the ambassadors and said, "Yes, indeed, I have everything anybody could possibly want. But at the same time I worry because I'll have to die one day and leave it all. I can't sleep at night for worrying about that!" The ambassadors thought it wiser to go home without this man's shirt.

At his wit's end, the king went hunting. He fired at a hare but only wounded it, and the hare scampered away on three legs. The king pursued it, leaving the hunting party far behind him. Out in the open field he heard a man singing a refrain. The king stopped in his tracks. "Whoever sings like that is bound to be happy!" The song led him into the vineyard, where he found a young man singing and pruning the vines.

"Good day, Majesty," said the youth. "So early and already out in the country?"

"Bless you! Would you like me to take you to the capital? You will be my friend."

"Much obliged, Majesty, but I wouldn't even consider it. I wouldn't even change places with the Pope."

"Why not? Such a fine young man like you…"

"No, no, I tell you. I'm content with just what I have and want nothing more."

"A happy man at last!" thought the king. "Listen, young man. Do me a favor."

"With all my heart, Majesty, if I can."

"Wait just a minute," said the king, who, unable to contain his joy any longer, ran to get his retinue. "Come with me! My son is saved! My son is saved! And he took them to the young man. "My dear lad," he began, "I'll give you whatever you want! But give me… give me…"

"What, Majesty?"

"My son is dying! Only you can save him. Come here!"

The king grabbed him and started unbuttoning the youth's jacket.

All of a sudden he stopped, and his arms fell to his sides.

The happy man had no shirt.

In economics there is a principle called The Law of Diminishing Returns. More is not better; often it is less. Those who can distinguish with Goldilocks between Too Little, Too Much, and Just Right and follow their insight, always holding to Just Right, will always be happy. All others will be tormented by Too Little or Too Much. This takes great wisdom, but only the wise are ever truly happy.

Those who persist will reach their goal. Those who keep their course have a strong will. This is absolutely so. Jesus said: "Ask, and it shall be given you; seek, and ye shall find; knock, and it shall be opened unto you: For every one that asketh receiveth; and he that seeketh findeth; and to him that knocketh it shall be opened." (Matthew 7:7-8). This is not a promise, it is the enunciation of a law. And not only will the persistent attain what they seek, in the seeking their wills become stronger, even invincible.

He who does not lose his center endures. This is because our center is our own divine nature that is itself the Tao, and only the Tao endures.

Those who embrace death will not perish, but have life everlasting. "Whosoever shall seek to save his life shall lose it; and whosoever shall lose his life shall preserve it," said Jesus (Luke 17:33). The death that Lao Tzu speaks of here is the death of the ego and of all limited, relative existence. Yogananda often said: "When the 'I' shall die, then shall I know 'Who am I?'" Again, this is backwards because the world is running in reverse. Anyway, it is only those who die that learn they are really immortal and cannot die.

Death comes in many forms, as does life. Some forms of death lead to further, deadlier death. But some forms lead to life. Death of spiritual consciousness yields only more death, but death of the ego, the false self, is itself the gate of life.

We can see from this entire section that the wise not only see the world entirely differently from everyone else, they also experience it utterly differently.

34. The Great Tao Flows Everywhere

The Great Tao flows everywhere, (like a flood) It may go left or right.

The myriad things derive their life from It, and It does not deny them.

When Its work is accomplished, It does not take possession.

It clothes and feeds the myriad things, yet does not claim them as Its own.

Often (regarded) without mind or passion, It may be considered small.

Being the home of all things, yet claiming not, It may be considered great.

Because to the end It does not claim greatness, Its greatness is achieved.

(Tao Teh King 34).

Here is the translation of Wu:

"The Great Tao is universal like a flood. How can It be turned to the right or to the left?

"All creatures depend on It, and It denies nothing to anyone. It does Its work, but makes no claims for Itself. It clothes and feeds all, but It does not lord it over them:

"Thus, It may be called 'the Little.'"

"All things return to It as to their home, but It does not lord it over them:

"Thus, It may be called 'the Great.'

"It is just because It does not wish to be great that Its greatness is fully realized."

You can see how different these are, often opposite to one another as the first verse of each translation shows. This is the problem with translating esoteric texts, especially those that are very ancient. This is why we must always base our spiritual life on our spiritual practice, our yoga, because that will never go wrong, whereas a text or translator may be completely erroneous. Therefore in all of these commentaries of mine I hope you are keeping it in mind that not only can the truth not be perfectly expressed in words, so also the approximate truth of scriptures may be completely missed or even suppressed or falsified by translators. That is why I am using eight translations as the basis for this commentary.

Ultimately it is up to the aspirant to decide what is true or false, valuable or worthless, in any spiritual text. That, again, is why it is so crucial that he develop his spiritual intuition through yoga meditation.

I am going to be commenting on Wu's translation because I believe it is closer to Lao Tzu's preceding teaching, and it is certainly in total harmony with the yogic understanding.

The Great Tao is universal like a flood. How can It be turned to the right or to the left? The Tao–Parabrahman, Dharmakaya, or Supreme Spirit (God)–is infinite, and therefore can neither be conditioned, influenced or directed in any manner, because that is contrary to Its nature. Just as we cannot dry water or color the sky, we can in no way control or direct the absolute Reality (and very little of relative existence, either). Therefore the wise person seeks to know the Tao as much as It can be known so he can conform himself to It. For it is when we go contrary to the Tao that we suffer and fall into confusion. Obviously the "knowing" I am speaking of is a direct, experiential matter and has nothing to do with the intellect, though afterwards the intellect can legitimately attempt to make some sense of it and apply it in a practical manner.

It is yoga we need for this, and any religion that is not essentially a yoga, but only a system of belief and conduct, is worthless. It is not true that yoga is not a religion–quite the opposite. Yoga is the only true religion there is. Originally every true religion was a system of how to know and ascend to infinite Reality. If we can find the yoga aspect of a religion then we have found the true form of that religion. If there is no yogic aspect, then the whole thing is false and we should have the wisdom to look elsewhere for truth.

All creatures depend on It, and It denies nothing to anyone. It does Its work, but makes no claims for Itself. It clothes and feeds all, but It does not lord it over them. The Tao is the Ground of Being. We exist because It exists. Everything to do with us, including our many births and deaths and their resulting effects on us, arises from the Tao. It responds to our will and action, denying us nothing.

Therefore our past, present and future conditions may arise from the Tao but they are utterly our "creation." The Tao never interferes or refuses. For that reason there are few more inappropriate questions than "Why does God…?" This is because God, the Tao, *does* nothing, but *allows* all things. All action is solely our doing. We are the sole creators and shapers of our destiny. All that we do is really a kind of echo: we send out the message and the Tao sends back exactly what we sent. The Tao does nothing, but It does respond. Yet the response in no way affects the Tao, so we can say that it does nothing since the reaction is a continuation of the acting. We act upon the Tao, but the Tao does not act upon us. And It remains unaffected. This makes no sense only because the Tao lies far beyond any human comprehension or experience. And that is the truth about our real nature which is the Tao. We really need to know this lest we mistake something for the Tao that is no such thing. When we finally get the sense of this we will realize that heretofore we have lived in total non-sense like *Alice in Wonderland* and *Through the Looking-Glass.*

If we do not like the way things work in relation to the Tao, we need to change ourselves, not the Tao. We must accommodate the Tao, or the

Tao will accommodate us and the ring-around-the-rosy will continue. That is why C. S. Lewis wrote that there are two kinds of people in this world: those that say to God: "Thy will be done," and those to whom God says "*Thy* will be done."

Since the Tao only responds, and that is Its sole "work," It cannot claim anything for Itself. We receive all from the Tao, but the Tao in no way controls or even influences us.

Thus, It may be called "the Little." It is common to speak of the Great Tao, but we will naturally draw on our experience to define that. And since great things have tremendous influence on us and control us and our environment we will mistakenly think the Tao is doing all things and ordering all things, that the Tao has a will and a purpose, that we are helpless in relation to It. But the opposite is true: the Tao is helpless in relation to us. We alone are the doer, we alone are responsible for the Tao's response. Thus the Tao is Little, even Nothing or No Thing in relation to us. We are all very Big in contrast to Its Smallness.

All things return to It as to their home, but It does not lord it over them. We are being inexorably drawn back to the Tao, to our point of origin, but it is not the Tao that is doing the drawing: we are. Whether we leave the Tao or return to the Tao: that is our concern and our willing and doing. We are in total charge at all times. That is why we must completely rethink every aspect of our life and existence, including our religion.

Thus, It may be called "the Great." Since the Tao is the only thing that exists, is that of which all things consist, the Tao is truly Great. In fact, "great" is a very feeble word; but since the Tao cannot be conceived or really spoken about, it does not matter much.

It is just because It does not wish to be great that Its greatness is fully realized. The very fact that the Tao is "beyond it all" proves Its infinite greatness. All relative things are nothing like the Tao and therefore are essentially nothing. The Tao, not being like anything, is therefore everything. That is Its nature, Its sublime simplicity.

Blackney renders this verse: "The wise man, therefore, while he is alive, will never make a show of being great: and that is how his greatness is achieved." This is so interpretive that it is more comment than translation, but nevertheless valuable for us, because all that we learn about the Tao should be applied to us and to anyone we might consider a person of wisdom. For the evolving individual becomes more and more like the Tao.

The child in the womb does not look at all like its parents or ancestors, and although there is a lot of talk about babies having someone's eyes, etc., the true likeness, especially psychologically, will not really be apparent until adulthood, though there will be hints, that nevertheless may lessen or vanish as the child grows. It is the same with the consciously evolving yogi. All kinds of phenomena may manifest and even miracles occur. But none of that means anything, for such things are not the Tao at all, just the responses of the Tao.

There is a story in India of a man who had a magical dye vat. A person said what color they wanted and the man dipped it in and brought it out the exact color desired. But one day a man said: "I want the color of the dye itself: your color." To learn the color of the Tao is the goal. So the more Tao-like we become, the higher we are evolving. But what is the Tao like? And how will we know? An outside observer cannot know, and the Tao-like person will never say that he is like the Tao, for he knows that is not enough: he must *be* the Tao.

This makes no sense to the non-yogis, but Lao Tzu did not write for them.

35. The Peace of Tao

> Hold the Great Symbol and all the world follows, follows without meeting harm, (and lives in) health, peace, commonwealth.
> Offer good things to eat and the wayfarer stays. But Tao is mild to the taste.
> Looked at, it cannot be seen.
> Listened to, it cannot be heard.
> Applied, its supply never fails.
> (Tao Teh King 35).

Hold the Great Symbol and all the world follows, follows without meeting harm, (and lives in) health, peace, commonwealth. This is impossible to interpret in an absolutely assured manner. First of all, who believes that Master Lao Tzu wanted people to carry around a symbol, and of what? Since it is called "Great Symbol" we can assume that he meant the Tao, which cannot be depicted but can be symbolized. However, the common yin-yang symbol seen everywhere was not formulated until centuries after Lao Tzu. So though we may not be absolutely sure of our interpretation, when we consider that words and concepts are symbols, Lao Tzu likely is urging us to live every moment with our understanding of the Tao, never leaving it out of any aspect of our life–that we should look at all things in the context of what we know of the Tao. In other words, our lives themselves should be expositions of the Tao. Since the Tao includes all existence, harmony and freedom from obstacles, if we become the living Tao then all things will come to us in a positive, strengthening, and peaceful way that will also be a benefit to all around us.

Offer good things to eat and the wayfarer stays. But Tao is mild to the taste. The obvious and the material easily attract deluded human beings like highly-flavored food. Therefore the master tells us that if we offer what the wayfarer, the wanderer in samsara, considers "good eating" he will be attracted. But just as soothing and mildly flavored food (the kind of food recommended in Bhagavad Gita 17:8) seems boring and without flavor to such people, so to the samsarins immersed in sensual materiality even the words about the Tao seem insipid, useless, and even foolish: what then to say of the Tao Itself? Its very existence is inconceivable and of no interest to them. It is certainly the same in religion. One time in a major city I saw a sign over the door of a large church: FREE HOT DOGS. Before that in another large city I saw outside a church a sign that said: "Let us cook Sunday breakfast for you!" We need not imagine the quality of such churches, or of those they would attract. Billions are racing in pursuit of the unreal, but how every few in comparison are walking the ways that lead to the Real.

Looked at, it cannot be seen. Listened to, it cannot be heard. This is understood easily by those mystics with inward vision, but is nonsense to all others. We must come to see the Unseeable, hear the Unhearable, touch the Untouchable and know the Unknowable.

Applied, its supply never fails. When we live the Tao we draw upon the infinite Being of the Tao which has no end (because It has no beginning). How is this? Because we have been part of the Tao all along. We need to awaken to this reality. That is why Saint Paul exhorts us: "Awake thou that sleepest, and arise from the dead," (Ephesians 5:14). The word translated "awake" is *egeiro*, which means "rise up." A lot of people wake up and loll in bed, but simple awakening not enough. We must arise in our consciousness and go back to our Source. We have no other destiny because we have no other nature.

36. The Rhythm of Life

He who is to be made to dwindle (in power) must first be caused to expand.
He who is to be weakened must first be made strong.
He who is to be laid low must first be exalted to power.
He who is to be taken away from must first be given.
This is the Subtle Light.
Gentleness overcomes strength; fish should be left in the deep pool, and sharp weapons of the state should be left where none can see them.
(Tao Teh King 36)

This is a very intriguing passage of the Tao Teh King, which is my way of saying that it seems impossible to determine what Lao Tzu meant by it! But I think we can extract the fundamental principles behind what is either advice or observation of human ways.

The main thing that will help us somewhat is the principle that getting implies losing. Whatever we gain must eventually be lost; whatever comes must eventually go; whatever change may occur must eventually resolve back into the previous state. In the ultimate sense, all manifestation must return to the unmanifest state that is the pure Tao. For if we have not had something from eternity, we never can have it, and so when reality begins to dawn we lose it.

Lao Tzu is certainly telling us that increase leads to decrease, strength leads to weakness, elevation leads to coming down, and gaining leads to losing. So to run obsessively after anything is to ensure our eventual experience of its opposite. Therefore we should live our lives intelligently and pursue that which is innately good, not merely pleasant or advantageous. For the truly good does not lead to evil, but only to increase of good. Why? Because good is the characteristic of the Tao. Evil is a distortion or denial of the Tao. Truth never leads to lies.

To understand these principles is no small thing. That is why Lao Tzu comments: "This is the Subtle Light," the insight that is possible only to the illuminated intellect which functions mostly on the highest intuitive level.

When Lao Tzu tells us that "gentleness overcomes strength" he is speaking an entire mode of life based on the understanding in the first part of this verse. Taoist writings frequently speak of the need to be yielding: not in the sense of being weak, conciliatory or wishy-washy, but in the sense of being flexible, acknowledging the realities of a situation, and shaping our actions accordingly. I once saw a sign that said: "Would you rather work harder or smarter?" Lao Tzu is saying that banging our heads again the door may eventually open it, but we may be too damaged to go through it. Rather, we must observe the nature and structure of the door and go about opening it in a manner that makes sense and succeeds.

We must also know when something needs changing and when it does not. To pursue foolish goals, even if they are attainable, can be more harmful than pursuing goals that cannot be reached. Many people regret it when they get what they strive for. So Lao Tzu tells us to consider well the fact that many times "fish should be left in the deep pool." In the West we say: "Let sleeping dogs lie" and: "Leave well enough alone." Fish belong and thrive in a deep pool. They belong there and we should not upset the natural, and therefore positive and sensible, order. (Taoists are traditionally vegetarian.)

"Sharp weapons of the state" and of private life "should be left where none can see them" and get wrong ideas. Saint Paul wrote: "All things are lawful for me, but all things are not expedient: all things are lawful for me, but all things edify not" (I Corinthians 10:23). The way of "power plays" are almost always a two-edged sword that cuts the wielders as well as the targets. Cunning and devious ways are dangerous things. The short-term advantage may seem good, but eventually grief and harm comes to those who employ them. Parents especially should protect their children from becoming enamored of the "quick-fix" and "looking out for 'number one'" approaches to life. I have seen both poor and rich fall into this trap and suffer, sometimes without any alleviation or remedy whatsoever.

It is extremely crucial for us to understand that Lao Tzu is not advocating passivity and the line of least resistance and surrender to negative forces and situations. He is urging us to gauge the truth of a situation, to weigh the consequences of all actions, and thus be able to live successfully in the truest and highest sense. Centered in the Tao, only good can result.

37. World Peace

> The Tao never "does," yet through it everything is done.
> If princes and dukes can keep the Tao, the world will of its own accord be reformed.
> When reformed and rising to action, let it be restrained by the Nameless pristine simplicity.
> The Nameless pristine simplicity is stripped of desire (for contention).
> By stripping of desire quiescence is achieved, and the world arrives at peace of its own accord.
> (Tao Teh King 37).

Mabry: "The Tao never 'acts' Yet nothing is left undone.
"If governments and leaders would keep It all things would of their own accord be transformed. Should desires arise from transformation I shall influence them through silent simplicity. Silent simplicity involves being free from desires.
"When you are without desire you are content And all the World is at peace."

The Tao never "does," yet through it everything is done. This is not contradictory as it seems at first sight. Rather, it is an indication that the Tao exists in a realm completely transcending that in which we presently find ourselves. The Tao is the Source of that relative state in which action and non-action are possible, but does not engage in either.

37. World Peace

If princes and dukes can keep the Tao, the world will of its own accord be reformed. At the time of Lao Tzu China was ruled by monarchs and aristocracy, but this applies to modern forms of government: if those who administer the government can maintain awareness of the Tao and conformity to Its nature, then everything else in society will be spontaneously corrected and made perfect. Do we think that Lao Tzu believed this would be done? If he did, why did he leave "the world" never to be heard from again? Yet he left behind this statement. I would speculate that although he knew there would be no mass adoption of the Tao in public life, this statement of his could inspire individual persons in public office to do their best to embody the Tao and their area of function at least would be reformed. Looking at the mess of the world and saying things are hopeless is not wisdom, for each one of us can work on straightening ourselves out, and that will benefit the world around us. In fact, we need not be anything official at all: just living our daily lives according to the wisdom of the Tao.

When reformed and rising to action, let it be restrained by the Nameless pristine simplicity. Presently there is a quality of perversity in all aspects of relative existence. One manifestation is the destructive nature of success and attainment. The moment something is gained the possibility of its loss begins to arise and cloud our possession of it. Also from that first moment there is the necessity to maintain or hold onto it and its preservation from erosion and dissolution. So "happiness" breeds anxiety, fear, pain and grief. Production of anything is the beginning of its destruction. Suffering never stops, it just changes in character and intensity, circling us like a wolf pack bent on attack.

Therefore Lao Tzu tells us that when any aspect of life does become reformed there is the very real danger that it will develop into yet another labyrinth of injustice and incompetence. This is because human beings have always thought that More Is Better, and therefore elaborated blessed simplicity into the curse of complexity that either cannot be maintained or will morph into something utterly alien from the original intentions. Nothing and no one is immune to this inherent virus.

The only preventive for this is to keep to the primal simplicity of the Tao at all steps and stages along the way of its establishment. This is not a matter of exterior regulation and direction through rules and authority, but of the continuous cultivation of the consciousness of Tao. There is no other means to keep the reform from becoming deformed.

The Nameless pristine simplicity is stripped of desire. Maintaining desirelessness while actively engaged in improvement is the only solution, for the Tao is dispelled by desire in any form. This may seem an impossible postulation, little more than a frustrating chase of a dog for its own tail, but it is not. Again, the Bhagavad Gita clearly and fully lays out the way to fulfill Lao Tzu's counsels. It approaches the matter from every possible aspect and clarifies both the situation and its correction. Meditation is always the primary element.

By stripping of desire quiescence is achieved, and the world arrives at peace of its own accord. I remember when as a child I heard a man speaking of a profound spiritual awakening he had experienced as a young man. "The world around me was new, the people were new, everything I saw was new… *I was new!*" The last clause is the key: everything was changed because he was changed. Or rather, it was not changed, he just saw it differently in a level of higher consciousness. That is why Sri Ramakrishna said that this ocean of sorrow we call the world is converted into a bazaar of joy when we awaken into the highest awareness that itself is God.

When our consciousness is changed, then everything is changed, both in the way we perceive it and in its subsequent unfoldment, for the world is really a sounding-board that reveals our inner status by changing to reflect it. That is why wild animals become tame in the presence of those that have attained the Tao. For the Tao is peace, harmony and clarity, and therefore the absence of desire.

Again we have to realize that this can only be achieved by the individual through his own effort, even if a group of people are engaged in the same aspiration and activity. Everything without exception is an individual matter. All our work must be on ourselves; then the world around us will be improved as we improve. Only the inside can change the outside.

38. Degeneration

The man of superior character is not (conscious of his) character. Hence he has character.

The man of inferior character (is intent on) not losing character. Hence he is devoid of character.

The man of superior character never acts, nor ever (does so) with an ulterior motive.

The man of inferior character acts, and (does so) with an ulterior motive.

The man of superior kindness acts, but (does so) without an ulterior motive.

The man of superior justice acts, and (does so) with an ulterior motive.

(But when) the man of superior *li* acts and finds no response, he rolls up his sleeves to force it on others.

Therefore:

After Tao is lost, then (arises the doctrine of) humanity.

After humanity is lost, then (arises the doctrine of) justice.

After justice is lost, then (arises the doctrine of) *li*.

Now *li* is the thinning out of loyalty and honesty of heart, and the beginning of chaos.

The prophets are the flowering of Tao and the origin of folly.

Therefore the noble man dwells in the heavy (base), and not in the thinning (end).

He dwells in the fruit, and not in the flowering (expression).
Therefore he rejects the one and accepts the other.
(Tao Teh King 38)

The man of superior character is not (conscious of his) character. Hence he has character. To be in touch with our true Self, our true nature which is the same as that of the Tao, is to be "of superior character." In Sanskrit there is an important adjective, *Sahaja*, which means that which is natural, innate, spontaneous and inborn. This and this alone is the Tao. And because it is absolutely natural and spontaneous, those who possess it never think of it and never identify with it because it is not external to them. For example, if you told fish about water they would doubt you. "What and where is this water?" they would object. "We have never seen it!" Why? Because it is the medium in which they exist. Therefore to them it is unperceivable.

So the illumined man does not think of himself as enlightened, but only as I Am.

The man of inferior character (is intent on) not losing character. Hence he is devoid of character.

One of the most pathetic things I ever saw was Alan Watts on television rubbing an ink slab while he gazed into the camera, trying to project the impression that he was enlightened in the midst of his activity. A bishop-friend of mine once remarked about a major Christian denomination: "They are terrified of making a mistake because they are infallible!" As the Upanishad says: "He who says 'I know,' does not know."

I have observed a lot of people pretending to be enlightened masters. Often it is quite funny, especially when they are Indian "gurus." But J. M. Barrie in the fourteenth chapter of *Peter Pan* depicts such people in the character of Captain Hook who is obsessed with "good form."

"Hook was not his true name. To reveal who he really was would even at this date set the country in a blaze; but as those who read between the lines must already have guessed, he had been at a famous public school; and its traditions still clung to him like garments, with which indeed

38. Degeneration

they are largely concerned. Thus it was offensive to him even now to board a ship in the same dress in which he grappled her, and he still adhered in his walk to the school's distinguished slouch. But above all he retained the passion for good form.

"Good form! However much he may have degenerated, he still knew that this is all that really matters.

"From far within him he heard a creaking as of rusty portals, and through them came a stern tap-tap-tap, like hammering in the night when one cannot sleep. 'Have you been good form to-day?' was their eternal question.

"'Fame, fame, that glittering bauble, it is mine,' he cried.

"'Is it quite good form to be distinguished at anything?' the tap-tap from his school replied....

"Most disquieting reflection of all, was it not bad form to think about good form?

"His vitals were tortured by this problem. It was a claw within him sharper than the iron one; and as it tore him, the perspiration dripped down his tallow countenance and streaked his doublet. Ofttimes he drew his sleeve across his face, but there was no damming that trickle.

"Ah, envy not Hook.

"...If Smee was lovable, what was it that made him so? A terrible answer suddenly presented itself–'Good form!'

"Had the bo'sun good form without knowing it, which is the best form of all?

"He remembered that you have to prove you don't know you have it before you are eligible for Pop [an elite social club at Eton].

"With a cry of rage he raised his iron hand over Smee's head; but he did not tear. What arrested him was this reflection:

"'To claw a man because he is good form, what would that be?'

"'Bad form!'

"The unhappy Hook was as impotent as he was damp, and he fell forward like a cut flower."

This is just what Lao Tzu is talking about.

The man of superior character never acts, nor ever (does so) with an ulterior motive. Every action of the superior person is an expression of cosmic order (ritam), of the truth of his true Self. He does what he does because it is the right and true thing. To do otherwise would be to violate his fundamental nature, and he has passed beyond that possibility. Saint John the Apostle affirms this when he says: "Whosoever is born of God doth not commit sin; for his seed remaineth in him: and he cannot sin, because he is born of God" (I John 3:9). The "seed" of the divine Self which has been fully awakened and developed in him makes wrong action impossible. Established completely in the I Am consciousness he has no other motive than To Be.

The man of inferior character acts, and (does so) with an ulterior motive. Being in the grip of ego and self-centeredness, the inferior person never acts outside that context. Therefore everything appearing noble, right, or good he might do is just the opposite because it springs from a wrong perspective and motivation. Just as the superior person cannot do wrong, the inferior person cannot do right. Everything he does is for "Me," an expression of pure narcissism.

The man of superior kindness acts, but (does so) without an ulterior motive. I knew a man who lived extremely frugally and gave everything he had to others. Though of a very wealthy background he lived in a virtual shack. He was renowned for his good deeds. But he was really a dead soul who had been told that was the way to act, so he did: to an extreme degree. But I never saw any real compassion or even simple kindness in him. He was a good-deeds robot and nothing more. On the other hand, I knew a man that lived just as frugally and intent on helping others, and since he was acting from a genuine, deep impulse of goodness and loving-kindness, he was a person of true and great virtue. This is important to understand, for today a great deal of very unworthy people are trying to hide their true character under a veneer of "caring" social action. The worse they are, the more "good" they do. It is the moral equivalent of charity done to get a tax break. Most things that glitter are not gold.

The man of 'superior justice' acts, and (does so) with an ulterior motive. Mabry: "A politician acts, but he has ulterior motives." Chan: "The man of superior righteousness takes action, and has an ulterior motive to do so." The people who have straightened themselves out simply live straight. but those who intend to straighten others out always have some motive in doing so, and it always leads back to them, not others. They always seek their own benefit, using others to attain it.

(But when) the man of superior li acts and finds no response, he rolls up his sleeves to force it on others. Blackney: "High etiquette, when acted out without response from others, constrains a man to bare his arms and make them do their duty!" Wu: "High ceremony fusses but finds no response; Then it tries to enforce itself with rolled-up sleeves." Byrn: "The 'moral' person will act out of duty, and when no one will respond will roll up his sleeves and uses force." Chan: "The man of superior propriety takes action, and when people do not respond to it, he will stretch his arms and force it on them." Legge: "(Those who) possessed the highest (sense of) propriety were (always seeking) to show it, and when men did not respond to it, they bared the arm and marched up to them." Feng and English: "When a disciplinarian does something and no one responds, he rolls up his sleeves in an attempt to enforce order." Mabry: "When a legalist acts and get no response, he rolls up his sleeve and uses force."

"Li" is a difficult word. As we have seen from these translations, it can mean etiquette, social norms, external propriety, discipline, and even legalism. All these are externals, and that is why they provoke external coercion and social bullying masquerading as justice and morality. The "just" man of the previous verse gets people to do what he wants by persuasion or even by fooling them into thinking that what he wants will benefit them. But the man of Li tries to coerce them even with brute force.

Lao Tzu is assuring us that anything which results in forcing others is worthless and even destructive. Why? Because it causes us to totally lose contact with the Tao, which is antithetical to manipulation or force. The sole purpose of the Tao is to liberate from within us the characteristics of the Tao that are our true nature. This can only come about spontaneously, inevitably.

In Section Eighteen, "The Decline of Tao," it says: "When the Great Tao ceased to be observed, benevolence and righteousness came into vogue. (Then) appeared wisdom and shrewdness, and there ensued great hypocrisy. When harmony no longer prevailed throughout the six kinships, filial sons found their manifestation; when the states and clans fell into disorder, loyal ministers appeared." Now Lao Tzu is going to give us another list of what arises when the Tao declines.

After Tao is lost, then (arises the doctrine of) humanity. Wu: "Failing Tao, man resorts to Virtue." Chan: "Therefore when Tao is lost, only then does the doctrine of virtue arise." Most translators prefer "virtue" to "humanity" in this verse. The idea is that when the Tao is lost, so also does spontaneous behavior in keeping with the Tao. Therefore an artificial code is substituted for it: external social and private "virtue," a code based on what others think it is, rather than an internal arising within the individual. This artificial (and therefore false) virtue must be learned, even imposed. Thus society ceases to be truly ordered, but rather regimented and rule-bound, essentially hypocritical and inwardly disordered. So outward rectitude prevails and secret vice pervades, leading to ultimate collapse of both society and the individual. The Soviet Union was a perfect example of this, as are all socialistic societies, for however they may begin, they end in totalitarian dictatorship. Fortunately in time they collapse, but the recovery from such evil is slow and hard.

After humanity is lost, then (arises the doctrine of) justice. Wu: "Failing Virtue, man resorts to 'humanity.'" Chan: "When virtue is lost, only then does the doctrine of 'humanity' arise." I have written about this a few times in other places. In the present day, moral corruption and inveterate selfishness are especially being covered up by "social action" and "good deeds." Certainly very good and worthy people do these things, but innocently, not with the ulterior motives of the inwardly self-serving.

Of course, "human rights" cover a multitude of social and political aberrations, often ploys to erode real human rights. Almost nothing that glitters is gold in this area.

After justice is lost, then (arises the doctrine of) li. Wu: "Failing humanity, man resorts to morality. Failing morality, man resorts to ceremony." Chan: "When humanity is lost, only then does the doctrine of righteousness arise. When righteousness is lost, only then does the doctrine of propriety arise." When natural inner goodness is lacking, then thoroughly external "goodness" begins to prevail in people's lives. This is, as Lao Tzu has just pointed out, evidence that not only is real goodness absent, very real wrongdoing and evil is rife in the unseen, hidden aspects of life. This has characterized many eras of social life in both East and West. China, the homeland of Lao Tzu, especially embodied this. Like any good writer, Lao Tzu was writing about what he knew from firsthand experience.

Religion is one of the main offenders in this. Presently, nearly all religion is externalized to the maximum degree in East and West. So also is yoga in the West, which has been almost totally reduced to nothing more than physical culture and emotional hype in the form of "chanting."

Now li is the thinning out of loyalty and honesty of heart, and the beginning of chaos. Wu: "Now, ceremony is the merest husk of faith and loyalty; It is the beginning of all confusion and disorder." Legge: "Now propriety is the attenuated form of leal-heartedness and good faith, and is also the commencement of disorder." ("Leal" means faithful, true, loyal, honest and genuine.) Chan: "Now, propriety is a superficial expression of loyalty and faithfulness, and the beginning of disorder." These translations themselves leave little need for comment, except that these things are the symptoms of a downward slide that will almost never be arrested or reversed until there is total collapse. Rather than looking at others, we need to look at our own hearts and lives and see if we, too, are on the slide.

The prophets are the flowering of Tao and the origin of folly. By "prophets" Lao Tzu does not mean true seers of the future and the inner side of things, but rather "oracles" of society who are followed unquestioningly and unthinkingly. This has been a phenomenon throughout history, so much so that history seems little more than a string of fools and follies. No wonder that Napoleon defined history as "a lie agreed upon." The truth is too unfaceable.

"Leaders" need followers, and intelligent and self-sufficient people never run in a herd. Therefore any mass movement is almost sure to be a mindless rushing to an unknown result that turns out to be the opposite of what was claimed or promised. Self-destruction is the keynote. It is true that history repeats itself because no one learns from it, but it also repeats itself because it is made up of the same unaware mobs that made history. For this reason Taoism is the most individualistic of the world's religions.

Therefore the noble man dwells in the heavy (base), and not in the thinning (end). He dwells in the fruit, and not in the flowering (expression). Therefore he rejects the one and accepts the other. Wu: "Therefore, the full-grown man set his heart upon the substance rather than the husk; Upon the fruit rather than the flower. Truly, he prefers what is within to what is without." It is a tragic fact that people often accept a symbol for a reality, a symptom for a cause, and only the wise seem able to discern the difference. Therefore Lao Tzu tells us that the mature spiritual person continually discriminates between the two and always takes the real thing.

In philosophy, religion and even yoga many people take the claims and ignore the contradictory actualities. They obsess on the teacher, the teaching and even the practice, and pay no attention to the results (or, rather, the lack of results). Many good people are trapped in the refusal to take a good look and come to the right conclusion.

But the wise do look and see. They consider only the results and not the claims. Further, they examine and see whether what seems real and a sign of progress will really end in the Goal or not. Experiences mean nothing if consciousness is not expanded and liberated. Some yogas give a continual "high" or exotic experiences and nothing else. At the end of the ride the yogi finds himself right where he started. It was entertaining, but useless. I have known sincerely dedicated people who took decades to figure out that it was only a light-and-sound show with no substance.

Those who insistently cling to the inner, continually examining the nature of their practice, will attain; the dreamers and hopers will not. It is crucial to realize that only our inner state is an indicator of the value or valuelessness of a belief or practice. "He whose happiness is within, whose delight is within, whose illumination is within: that yogi, identical in being with Brahman, attains Brahmanirvana" (Bhagavad Gita 5:24). "The yogi is superior to ascetics (tapaswins), and considered superior to jnanis and superior to those engaged in Vedic rituals (karmakanda). Therefore be a yogi" (Bhagavad Gita 6:46).

39. Unity Through Complements

There were those in ancient times possessed of the One.
Through possession of the One, the Heaven was clarified.
Through possession of the One, the Earth was stabilized.
Through possession of the One, the gods were spiritualized.
Through possession of the One, the valleys were made full.
Through possession of the One, all things lived and grew.
Through possession of the One, the princes and dukes became the ennobled of the people.
That was how each became so.

Without clarity, the Heavens would shake.
Without stability, the Earth would quake.
Without spiritual power, the gods would crumble.
Without being filled, the valleys would crack.
Without the life-giving power, all things would perish.
Without the ennobling power, the princes and dukes would stumble.
Therefore the nobility depend upon the common man for support, and the exalted ones depend upon the lowly for their base.

That is why the princes and dukes call themselves "the orphaned," "the lonely one," "the unworthy."

> Is is not true then that they depend upon the common man for support?
> Truly, take down the parts of a chariot, and there is no chariot (left).
> Rather than jingle like the jade, rumble like the rocks.
> (Tao Teh King 39)

There were those in ancient times possessed of the One. Just as in the East it is understood that life (spirit) existed before matter, so also it is known that humanity did not begin as some semi-conscious beings, but that the first humans were the highest evolved of those that had retained human form from the previous creation cycle. Not only that, the earth was in such a state of high vibration that spiritual guides worked along with human beings in the re-establishing of human civilization. At that time the material creation also perfectly reflected its source, which was the infinite consciousness of the One: the Tao.

Through possession of the One, the Heaven was clarified. The material creation, on the other hand, did begin in tremendous flux and change as the "cosmic soup" began to shape itself into the universe. However, in time perfect order was manifested since the creation itself is part of the Tao, and the Tao is Perfect Order.

Through possession of the One, the Earth was stabilized. In the same way the earth itself became habitable and no longer subject to the upheavals that had characterized its existence previously. This, too, was a mirroring of the Tao.

Through possession of the One, the gods were spiritualized. The sentient beings, both incarnate and discarnate, began to function in the manner calculated to evolve and ultimately liberate them into higher realms of existence and life. This included the guardian spirits whose evolution consisted in guiding the sentient beings through subliminal direction.

Through possession of the One, the valleys were made full. Vegetation and animal life abounded in places suitable for their survival.

Through possession of the One, all things lived and grew. In time human beings appeared, not through evolution of form but as the specific, unique creation of those guiding and supervising intelligences known in the East as the Creator Mothers (Matrikas) and in the Bible as the Elohim, a term implying several female entities.

Through possession of the One, the princes and dukes became the ennobled of the people. After more time, humans began to more and more live interdependently and society emerged along with culture and government. This necessitated leaders which at that time rose to their position by the recognition of their superior abilities by the people themselves and not through personal ambition.

That was how each became so. Naturally, this all took incalculable time and was of tremendous complexity. But what happens when the Tao begins to fade in Its influence and in the consciousness of human beings?

Without clarity, the Heavens would shake. Without stability, the Earth would quake. Without spiritual power, the gods would crumble. Without being filled, the valleys would crack. Without the life-giving power, all things would perish. Without the ennobling power, the princes and dukes would stumble. Degeneration is the key word for that which follows the weakening of the Tao's influence in organic and inorganic life

Therefore the nobility depend upon the common man for support, and the exalted ones depend upon the lowly for their base. In human society worthiness is no longer recognized, so leaders depend on the cooperation of the general populace without regard to their qualifications. In fact, as human life degrades, it is the strong and ruthless that come to rule over a society that fears them and yet depends on them for order and safety (often without obtaining either order or safety). Then wars arise between the leaders and the populace is sacrificed accordingly.

That is why the princes and dukes call themselves "the orphaned," "the lonely one," "the unworthy." Yes, they call themselves that in a formal, ceremonial way, but of course they neither mean it, nor do they act accordingly.

Is is not true then that they depend upon the common man for support? Is it not strange that tyrants depend upon the people they enslave and repress? Without them these potentates would be nothing and powerless. So at all times it is the people who empower their rulers and officials, though to their detriment and even destruction. Ironic, is it not?

There is a spiritual side to this which can benefit us. In the individual there are also elements that obey and others that rule. In the life of the yogi the highest spiritual states depend on the elementary observances of moral and ethical conduct. No one ever is above the basics of right thought, speech and conduct. The greatest mystic in the world is totally dependent upon the fundamental principles of spiritual life which include codes of conduct in the simplest level of his life.

Truly, take down the parts of a chariot, and there is no chariot (left). Chan: "Therefore enumerate all the parts of a chariot as you may, and you still have no chariot." Spiritual life and its fruition in enlightenment is not a simple, single entity, but rather it consists of many indispensable elements, all of which are interdependent. It is like a tree. A tree consists of bark, wood, roots, branches and leaves. All together they make up a tree; but take one away and the tree dies and decays and in time there is no tree. The tree cannot exist independently of any element. Spiritual life is the same. Therefore the spiritual aspirant must ensure that not a single facet of spiritual life is omitted or neglected. Otherwise he fails in his quest for higher consciousness.

Rather than jingle like the jade, rumble like the rocks. In China at the time of Lao Tzu jade was perhaps the single most prized substance for objects of art. Single, large lumps of jade were very rare, so jade objects were relatively small, and if put together in a container they would strike against one another, tinkle or jingle and would certainly crack if handled roughly. On the other hand, boulders crash and rumble and are virtually unbreakable and immovable. So Lao Tzu is telling us not to be like jade, however attractive or precious society may consider it to be, but rather be like stone: substantial, strong and endurant.

40. The Principle of Reversion

> Reversion is the action of Tao.
> Gentleness is the function of Tao.
> The things of this world come from Being,
> And Being (comes) from Non-being.
> (Tao Teh King 40)

Reversion is the action of Tao. Wu: "The movement of the Tao consists in Returning." Byrn: "All movement returns to the Tao."

A serpent swallowing its own tail is an ancient symbol of the continual cycle of return in existence: perpetual creation and dissolution, projection and withdrawal. So it would be a mistake to think that Lao Tzu means only the return of the form into the formless. Rather, he means the return into the formless followed by the return from the formless into form. Because the Tao is One at all times, this Unity moves in perpetual outward/inward movement. It is like the pendulum of a clock. It swings from one side to another, yet is itself always exactly the same. So the Tao is ever the same yet ever-changing because that is Its nature. This is one instance in which the question "Why?" is only answered by "Because."

Gentleness is the function of Tao. Wu: "The use of the Tao consists in softness." Feng and English: "Yielding is the way of the Tao." Since the Tao is ever in a process of change, in the same way the knower of the

Tao is ever flexible, ever able to change, to evolve, yet always established at the unmoving, unchanging center that is the Tao.

The things of this world come from Being, and Being (comes) from Non-being. Creation and all it contains come from the state that is manifestation, from the condition known in India as "the Day of Brahma." But that state arises from non-manifestation known as "the Night of Brahma." Again, we have a perpetual cycle, a movement between manifest and unmanifest. Yet, behind it all is That which transcends all these dualities: the Tao.

41. Qualities of the Taoist

When the highest type of men hear the Tao (truth), they try hard to live in accordance with it.

When the mediocre type hear the Tao, they seem to be aware and yet unaware of it.

When the lowest type hear the Tao, they break into loud laughter–if it were not laughed at, it would not be Tao.

Therefore there is the established saying: "Who understands Tao seems dull of comprehension; who is advanced in Tao seems to slip backwards; who moves on the even Tao (Path) seems to go up and down."

Superior character appears like a hollow (valley);
Sheer white appears like tarnished;
Great character appears like infirm;
Pure worth appears like contaminated.
Great space has no corners;
Great talent takes long to mature;
Great music is faintly heard;
Great form has no contour;
And Tao is hidden without a name.

It is this Tao that is adept at lending (its power) and bringing fulfillment.

(Tao Teh King 41)

When the highest type of men hear the Tao (truth), they try hard to live in accordance with it. Chan: "When the highest type of men hear Tao, they diligently practice it." We must remember that the Tao is Being Itself, and not a set of philosophical postulates or rules of behavior. The only way to embody or manifest the Tao is to become attuned to Cosmic Reality and Order through profound self-investigation or Atmavichara. The process is meditation which brings us into alignment with the universal Tao.

When the mediocre type hear the Tao, they seem to be aware and yet unaware of it. Considering that most people are sleepwalkers through life, it can only be expected that they will be both aware and unaware of the Tao simultaneously. There are seven other renderings of this sentence, and each one has a nuance of its own, so I include them all.

Blackney: "The mediocre person learns of it and takes it up and sets it down." The middling type of person examines the truth of the Tao superficially out of middling curiosity–never with the serious intent of benefitting from It. Then, having examined it enough to satisfy him, he drops the subject–which satisfies him even more.

Byrn: "When an average person hears of the Tao, he believes half of it, and doubts the other half." Whatever appeals to his desires or makes sense to him intellectually, that he announces he can accept, but the other he rejects. Both his acceptance and his rejection are utterly desultory in character; there is no conviction or earnestness in them.

Chan: "When the average type of men hear Tao, they half believe in it." If they do accept the Tao, they are only lukewarm about it, not hot or cold. They believe, but only half-heartedly. Consequently there is no result in their thought or life.

Feng and English: "The average student hears of the Tao and gives it thought now and again." This is one of the most common reactions to any kind of higher truth. Once in a while the philosophical dilettante toys with the idea of the Tao and may even decide that "one day" he will look into it more seriously. But he never does.

Legge: "Scholars of the middle class, when they have heard about it, seem now to keep it and now to lose it." Now and again they conform

41. Qualities of the Taoist

to the truth of the Tao, and now and again they do not. It is thoroughly whimsical and rootless.

Mabry: "When ordinary people hear about the Tao they can take it or leave it." And they usually leave It at the initial hearing or they fiddle with It for a bit and then drop it and move on aimlessly.

Wu: "When a mediocre scholar hears the Tao, he wavers between belief and unbelief." There are those that simply cannot make up their mind about the Way of the Tao; they do and they don't, they will and they won't.

The conclusion of these eight interpretations is the same: Nothing comes from mediocrity.

When the lowest type hear the Tao, they break into loud laughter–if it were not laughed at, it would not be Tao. Chan: "When the lowest type of men hear Tao, they laugh heartily at it. If they did not laugh at it, it would not be Tao." One day in my early teens a lady said to me: "Show me your friends and I will tell you who you are." At first it shocked me, seeming snobbish, but reflection convinced me she was right. Many (many) years later a former bank-robber friend of mine told me: "You can judge a man by his enemies as well as by his friends." I had never thought of it that way, but saw immediately that he was right, especially since I had been acting on that principle for years without formulating it. In the same way we can distinguish truth from untruth just by watching the response of people to it. The liars and frauds will denounce truth and embrace lies. The malicious will reject that which is beneficial and eagerly embrace that which is harmful. Living in a mirror, they see everything backwards. The good and the true, however, recognize goodness and truth when they encounter it, and act accordingly. So if fools did not laugh at the Tao it would not be wisdom and would not be real.

These foregoing statements regarding response to the Tao have a twofold value: they both tell us how to recognize the Tao and how to recognize the superior, mediocre and worthless individuals by their response to It. This is why the great twentieth-century Catholic philosopher Dietrich von Hildebrand spoke so often of "response" as a key to a person's character.

Therefore there is the established saying: "Who understands Tao seems dull of comprehension; who is advanced in Tao seems to slip backwards; who moves on the even Tao (Path) seems to go up and down." Not everyone laughs at the Tao; quite a few detest and defame It. So knowers of the Tao seem stupid or crazy, to be destined for some kind of awful crackup or other fate, and to be unstable, unsure and unreliable.

Byrn: "Thus it is said: The brightness of the Tao seems like darkness, the advancement of the Tao seems like retreat, the level path seems rough." Regarding this the Bhagavad Gita says: "The man of restraint is awake in what is night for all beings. That in which all beings are awake is night for the sage who truly sees" (Bhagavad Gita 2:69).

Feng and English: "Hence it is said: The bright path seems dim; going forward seems like retreat; The easy way seems hard." This is the sad condition of those who wander in ignorance: everything is seen by them completely backwards. Their minds are truly like a photographic negative: that which is dark appears light and that which is light appears dark. Consequently the blessed and easy path to higher consciousness seems doomed and difficult, beyond their abilities to even begin, much less complete. The dark and miserable path to ever darker consciousness seems light, beautiful, assured and easy. It is all a matter of dominant mental polarity, positive or negative. Saint Paul wrote: "For we are a sweet savour of Christ, in them that are saved, and in them that perish: To the one we are the savour of death unto death; and to the other the savour of life unto life" (II Corinthians 2:15-16). This is a terrible state of mind, yet it is the norm in this negative world we call "society."

Superior character appears like a hollow (valley). This is not really hard to understand. Since Reality contains nothing of the the illusion and delusion in which people commonly live, everything about it seems nothing–even non-existent–to those people who live in the condition of anti-life. Positive virtue seems to be negative emptiness, wisdom seems to be folly, happiness seems to be misery and life itself seems like death to them, whereas they pursue and embrace death and call it life. That is why Mabry renders this: "The greatest good seems to us empty." And Wu: "High Virtue looks like an abyss."

Sheer white appears like tarnished. There are some people who cannot be content if they are not discontent and disapproving. They see faults in everything. One of the most negative people I ever knew did this physically. She would go into a store and pick up anything and instantly see the tiniest flaw. Because of this, people often asked her to go shopping with them so they would buy something without any defect. On one level such keen perception is good, but in her case it was a manifestation of a predisposition to find fault with everything. As Saint Paul said: "Unto the pure all things are pure: but unto them that are defiled and unbelieving is nothing pure; for even their mind and conscience is defiled." (Titus 1:15).

I knew a little boy that got his face all smudgy while playing, and he saw it in a mirror when he came in the house. Later after he had washed his face, he looked in the mirror and said: "Oh, we must have a new mirror." Many people merely see their own "face" in everything around them. To the unclean all things are unclean; and negative people often hate virtue and denounce it as evil. Blackney: "The purest innocence seems like shame." Chan: "Great purity appears like disgrace." Mabry: "True purity seems stained." Wu: "Great whiteness looks spotted."

Great character appears like infirm. Pure worth appears like contaminated. Blackney: "Established goodness seems knavery." Wu: "Abundant Virtue looks deficient." It is common for thugs to consider virtuous people to be weak and foolish. This was a prime trait of the Nazis. Forgiveness was especially abhorrent to them, since the whole movement was based on resentment and hatred. So people who are truly virtuous are always denounced by such people as crazy, fanatical, mean-spirited, negative, etc., etc., etc.

How should we react to this kind of thing? In the *Gospel of Sri Ramakrishna* we find this:

"The conversation was about worldly men, who look down on those who aspire to spiritual things. The Master was talking about the great number of such people in the world, and about how to deal with them.

"MASTER (to Narendra): How do you feel about it? Worldly people say all kinds of things about the spiritually minded. But look here! When an elephant moves along the street, any number of curs and other small animals may bark and cry after it; but the elephant doesn't even look back at them. If people speak ill of you, what will you think of them?

"NARENDRA: "I shall think that dogs are barking at me.

"MASTER (Smiling): Oh, no! You mustn't go that far, my child! *(Laughter).* God dwells in all beings. But you may be intimate only with good people; you must keep away from the evil-minded. God is even in the tiger; but you cannot embrace the tiger on that account. *(Laughter).* You may say, Why run away from a tiger, which is also a manifestation of God? The answer to that is: 'Those who tell you to run away are also manifestations of God–and why shouldn't you listen to them?'"

Great space has no corners. Byrn: "The true square seems to have no corners." Feng and English: "The perfect square has no corners." Corners consist of two lines joined at right angles to one another. But the Great Space that is the Tao is a unity, therefore there can be no corners. Furthermore the two lines of a corner are "moving" in different directions, and in the Tao there are no contradictory movements. Rather, everything moves in a circle which is both unity and wholeness. In this material world a perfect circle never occurs naturally, which is why the Egyptians used a winged circle to represent the unfettered spirit. However, things do move in an ellipse such as the orbits of planets. Because of this the Shiva Linga is elliptical in shape to represent the Golden Egg (Hiranyagarbha) of the cosmos, in which, as said, everything moves elliptically. This idea of all this is that the Tao transcends the multiform configurations of relative existence, especially that of matter.

Great talent takes long to mature. Evolution is the only mode of development possible in this world or any other, and evolution and growth of any kind require time before the process is completed. Unfortunately in modern times we want everything to be instant. Shoddy buildings go up quickly, but solid, well-built structures take much more time. It is the same with learning. Whenever I go to an alternative therapist (including a chiropractor), if I see certificates on the wall showing completion of a weekend seminar in "electric acupuncture" or similar nonsense, I know I am in the den of a shameless quack.

The unfoldment of our innate potential takes time, just as Byrn translates this phrase: "The best vessels take the most time to finish." No, it need not be lifetimes, but it is likely that it will require decades. This is especially true in the evolution of consciousness.

Great music is faintly heard. Either this means that the "music" of the Tao is so subtle that it is experienced only in those levels where sound is virtually silence, or that ordinary people hear it but faintly, have no idea what it is and therefore lose [or never have] interest.

Blackney "Great music is soft sound," indicating its subtlety. Byrn: "The greatest sounds cannot be heard" by the ear, but perceived in levels in which the sound has become a *bhava*, a movement or state of consciousness. Feng and English: "The highest notes are hard to hear" because of the limitation of the "ears" of the perceivers unless they are finely honed and tuned by diligent and prolonged development. Mabry: "Celestial music is seldom paid much heed" except by those that are themselves celestial in the sense of being more spiritual than material. Wu: "Great sound is silent," yet is the source of all lesser sound. (See the section entitled "The 'genealogy' of sound" in Appendix One of *Soham Yoga*.)

Great form has no contour. Blackney: "The great Form has no shape." The Tao has no form, as is shown in the following incident from *Autobiography of a Yogi*.

"Sitting on my bed one morning, I fell into a deep reverie.

"'What is behind the darkness of closed eyes?' This probing thought came powerfully into my mind. An immense flash of light at once manifested to my inward gaze. Divine shapes of saints, sitting in meditation posture in mountain caves, formed like miniature cinema pictures on the large screen of radiance within my forehead.

"'Who are you?' I spoke aloud.

"'We are the Himalayan yogis.' The celestial response is difficult to describe; my heart was thrilled.

"'Ah, I long to go to the Himalayas and become like you!' The vision vanished, but the silvery beams expanded in ever-widening circles to infinity.

"'What is this wondrous glow?'

"'I am Ishwara. I am Light.' The voice was as murmuring clouds.

"'I want to be one with Thee!'

"Out of the slow dwindling of my divine ecstasy, I salvaged a permanent legacy of inspiration to seek God. 'He is eternal, ever-new Joy!' This memory persisted long after the day of rapture."

The Tao is Light Itself in the highest sense.

And Tao is hidden [and] without a name. The Tao is everywhere and everything, yet It is hidden to nearly everyone. The "hiding" is not on the part of the Tao, but is the active delusion of the individual who hides from seeing the Tao. When anyone turns toward the Tao and seeks its perception (for the Tao is not "found," since It is ever-present), refining his inner instruments of perceptions (jnanendriyas) through meditation and ascesis, the Tao is no longer hidden. "   He who sees the Supreme Lord existing in all beings equally, not dying when they die–he sees truly. Truly seeing the same Lord existing everywhere, he injures not the Self by the lower self. Then he goes to the Supreme Goal. When he perceives the various states of being as resting in the One, and their expansion from that One alone–he then attains Brahman" (Bhagavad Gita 13:27-28, 30).

The Tao can be referred to by many names, but none encompass the Tao because It is never an object, but is the Eternal Subject.

It is this Tao that is adept at lending (its power) and bringing fulfillment. Chan: "It is Tao alone that skillfully provides for all and brings them to perfection." Mabry: "It is the Tao alone that nourishes and completes things." The Tao is all in all, the sole power of evolving perfection. It does all things within all beings, yet Itself is unacting and unattached.

In the Bhagavad Gita the Tao speaks through Krishna the enlightened teacher, saying: "I know the departed beings and the living, and those who are yet to be, but none whatsoever knows me.… Know that states of being proceed from me. But I am not in them–they are in me" (Bhagavad Gita 7:26, 12).

"I am that which is the seed of all beings. There is nothing that could exist without existing through me–neither animate nor inanimate. There is no end to my divine manifestations. But this has been declared by me to exemplify the extent of my manifestations.... But what is this extensive knowledge to you? I ever support this whole world by just one portion of myself" (Bhagavad Gita 10:39-40, 42).

42. The Violent Man

Out of Tao, One is born; out of One, Two; out of Two, Three; out of Three, the created universe.

The created universe carries the *yin* at its back and the *yang* in front; through the union of the pervading principles it reaches harmony.

To be "orphaned," "lonely" and "unworthy" is what men hate most. Yet the princes and dukes call themselves by such names. For sometimes things are benefited by being taken away from, and suffer by being added to.

Others have taught this maxim, which I shall teach also: "The violent man shall die a violent death."

This I shall regard as my spiritual teacher.

(Tao Teh King 42)

Wu: "Tao gave birth to One, One gave birth to Two, Two gave birth to Three, Three gave birth to all the myriad things."

Tao gave birth to One. The important thing to realize here is that the Tao transcends both unity and diversity, yet is the source of both. In the same way It transcends existence and non-existence. As the Rig Veda says of the Tao (Brahman): "His shadow is immortality" (10:12:2). Although it is true that all things have come from the One, we must keep in mind that the One came from the Tao, the ineffable and inexpressible. There was a time when the One existed only as a potential extension within the Tao, then It emerged from the Tao only to once more return to the Tao. To concentrate on the One to the exclusion of the Tao is profound ignorance.

We find everyone obsessed with unity, duality and trinity, but these are only appearances of the Tao, nothing in themselves. The Tao is all things simultaneously, and at the same time is No Thing. Of course we do not understand it. Only when we merge with the Tao will misunderstanding cease.

One gave birth to Two. Oneness is impossible in relative existence; there must always be two. So the moment the One emerges from the Tao It splits in two and becomes the Duality which so absorbs our attention from life to life.

Two gave birth to Three. In the eternal moment in which the One divides into Two, a Third manifests. In other words, the One evolves into Two and the Two instantly evolve into Three. In a Christian perspective we would say that the Transcendent Absolute, the Father, manifests the Son who immediately manifests as Son and Holy Spirit.

Three gave birth to all the myriad things. All that exists in relativity is a manifestation of the Absolute extended into the Three, the Trinity. Everything partakes of the essential being of the Trinity and so are reflections of the Trinity. The physical is a revelation of the metaphysical.

The created universe carries the yin at its back and the yang in front; through the union of the pervading principles it reaches harmony. Wu: "All the myriad things carry the Yin on their backs and hold the Yang in their embrace, deriving their vital harmony from the proper blending of the two vital Breaths." Byrn: "All things carry Yin yet embrace Yang. They blend their life breaths in order to produce harmony."

Yin and yang can have many different meanings in more than one Chinese school of thought. In this instance fortunately it is simple. Yin is the force which is diffuse, unfocused and tending to formlessness. It is the basic condition of the universal energies. Yang is the force which is cohesive and focused, tending to solidity and form. The entire range of relative existence embraces both of these seemingly contradictory forces and everything moves back and forth between these two modes of manifestation.

All the myriad things carry the Yin on their backs and hold the Yang in their embrace,.... Yin is the unseen basis of all things and remains their ground into which they are always tending to return, although they always show their yang side, the only side with which we can ordinarily interact. So the formless is always at the back of the form. Yin and yang are present wherever we may be.

...deriving their vital harmony from the proper blending of the two vital Breaths. Yin and Yang are the breath streams of the ever-moving universe, the inhalation and exhalation of the Tao, known to the yogis as prana and apana. The predominance of one or the other determines how we perceive them and how they affect us, at least potentially. Nothing in our environment is either purely one or the other, but all are a combination of yin and yang. There really is nothing but yin and yang, which means there really is nothing but the Tao.

To be "orphaned," "lonely" and "unworthy" is what men hate most. Yet the princes and dukes call themselves by such names. For sometimes things are benefited by being taken away from, and suffer by being added to. Wu: "What is more loathed by men than to be 'helpless,' 'little,' and 'worthless'? And yet these are the very names the princes and barons call themselves. Truly, one may gain by losing; And one may lose by gaining."

In section thirty-nine we were told that since the nobility depend upon the common people they give themselves such epithets to make the people think they are somehow like them or are aware that they could become so easily. It is of course a pathetic affectation, like all such manipulative ploys. But here another side is pointed out: the awareness of even the exalted that Heaven, the Tao, may change their status into one undesired, but that it can be to their own benefit. And of course Lao Tzu is in this way pointing out that all men can be benefited by losing and harmed by gaining.

Many have at first been pained by loss, only to find that the loss opened the way to greater gain. Some people find that their losing gave them freedom they could never have otherwise had. That is why kings have renounced their thrones and princes have fled them. Money and

42. The Violent Man

possessions not only often bring misery and frustration, they can destroy spiritual life.

I knew a man who became a fervent yogi. Time went on, and things got better and better for him. Then one day a relative died and left him an apartment house. After a while he had three more apartment houses, but had along the way totally abandoned his search for God. His misery was great, but the world had entered his heart and there was no hope of his turning back in this lifetime.

Others have taught this maxim, which I shall teach also: "The violent man shall die a violent death." This I shall regard as my spiritual teacher. Wu: "What another has taught let me repeat: 'A man of violence will come to a violent end.' Whoever said this can be my teacher and my father." Violence is more than physical action, and this maxim includes all forms, inner and outer. Jesus simply said: "All they that take the sword shall perish with the sword" (Matthew 26:52).

43. The Softest Substance

> The softest substance of the world goes through the hardest.
> That-which-is-without-form penetrates that-which-has-no-crevice.
> Through this I know the benefit of taking no action.
> The teaching without words and the benefit of taking no action are without compare in the universe.
> (Tao Teh King 43)

Here, too, yin and yang are being considered, because we often mistake which of two contradictory forces is the strongest and therefore make mistakes in our decisions and expectations.

"It's a dog-eat-dog world," "Get them before they get you," its variation: "Do it to others before others do it to you" and "Look out for Old Number One" are utterly fallacious slogans thrown around constantly, especially by criminals of varying degree. The real nature and meaning of Survival Of The Fittest is never understood, because people seem incapable of realizing that the strongest are not at all the fittest to survive. Often oppressors have only been remembered by those they oppressed. Shelley certainly got it right:

> I met a traveller from an antique land
> Who said: Two vast and trunkless legs of stone
> Stand in the desert. Near them, on the sand,
> Half sunk, a shattered visage lies, whose frown,

43. The Softest Substance

And wrinkled lip, and sneer of cold command,
Tell that its sculptor well those passions read
Which yet survive, stamped on these lifeless things,
The hand that mocked them and the heart that fed:
And on the pedestal these words appear:
"My name is Ozymandias, king of kings:
Look on my works, ye Mighty, and despair!"
Nothing beside remains. Round the decay
Of that colossal wreck, boundless and bare
The lone and level sands stretch far away.

The meek and often despised are the only ones who look at that colossal wreck and read the words. They alone even know the name Ozymandias.

The softest substance of the world goes through the hardest. Byrn: "That which offers no resistance, overcomes the hardest substances." Jesus, Confucius and Lao Tzu followed the path of non-resistance, and only because of our admiration for them do we remember their persecutors. Who today would have ever heard of Pilate if not for his shameful refusal to exonerate Jesus and ordering his crucifixion? Gandhi in our very own time proved the power of non-violence. "A soft answer turneth away wrath" (Proverbs 15:1). Sometimes it does not work that way, and instead the suffering of the good is their sole weapon. Making ourselves soft and non-resistant is the path of power.

That-which-is-without-form penetrates that-which-has-no-crevice. Mabry: "That which is without substance can enter even where there is no space." Refinement and subtlety of mind and perception is another valuable tool for ultimate success. Spiritual evolution is the only way to overcome the chaos and misery of mere materiality. It is the spiritual adepts that are the surest survivors. Some have even been killed and returned to life.

In my teen years I met an elderly man in Louisiana who had been present in 1890 when members of the Klan came to their church which even in the nineteenth century was condemning racial segregation and holding integrated meetings. Laughing, they described how the night before they had killed the founder of the church by beating him to death and had thrown his body into the swamp quicksand so he could not have the honor of a funeral. This grieved the church people tremendously, yet, being genuine pacifists, they meekly listened to the klansmen and let them go unchallenged (and unreported). Prayer was their sole recourse. A little over a week later, the founder came quietly walking into the home of one of the faithful, saying that he had indeed died, but had been sent back into his body, crawled out of the quicksand and stood before him alive. He could say with his Master, Jesus: "I am he that liveth, and was dead; and, behold, I am alive" (Revelation 1:18).

Then he sat down and wrote the following which later was made into a beautiful hymn:

> Who will suffer with the Savior?
> Take the little that remains
> Of the cup of tribulation
> Jesus drank in dying pains?
>
> Who will offer soul and body
> On the altar of our God?
> Leaving self and worldly mammon,
> Take the path that Jesus trod?
>
> Who will suffer for the gospel,
> Follow Christ without the gate?
> Take the martyrs for example,
> With them glory at the stake?
>
> Oh, for consecrated service
> 'Mid the din of Babel strife;
> Who will dare the truth to herald,
> At the peril of his life?

Soon the conflict will be over,
Crowns await the firm and pure;
Forward, brethren, work and suffer,
Faithful to the end endure.

Lord, we fellowship Thy passion,
Gladly suffer shame and loss;
With Thy blessing pain is pleasure,
We will glory in Thy cross.

The Klan never bothered any members of that church again.

In the twentieth century the Venerable Master Hsu Yun was beaten to death by the Chinese Communists, but he returned to life and lived to the age of one hundred and nineteen years unmolested. He is even now a living presence in the world for the awakening of many.

Through this I know the benefit of taking no action. Blackney: "By this I know the benefit of something done by quiet being." "He who perceives inaction in action and action in inaction–such a man is wise among men, steadfast in yoga and doing all action" (Bhagavad Gita 4:18). Only that which is done in full consciousness of the divine Self, the Tao, can prevail, because it is the truth of things, the proof of the Sanskrit motto: Only Truth Prevails, or: Only Truth is Victorious: *Satyam Eva Jayate.*

The teaching without words... There are two forms of this. The first is the teaching conveyed through example. In my late teens I was very impressed when I heard a minister tell a congregation that their neighbors should know all the teachings of their church simply by living next door to them without ever speaking about religion. Such an idea implied people whose entire life was shaped by their faith. I was used to churches that made absolutely no difference in their members, and any attempt to do so would have been denounced as interference and fanaticism. Most church members seemed proud of the fact that they were just like everyone else, including those that had no religion. What the value of those churches were I could never figure out. Eventually I realized it was because they had no value to figure out.

Fortunately, later in life I came across the spiritual traditions of the East (including Eastern Christianity) that did make a great difference in the lives of those who not only believed in their value but ordered their lives according to their beliefs and principles. Of course, they were all labeled crazy, fanatics, devil-worshippers and even drug addicts by the ordinary American churchgoers around them. Among both the leaders and the followers of those oriental philosophies, and even more so among those in the countries of their origin, I met people whose entire being embodied their wisdom.

Great individuals such as Gandhi teach every moment of their lives. In India I have met and spent time with men and women who were living scriptures. Certainly the ideals of Indian religion could be learned by just associating with them. I have already several times mentioned Swami Sivananda of Rishikesh whom I can say without exaggeration was what the Eastern Christians call "a heavenly man and an earthly angel." Such people are ever with God, and so are those who associate with them. The mere sight of them can awaken spiritual consciousness. In their presence profound understanding can arise spontaneously from within.

The benefit of taking no action. Chan: "The advantage of taking no action." Feng and English: "Work without doing." Wu: "The fruits of Non-Ado." There is great wisdom and benefit in knowing when we should act and when we should not act. Much is accomplished both by acting and not acting. We just have to know the right time for each. The Chinese understood for thousands of years that hermits who seemed to being doing nothing were among the most beneficial members of society. Their inactivity tempered the worker ant attitude of aggressive business and government. At the same time, their speaking from the perspective gained by their stepping back from ordinary life brought great benefit to those who consulted them. Throughout history in both east and west the leaders of society have asked the counsel of those who have withdrawn from the common order of things. Both their example and words led many to understand how to better to live their lives in the company of busy mankind. Plato insisted that without such contemplatives and solitaries, a healthy society was impossible.

44. Be Content

Fame or self: which is more important? Your possessions or your person: which is worth more to you? Gain or loss: which is worse?

Therefore, to be obsessed with "things" is a great waste, the more you gain, the greater your loss.

Being content with what you have been given [Wu: To know when you have enough], you can avoid disgrace. Knowing when to stop, you will avoid danger. That way you can live a long and happy life.

(Tao Teh King 44, Mabry's translation)

Fame or self: which is more important? In this world of externalized consciousness, people are much more interested in what people only think they are rather than what they really are. Further, they will compromise, degrade and even falsify themselves so others will have the opinion of them they desire. This is incredibly dangerous, because in time such people will completely lose touch with their true character. I have known people who believed they were what people considered them to be, lacking any self-awareness whatsoever. Needless to say, these were thoroughly characterless people, hardly even two-dimensional personalities. Some were one-dimensional, just being a husk with a name, a mask with no one really behind it.

Your possessions or your person: which is worth more to you? I think we know the general answer to that: possessions alone matter. There are even those who pride themselves on frugality or austerity whose lack of possessions are most important to them. And there are those engaged frantically in what is known as "conspicuous non-consumption." So whether there is a desire for more or less, material possessions define most people, both to themselves and others. These people, as well as those discussed in the previous section, have not just lost their soul, they have tossed it away for the sake of appearance. As Galsworthy satirically put it: "What does it profit a man to gain his soul and lose his possessions?"

Gain or loss: which is worse? This has already been discussed in Section 42 where it is said: "Truly, one may gain by losing; And one may lose by gaining." So now we are being urged to look at the consequences of gain and loss in regard to our personal integrity, not to make a blanket evaluation of the two.

Therefore, to be obsessed with "things" is a great waste, the more you gain, the greater your loss. To be possessed by possessions is to be lessened by them the more they are gained. Here, too, people can be reduced to mere husks, their life energies drained away by their money and possessions. Once a friend and I encountered a very wealthy but obnoxious young man. When the man left, my friend commented to me: "If he wasn't a 'rich kid' he would be nothing." The spectacle of such people is terribly sad. Jesus was actually giving practical psychological advice when he told the rich young man: "Go, sell what you have and give to the poor, and you will have treasure in heaven" (Matthew 19:21).

Being content with what you have been given Wu: "To know when you have enough, you can avoid disgrace." There is no doubt that the stress of getting more and more can ruin physical and mental health, what to speak of the anxiety about keeping what has been gained. Having just the right amount and being content with it contributes to general well-being. So many people come to ruin personally and socially when this is not known or not followed.

Knowing when to stop, you will avoid danger. This applies to all aspects of life, not just material welfare. There is nothing in human life that cannot become a curse when overdone. Knowing what is necessary and never going beyond that is the formula for success and happiness.

(Though there is the lazy insistence by those who do not want to fulfill their spiritual obligation: "You can go too far, you know!")

That way you can live a long and happy life. And be a valuable example to others.

45. Calm Quietude

> The greatest perfection seems imperfect, and yet its use is inexhaustible.
> The greatest fullness seems empty, and yet its use is endless.
> The great straightness looks like crookedness.
> The greatest skill appears clumsy.
> The greatest eloquence sounds like stammering.
> Restlessness overcomes cold, but calm overcomes heat.
> The peaceful and serene is the norm of the world.
> (Tao Teh King 45–Wu translation)

What we are given here, and which has confused and stymied many translators, is a diagnosis of the way the world of human experience looks to those immersed in delusion and confusion. Being truly negative and therefore seeing everything opposite to the way they really are, ordinary people will naturally go toward the false and the harmful and suffer as a consequence. The more intense their search for these things, the greater their misery, so much so that many of them crown their self-destruction with the ultimate folly of suicide. Frantically seeking peace and happiness, they run from the very things that will give them what they seek. Regarding enemies as friends and friends as enemies, what can result but what the Bhagavad Gita calls *Mahato Bhayat*, the Great Terror or Great Fear? Abhorring the great joy and peace that is the Tao, what hope is there? Lao Tzu is trying to shake us awake.

The greatest perfection seems imperfect, and yet its use is inexhaustible. Blackney: "Most perfect, yet it seems imperfect, incomplete: Its use is not impaired." First of all, the entire universe being a manifestation of the Tao, it is perfect. The imperfection we see is due to both ignorance and limitation of experience, potential and actual. Since the universe is a mixture of black and white as shown in the yin-yang symbol, which includes karmic forces positive and negative, naturally we see conflict and confusion in the universe. And it is there, only it is not a flaw but a working out of the potential perfection of creation which is moving toward the inevitable manifestation of that perfection. When that happens, the universe dissolves (in a precise manner) and remains unmanifest for as long as it was manifest; then it returns to manifestation.

Creation is inexhaustible, occurring again and again eternally. It had no beginning and it will have no end because it is a manifestation of the beginningless and endless God. The Bhagavad Gita describes it this way: "The worlds up to Brahma's realm are subject to rebirth's return,.... They know the true day and night who know Brahma's Day a thousand yugas long and Brahma's Night a thousand yugas long. At the approach of Brahma's Day, all manifested things come forth from the unmanifest, and then return to that at Brahma's Night. Helpless, the same host of beings being born again and again merge at the approach of the Night and emerge at the dawn of Day. But there exists, higher than the unmanifested, another unmanifested Eternal which does not perish when all beings perish. This unmanifest is declared to be the imperishable, which is called the Supreme Goal, attaining which they return not. This is my supreme abode" (Bhagavad Gita 8:16-21). It is the Tao.

The greatest fullness seems empty, and yet its use is endless. Blackney: "Filled, and yet it seems an empty void: it never will run dry." "Where is this God of yours? Where is he to be found, to be seen?...." So runs the old objection. In India they say that if fish were told about water they would make the same objection: Where is it and how can you see it? Kabir wrote about such unphilosophers: "Verily it makes me smile to hear of a fish in water athirst!"

Thomas Hardy wrote the following poem, "New Year's Eve," satirizing the "rational" and "scientific" that miss the point.

"I have finished another year," said God,
    "In grey, green, white, and brown;
I have strewn the leaf upon the sod,
Sealed up the worm within the clod,
    And let the last sun down."

"And what's the good of it?" I said.
    "What reasons made you call
From formless void this earth we tread,
When nine-and-ninety can be read
    Why nought should be at all?

"Yea, Sire; why shaped you us, 'who in
    This tabernacle groan'–
If ever a joy be found herein,
Such joy no man had wished to win
    If he had never known!"

Then he: "My labours–logicless–
    You may explain; not I:
Sense-sealed I have wrought, without a guess
That I evolved a Consciousness
    To ask for reasons why.

"Strange that ephemeral creatures who
    By my own ordering are,
Should see the shortness of my view,
Use ethic tests I never knew,
    Or made provision for!"

> He sank to raptness as of yore,
>   And opening New Year's Day
> Wove it by rote as theretofore,
> And went on working evermore
>   In his unweeting way.

The great straightness looks like crookedness. Blackney: "The straightest, yet it seems to deviate, to bend." I well remember the time I played a recording of some exquisite singing by a group of people with no musical training for my great uncle Riley Maxey. At the end both my grandmother (his sister) and I expressed our amazement. But Uncle Riley pulled a sour face, looked at us and pronounced: "There's something fishy about that!" My grandmother looked at me, smiled and shook her head. Nothing more was, or could be, said. A bent mirror gives a distorted image and so does a bent mind. As a result, personal experience often counts for very little and we must realize that someone's sincere assertion about something may have little value as well, and that includes our own opinion. Caution is always wisdom.

For some people clarity is confusion and truth sounds like lies. Conversely, for them confusion is clarity and lies are truth. This is a state of thorough negativity. Here, too, the supposed rationalists and scientists (including the Amazing Randy who is amazingly unamazing) have their input–often unasked and certainly without real relevance or factual reality.

It is essential that we both think and live in a straight line; but we can be assured that many people will see us as bent and deviating from reason and reality. I have known parents who had no objection to their children engaging in heavy drug use and immorality, but truly did go ballistic when their children turned around, cleaned up their lives and took up yoga meditation. People commonly think that morality is not only harmful but mental illness, that freedom is slavery and the quest for a higher life and consciousness is purposeless and a dead end. Once we step out of that crowd we can be assured of their opposition and censure. We must be prepared for that and learn to calmly hold to our principles and convictions despite protestations, threats and even active persecution.

The greatest skill appears clumsy. Many great geniuses have been considered fools and incompetent and their work garbage. This is true in every field including science that is often a haven of bigotry and resistance to progress. The wise appear fools and the fools appear wise. That is the world in which we live.

The greatest eloquence sounds like stammering. "What you say is nonsense," "You make no sense," "Your ideas are contrary to all reason," and so on and on and on. Many times I have seen people who were awakened and helped by spiritual books give away copies to their friends only to have those friends viciously denounce and mock them in return. I cannot count the number of people who have told me as they mailed a book or letter to a good (or best) friend: "He/She was always more interested in these kind of things than I was.... We used to talk for hours about spiritual subjects." Then BANG came the response in the form of a phone call or letter filled with contempt and hostility. My friends would be completely shocked and bewildered. They did not realize that those who love to talk and theorize about something almost always hate encountering it as a reality. "Oh, how I wish...," they lament, only to explode when the possibility of their wish being fulfilled confronts them. I knew a woman who lamented the lack of a certain kind of spiritual group in her town. When such a group was formed she attended once and in two or three weeks moved to a distant state to get away from having to be a part of it. Another acquaintance of mine began making plans to move out of the country (!) when what she claimed to always have wanted spiritually suddenly was made available.

Restlessness overcomes cold, but calm overcomes heat. Blackney: "Movement overcomes the cold, and stillness, heat." The molecules of cold objects move slowly, but those of warm or hot objects move quickly. Molasses and wax are often cited as proof of this. Getting busy and engaging in meditation and spiritual disciplines and practices is the way to overcome the inertia and resistance often encountered when we try to lead a spiritual life. Cutting back or slacking off is disastrous. In

Sanskrit spiritual practices are called tapasya, the generating of heat. On the other hand, when mental fever and passions erupt, being calm and relaxed is the remedy. In acupuncture some points are increased in energy levels and others are decreased. In the same way judicious action and judicious inaction can ensure spiritual health.

The peaceful and serene is the norm of the world. Blackney: "The wise man, pure and still, will rectify the world." The ideal world is peaceful and serene, in fact that is its real nature though outer and internal disorder makes it seem just the opposite. Blackney's translation is very meaningful for us. Being pure and still is the way of setting things right. Not only will it help us, it will help the world, for after all we are a part of this world. Everyone believes that the world affects them, but overlook the fact that they affect the world. For example, terrible and destructive upheavals in nature are the result of the thought and deeds of the people in those areas. The world is a mirror that reflects the group karma of humanity.

> Let there be peace on earth
> And let it begin with me.

46. Racing Horses

When the world lives in accord with Tao, racing horses are turned back to haul refuse carts.
When the world lives not in accord with Tao, cavalry abounds in the countryside.
There is no greater curse than the lack of contentment.
No greater sin than the desire for possession.
Therefore he who is contented with contentment shall be always content.
(Tao Teh King 46)

When the world lives in accord with Tao, racing horses are turned back to haul refuse carts. From this we certainly know what Lao Tzu thought of gambling and "sport." It also illustrates the principle that things should be put to practical use and not exploited for the entertainment of people too idle or empty-headed to be living meaningful lives. Certainly Lao Tzu would subscribe to our early American maxim: "Eat it up; wear it out; make it do or do without."

When the world lives not in accord with Tao, cavalry abounds in the countryside. Unfortunately, when the Tao is ignored race horses are not the worst to be encountered: the game of war is rampant. Preparing for war, engaging in war and recovering from war are favorite pastimes of the morally insane rather than the sad necessities they often are in this skewed world. This statement also deplores the social aggression and coercion that abound everywhere, both passive and active. The willingness to exploit and even injure others for personal benefit is another form of madness quite acceptable in the minds of those who very contentedly aver: "It's a dog-eat-dog world." They do not realize they are calling themselves dogs if they plan to engage in the "eating"! Getting ahead at the price of other's loss, and the loss of one's own integrity, is considered hard-headed wisdom, bedrock practicality. No wonder Lao Tzu was on the road to escape "civilization" when he wrote down the Tao Teh King.

There is no greater curse than the lack of contentment. Some years ago I met a woman whose life seemed to be perpetually miserable. Naturally I assumed it was from past karma, but a very wise man I consulted about the situation simply said: "She makes herself miserable wherever she is." It is also tragic that we will not shake off the foolish delusion that contentment is derived from "stuff." Gain, as the Tao Teh King says, is often nothing but loss.

Wu translates this: "There is no calamity like not knowing what is enough." That is certainly the great calamity of the "developed" countries of the world.

Blackney has an interesting perspective on this. He renders it: "No sin can exceed incitement to envy." It is true that many people strive for gain, not with the intention of enjoying it, but of making other people jealous of them.

I knew a brilliant man who did not pursue a career in physics, which he loved, but instead became a movie producer in Hollywood so the people that made fun of him in school and called him "the brain" would respect and envy him. The result was total misery. He perpetually smoked with trembling hands and hated everything in his life, including his wife and children.

One of my aunts absolutely could not enjoy having something (and she had a lot) unless she felt that it made someone jealous. She lived in a mansion made of imported Italian brick with a great staircase and stained glass window as in *Gone With the Wind* and a huge ballroom taking up the entire third floor. Her husband normally deposited tens of thousands of dollars in the bank at a single time. The family never spent a single evening at home in their fabulous home, but wandered around, shopping and driving far afield to eat in special restaurants. Finally she insisted they abandon the mansion and move back to her small home town so she could show off her money to those she had known in childhood and adolescence. But no one in the town cared about her wealth and they were completely indifferent to the things she did to provoke envy, so after two or three years she had to move back to the Big City and continue being discontent unless she could brag about how jealous someone was of her.

No greater sin than the desire for possession. Just to get for the sake of getting is a major part of many people's lives who really just exist rather than live. Empty lives, hearts and heads often motivate the getting and spending that Wordsworth laments in "The World Is Too Much With Us."

Wu renders this: "There is no evil like covetousness." I assume he means the drive to get everything that others have even if it is not really wanted. We have all seen that, too.

Mabry sums it all up: "Nothing breeds trouble like greed." Chan: "There is no greater disaster than greed."

Therefore he who is contented with contentment shall be always content. This is the secret: to seek contentment within rather than to scramble after outer things and situations that only breed discontent. This is, I think, the best translation because it leads us back to the seat of the problem: our own minds and hearts.

However there is value in these three others: Wu: "Only he who knows what is enough will always have enough." Mabry: "Only one who is content with what is enough will be content always." Feng and English: "Therefore he who knows that enough is enough will always have enough."

The solution to the entire matter is within us..

47. Pursuit of Knowledge

> Without stepping outside one's doors, one can know what is happening in the world.
> Without looking out of one's windows, one can see the Tao of heaven.
> The farther one pursues knowledge, the less one knows.
> Therefore the Sage knows without running about, understands without seeing, accomplishes without doing.
> (Tao Teh King 47)

Though we know him mostly through his novels and short stories, Mark Twain (Samuel Clemens) was also a philosopher who wrote very interestingly on the everyday aspects of human life that we almost never think about. I was really impressed by one essay in which he said that those who knew and understood themselves could know and understand every human being. His reasoning was that we all consist of the same elements, the differences between us being determined by the quality and degree of those elements as well as how much or little we express them. The colors of a painting are basically the same as those in other paintings, but the arrangement, amount and shade can vary infinitely. So it is with us. Knowing ourselves we can know others. This may be part of the reasoning of Lao Tzu.

Without stepping outside one's doors, one can know what is happening in the world. This is certainly true for a very astute person, assuming that the outside world comes to him by contact with other people in his home and observation of the material objects that also enter there. However, if we enlarge "one's doors" to include the town in which he lives and maybe a bit of the countryside, then any intelligent and perceptive person can see and understand through the various elements of his environment what is happening in the world, or at the least the world of his nation.

We must remember that the world of Lao Tzu had no newspapers, radio, television or all the means of information and communication without which we now cannot imagine living for a day. So he is speaking of someone who would be a kind of social and philosophical Sherlock Homes who could know the whole by studying the part.

Without looking out of one's windows, one can see the Tao of heaven. Frankly, I cannot image anyone being able to know the Tao of heaven without spending a great deal of time in the confines of one's house, for only there can meditation and study be engaged in intensely.

The farther one pursues knowledge, the less one knows. I believe this is especially true at this point in time. While I was in my teens I realized that a worthwhile school or university should be little more than a gigantic library with a staff of qualified advisors to guide the student in a personal pursuit of knowledge according to his inclination or need. In 1963 after I returned from my first trip to India I met one of the country's leading computer experts. At that time computers were immense things with whirling tape reels that cost a fortune to install and maintain. But he told me that the day of home computers was coming, and when it did schools would be obsolete. So it has proven, though nearly everyone is lagging behind and students still are imprisoned in the educational gulags. I knew a child who learned to read at the age of two through an computer program called Reader Rabbit. Bank Street Writer was a word processor intended for use by kindergarten students. There is no need to travel hundreds and thousands of miles for a good education. It is right at hand in the home.

After beginning to write on this verse I went online to investigate what was available for home study through the internet. There were many programs available. One had a video of an American teenager who

47. Pursuit of Knowledge

grew up in China but through the internet had a thoroughly American education. Now he attends the university that sponsored the internet education he received all the way from the early grades through high school. (Many universities now offer online degree programs.) So Lao Tzu's ideals about learning can be better realized now than in his day.

The philosophical meaning of this verse is that the further we go from ourselves for knowledge (in the highest sense) the less we will know, for infinity, the Tao, is within.

Therefore the Sage knows without running about, understands without seeing, accomplishes without doing. The yogi especially travels far, understands and accomplishes within what the "outsiders" can never imagine. All of his activity is in a realm undreamed of by others. Swami Sivananda in one of his letters wrote: "I always travel throughout the world, and those who are quick catch me." The lives of great yogis prove this to be true. Sitting in caves the yoga adepts know what is going on throughout the world. A man once told me he traveled thousands of miles to meet a great mystic only to find that the saint knew all about him and told him he had been looking in on him for a long time, and mentioned the various things that had been going on with him: inner things that only one who knew his heart and mind could have known. Those who lived with him had no idea of the things the mystic knew.

48. Conquering the World by Inaction

> In the pursuit of learning, every day something is acquired.
> In the pursuit of Tao, every day something is dropped.
> Less and less is done until non-action is achieved. When nothing is done, nothing is left undone.
> The world is ruled by letting things take their course. It cannot be ruled by interfering.
> (Tao Teh King 48–Feng and English translation)

In the pursuit of learning, every day something is acquired. In the pursuit of Tao, every day something is dropped. Byrn: "One who seeks knowledge learns something new every day. One who seeks the Tao unlearns something new every day." We must realize that "learning" and "knowledge" here mean the accumulation of the trivia that passes for learning and knowledge but are really the fluff of an idle mind. Worldly people cram their minds full of pointless ideas and facts in a desperate attempt to cover their inner and outer emptiness. I once had a conversation with a man who told me with great satisfaction that his entire life was on a completely different track from it had been previously. This he told me was because: 1) he had gotten a divorce, 2) had taken a course in Ancient Wisdom, 3) he was learning to play the saxophone, and 4) he was going on a cruise. What a life change! Running in the hamster wheel of their lives, people are occupied and blinded to the pathetic pettiness of their lives and minds.

But those who seek the Tao are the opposite. They shrug off the nonsense they were indoctrinated with as children and adults and simplify their existence so the horizons of their life will be clear and ready for seeing the Tao. They turn from "reality" to the Real, from "truth" to the True, from "knowledge" to Knowing, from "living" to Life. It takes a courageous mind to be willing to discover what is actually true and what is false, what is worthwhile and what is worthless. Such an outlook certainly estranges us from the false realm of ordinary life. As Shelley wrote:

Lift not the painted veil which those who live
Call Life: though unreal shapes be pictured there,
And it but mimic all we would believe
With colours idly spread–behind, lurk Fear
And Hope, twin Destinies; who ever weave
Their shadows, o'er the chasm, sightless and drear.
I knew one who had lifted it–he sought,
For his lost heart was tender, things to love,
But found them not, alas! nor was there aught
The world contains, the which he could approve.
Through the unheeding many he did move,
A splendour among shadows, a bright blot
Upon this gloomy scene, a Spirit that strove
For truth, and like the Preacher found it not.

Less and less is done until non-action is achieved. When nothing is done, nothing is left undone. This may sound like nonsense, but if we look at it carefully it will make total sense. The wise person becomes less and less intent on busyness and gets down to business: the knowing of the Tao. He eliminates activity that is nothing but distraction or insincere fulfillment of shallow social expectations. He does not become idle, but has no involvement with activity that is to no worthwhile purpose or which produces no desirable or lasting result.

Only that which has genuine benefit interests him. As far as the world is concerned he does nothing and wastes his time. A friend of mine was constantly pestered by her mother if she tried to read a book. "Why don't you *do* something?" her mother would say. Once when traveling on a bus I heard a woman complaining to someone about how her son had a good job that made money but was always listening to music or reading. "And this week he's going to an opera, even though he's been to that one before," she complained. "But it's not the story, it's the music," said her companion. "Well, I don't see it!" retorted the disgruntled mother. Naturally I had to get a look at the offender, so I dawdled around and witnessed the meeting of mother and son. He was dressed in suit, tie and overcoat, obviously prosperous and obviously intelligent. She kept looking at him and though he had two heads and after she managed to gripe about "that opera" and his life in general he got her into a taxi and away they went for what I felt sure would be a horrible visit for both of them.

When we no longer waste our time and life we accomplish a great deal: everything, in fact.

The world is ruled by letting things take their course. It cannot be ruled by interfering. Byrn: "Mastery of the world is achieved by letting things take their natural course. You cannot master the world by changing the natural way." Does this mean we do nothing? No; it means we do what needs to be done and then let the cosmos respond as it will. All our lives we have been seeing people force things in their life rather than realizing that they have to let the tides of the world determine the result. Usually, if they bully the universe into doing what they want the result is disastrous or completely nil. They only end up with wasted time and energy.

Montessori education (real Montessori, that is) is a perfect example of Lao Tzu's principle. Children are never required to study something. Rather it is presented to them and if they are ready for it they respond with interest, otherwise not. We must deal with the world in the same way. In spiritual matters this is especially crucial. Consider Lao Tzu; he said what he had to say and then passed on leaving the result up to those who encountered his wisdom. Buddha embodied this, also. And so do all viable spiritual teachers.

49. The People's Hearts

>The Sage has no interests of his own, But takes the interests of the people as his own.
>
>He is kind to the kind; he is also kind to the unkind; for Virtue is kind.
>
>He is faithful to the faithful; he is also faithful to the unfaithful: for Virtue is faithful.
>
>In the midst of the world, the Sage is shy and self-effacing.
>
>For the sake of the world he keeps his heart in its nebulous state.
>
>All the people strain their ears and eyes: the Sage only smiles like an amused infant.
>
>(Tao Teh King 49–Wu's translation)

The Sage has no interests of his own, But takes the interests of the people as his own. Living in wise simplicity and free from ego, the sage is sensitive to the difficulties and needs of others and does what he can to quietly and unobtrusively (even invisibly) assist them. Possessing peace and contentment himself, he feels for those who have none. Sometimes he must simply observe and care, but as much he can he tries to alleviate all care and need in others. I have known such people, mostly in India where there was a great deal to feel compassion about.

He is kind to the kind; he is also kind to the unkind; for Virtue is kind. We tend to have the idea that it is all right to be pleasant to the pleasing and unpleasant to the unpleasing. "They asked for it," or "They deserved it," we say in justification. But we are only revealing our lack of virtue. For as Lao Tzu tells us, virtue is unfailingly kind.

He is faithful to the faithful; he is also faithful to the unfaithful: for Virtue is faithful. It is considered acceptable to lie to liars and cheat cheaters, to let the unmerciful suffer and the selfish stingy continue in need. But Lao Tzu says otherwise. No matter what a person is not, we must not mirror his lack or defect. We must be what he should be, no matter what. This is not easy, for being virtuous does not much appeal when dealing with the unvirtuous. But the virtuous are always virtuous. Of course they are not foolish, and do not let themselves be made fools of. But they are consistently gentle and kind, even if firm and uncompromising.

In the midst of the world, the Sage is shy and self-effacing. "Shy" may not be such a good translation; reticent, modest and retiring is the idea. No sage is a zero, a wimp or a bore. Lao Tzu does not mean mean that. Rather, the sage is unassuming and quiet. Preferring to be completely offstage rather than on center stage, he is not antisocial but fits the description of a wise man given in the Bhagavad Gita: "Absence of pride, freedom from hypocrisy, harmlessness, fortitude, rectitude, purity, constancy and self-control, detachment from the objects of sense, absence of egotism, keeping in mind the evils of birth, death, old age, disease, and pain, non-attachment, constant even-mindedness in desired and undesired events, living in secluded places, having distaste for association with many people, establishment in the knowledge of the Supreme Self, keeping in mind the goal of knowledge of the truth–this is said to be true knowledge. The contrary is ignorance" (13:7-11).

For the sake of the world he keeps his heart in its nebulous state. That is, he meets everything without preconception or prejudice, able to see it as it is. His mind is in a sense ever new in its experience of the world. This is why saints are mistakenly thought to be childlike and childish people are mistakenly thought to be saints. Just as wax or clay must be kept warm and malleable for the sculptor's use, so the mind and heart of the sage is able to receive a full and perfect impression of anything or anyone he encounters. Since he lets nothing interfere with his perception, including any thoughts or attitudes regarding himself, his mind is more than a mirror, it is a source of understanding and knowledge regarding all things. It is not passive but supremely active in an incomprehensible manner. Consequently Lao Tzu concludes:

All the people strain their ears and eyes: the Sage only smiles like an amused infant. The sage does not try to be a sage–he does not try to be anything. Rather, by cultivating non-trying and non-thought he is totally himself and practically speaking omniscient. All things are a source of happiness to him. His smile is the smile of an amused infant. This is not mere poetics. Swami Sivananda had just such a smile, which I will never forget, and which I have never seen the like of in all the intervening years. He was one whom Krishna meant when he said about the man of illumination: "When he leaves behind all the desires of the mind, contented in the Self by the Self, then he is said to be steady in wisdom. He whose mind is not agitated in misfortunes, freed from desire for pleasures, from whom passion, fear and anger have departed, steady in thought–such a man is said to be a sage. He who is without desire in all situations, encountering this or that, pleasant or unpleasant, not rejoicing or disliking–his wisdom stands firm" (Bhagavad Gita 2:55-57).

50. The Preserving of Life

From birth to death, three people out of ten are celebrators of Life. Three people out of ten are advocates of Death. The rest simply move numbly from cradle to grave. Why is this? Because they are overly protective of this life.

It is said that one who knows how to protect his life can walk freely without fear of the wild buffalo or tiger. He may meet an army bravely with neither sword nor shield. For the buffalo will find no place to sink its horns, the tiger finds no place to dig his claws, weapons find no soft place to pierce. Why? Because there is no place for death in him.

(Tao Teh King 50–Mabry translation)

In the twentieth century William Arthur Dunkerley, writing under the name of John Oxenham, wrote the following poem.

To every man there openeth
A Way, and Ways, and a Way,
And the High Soul climbs the High Way,
And the Low Soul gropes the Low,
And in between, on the misty flats,
The rest drift to and fro.
But to every man there openeth
A High Way, and a Low.
And every man decideth
The way his soul shall go.

He was writing a long time after Lao Tzu, but his insight was the same. Perhaps he was a Taoist in a previous life.

The thirds

According to Lao Tzu, the human race can be divided into three groups.

The first are those who come out of the womb planning to live life. They may be wise or foolish in the way they go about it, the results along the way may be every kind imaginable, and their personal style may cover the entire spectrum of possibilities, but they *live*.

The second are self-destructive, determined to spend their life rushing toward its end in as direct a way as possible. As children they always have a bandage, a bruise or a scab or sometimes a cast on an arm or leg. All the childhood diseases in their most virulent forms occupy them in turn. Allergies are their first love. Their bodies are self-killing machines. These people do everything in life to injure, maim, distort, corrupt and ultimately destroy themselves. Some manage after only a few years of life and others take longer than most people live. They do not do this for enjoyment but for the misery of it. Self-loathing may motivate them or simple idiocy, but pain and agony will be the order of the day. These people cannot possibly be helped. Any good that comes into their life is seized and immediately transmuted into a tool for chaos and suffering, both for themselves and others. Any truth that accidentally get through into their heads is also instantly transformed into a form of delusion, fuel that makes their hell-fire burn more intensely. They run through life slashing and burning–usually themselves, but others are certainly going to be involved along the way. These people also may band together and raise more hell than could be done separately. The world itself is in peril from these. The only good thing about them is that they do eventually end by *dying*.

The third simply zombie their way through the world in a kind of comatose subsistence. They think nothing, they plan nothing, they do nothing and they are nothing. But they make great consumers and citizens and community workers and joiners and demonstrators for causes–causes which they cannot talk about or answer questions about because they do not really know anything about them. As I say, they just zombie along. They also raise children just like themselves and are absolutely average and normal in the most deadly sense. They also follow fads and fashions, not avidly but totally reflexively, unquestioningly. They really relate to brand names and like them on their clothing. As the poet says, in between on the misty flats they drift to and fro. Until they disappear. They don't live and they don't actually die, they kind of fade away or vaporize. People often do not know they are gone for years, if ever. They are forgotten before they are gone. As Lao Tzu explains they guard their life, they take safety measures, but never chances or risks, they get all their immunizations and follow all the rules. They are so protected nothing ever affects them, their whole environment is a kind of bubble that nothing much ever gets through, and certainly nothing upsetting or confusing. As I say, they just drift along until they are lost sight of.

The immortals

Lao Tzu finally tells us that there are those who are at all times alive, so much so that neither death nor the things that lead to death seem to be aware of them. What is to be done is done by them with no injury whatsoever. There was a modern saint in Egypt named Abdul Messiah, Servant of Christ. He was an Ethiopian monk who lived in the desert and was the friend of all the desert wildlife including cobras who shared his cave with him. During World War II he used to walk nonchalantly between the Allies and the Axis forces that were shooting and tossing bombs and fire at each other. Bullets were flying and bombs were bursting and there was Abdul Messiah calmly walking on completely untouched. He was the kind of person Lao Tzu is describing. "Even as a man casts off his worn-out clothes and then clothes himself in others which are new, so the embodied casts off worn-out bodies and then enters into others which are new" (Bhagavad Gita 2:22). An immortal never really dies, just changes his clothing and then after a while he stops doing even that and does nothing but *live*.

51. The Mystic Virtue

Tao gives them birth, Teh (character) fosters them.
The material world gives them form. The circumstances of the moment complete them.
Therefore all things of the universe worship Tao and exalt Teh.
Tao is worshipped and Teh is exalted without anyone's order but is so of its own accord.
Therefore Tao gives them birth, Teh fosters them, makes them grow, develops them, gives them a harbor, a place to dwell in peace, feeds them and shelters them.
It gives them birth and does not own them, acts (helps) and does not appropriate them, is superior, and does not control them.
This is the Mystic Virtue.
(Tao Teh King 51)

Tao gives them birth, Teh (character) fosters them. It is essential that we realize we take our being from the Tao, that we are not one thing and the Tao another. Actually, the Tao is all things. Being a part of the Tao it is inherent in us to live in accordance with the Tao, but in our many previous lives we have usually gotten more and more out of phase with the Tao until our lives virtually oppose the Tao and seem to be something completely outside the Tao, even irreconcilable with the Tao. This is an illusion, but it can produce many very real and painful results.

In our origin we are identical, but each of us develops as uniquely as snowflakes form. The Tao is infinite, and it is its infinity that is manifesting in all this never-repeating variety. Teh, character or quality, is an aspect of the Tao, and it keeps us fluid as we evolve through a kaleidoscope of forms. We remain the same in essence, but continually differ in expression, rather like an artist's brush and paints. Tao is the great Artist, the great Playwright, the great Stage Manager and Director. As we move up the evolutionary ladder, the characteristics we develop gradually refine until all distortion, conflict or deficiency disappear and we are revealed as perfect images of the Perfect. All this is totally intended in the divine plan and is therefore totally natural. The only reason our perfection cannot be manifested without a struggle is our habits and conditionings from prior lives that go contrary to it. Cleaning up the spots and ironing out the wrinkles is the purpose of the interior mystical life which is the foundation of Taoism.

The material world gives them form. The circumstances of the moment complete them. Wu: "Matter shapes them, Environment perfects them." Coming into the material plane we take upon ourselves many forms in succession, and each moment of those incarnations affects us, as does our response to them. And this we call karma. Karma is usually thought of as something to be rid of, but in fact karma is the impelling force of evolution. Rebirth is not bondage; ignorance is bondage. We need to develop wisdom: awareness of and conformity to the Tao. When that is done, rebirth becomes a wonderful source of growth and expansion that leads to freedom from any need for further rebirth. Then we dwell in higher and higher worlds until we transcend them all and can remain beyond them or enter into them at will. This is freedom.

Therefore all things of the universe worship Tao and exalt Teh. The worship all things render to the Tao is their life within the Tao which is totally spontaneous, an expression of their nature as part of the Tao. They particularly do this by developing an infinite variety of forms, qualities and characteristics. In this way they not only exalt Teh by are themselves exalted by it.

51. The Mystic Virtue

Tao is worshipped and Teh is exalted without anyone's order but is so of its own accord. As just said, this all occurs spontaneously and is an expression of the very nature of things.

Therefore Tao gives them birth, Teh fosters them, makes them grow, develops them, gives them a harbor, a place to dwell in peace, feeds them and shelters them. Everything arises from Tao and Teh.

It gives them birth and does not own them, acts (helps) and does not appropriate them, is superior, and does not control them. Mabry renders this: "The Tao gives birth, but does not possess; acts, but does not take credit; guides, but does not control." This is not just a statement of fact but is meant to give us insight into how we should be doing our part in the evolutionary life within the Tao. We should not think to possess or attribute to ourselves that which we produce. We should not identify with our actions and think that we are acting independently of the Tao. We should not violate the freedom and nature inherent in all things, but work with them so they will unfold naturally and not be forced, for that will lead to distortion, misery and destruction. Certainly other people should only be guided and never controlled or persuaded. And then they should be left alone. If they do or do not accept guidance they should be left in peace.

This is the Mystic Virtue. Mabry: "This is the mystery of goodness." Everything outside this is not good or benevolent but egotism and a sure path to disharmony and suffering, blindness to the Tao and interior death.

52. Stealing the Absolute

There was a beginning of the universe which may be regarded as the Mother of the Universe. From the Mother, we may know her sons. After knowing the sons, keep to the Mother. Thus one's whole life may be preserved from harm.

Stop its apertures, close its doors, and one's whole life is without toil.

Open its apertures, be busy about its affairs, and one's whole life is beyond redemption.

He who can see the small is clear-sighted; he who stays by gentility is strong.

Use the light, and return to clear-sightedness. Thus cause not yourself later distress. This is to rest in the Absolute.

(Tao Teh King 52)

There was a beginning of the universe which may be regarded as the Mother of the Universe. The Tao embraces everything, but its center is in the transcendental realm beyond all relativity. In this field of transcendent consciousness that is the Tao, there arises a single point (bindu) from which the entire range of relative existence streams forth and into which everything returns. This point is called the *Brahmayoni*, the Womb of God, in Indian philosophy. It is itself the Mother, the Birth-giver and Life-giver of all.

In nineteenth-century France the Virgin Mary appeared to a peasant girl. When the girl asked who she was, the Virgin answered: "I *am* the

Immaculate Conception." This seemed utter nonsense to the adherents of exoteric Christianity, but to those who understood esoteric Christianity it made complete sense. The Virgin Mary is the perfect imaging of the Mother aspect of Divinity. Being one with that aspect, she both speaks and acts as the Mother of All. At the time of her appearance there was a lot of agitation about the newly-introduced dogma of the Immaculate Conception which stated that the Virgin Mary had been absolutely free of Original Sin from her conception. (It has nothing to do with the Virgin Birth, as non-Catholics usually assume.) Because of the complete lack of esoteric understanding no one in the Roman Catholic Church realized that the Virgin herself had corrected the prevailing ideas about the Immaculate Conception. She indicated that it had nothing to do with Original Sin, which is a myth, or her personal conception, but it was exactly what Lao Tzu spoke about in this verse thousands of years before. Symbolically speaking, in and through the Brahmayoni all things are conceived and given birth.

From the Mother, we may know her sons. After knowing the sons, keep to the Mother. Thus one's whole life may be preserved from harm. "Out here" in the vastness of Relativity, we have little or no understanding of anything around us. But if we cultivate our interior consciousness we can perceive our own inner makeup which is a microcosmic reflection of Creation, the Macrocosm. When this is done we will come to understand the Mother and her nature which is shared by all her "children"–everything that exists. Knowing the Mother, we will know her children. But we must keep close to the Mother, the Origin, and not get lost in the virtually infinite labyrinth of relative existence. For otherwise we will forget who we and they really are, where we all came from and to whom we must eventually return. Close to the mother, we will be preserved from the Great Fear.

Stop its apertures, close its doors, and one's whole life is without toil. Wu: "Block all the passages! Shut all the doors! And to the end of your days you will not be worn out." This seems pretty ferocious, but what it means is very mild when we understand both what it means and how to manage it. As with just about any philosophical matter, the Bhagavad Gita illuminates the situation and shows us to do the needful. The entire fifth chapter of the Gita is devoted to this subject and I recommend you read it through.

Basically the question is how to touch the world and not be touched by it in return. Speaking of the person skilled enough to accomplish this, the Gita says: "He acts untainted by evil as a lotus leaf is not wetted by water" (5:10). How simple!

Sri Ramakrishna put it this way: "I ask people to live in the world in a spirit of detachment, If you break the jack-fruit after rubbing oil on your hands, its sticky juice will not smear them. If the 'unripe' mind dwells in the world, the mind gets soiled. One should first attain knowledge and then live in the world. If you put milk in water the milk is spoiled. But this will not happen if butter, churned from the milk, is put in water." In India spiritual practice is often referred to as being like churning butter from milk. If you pour milk into water it will be diluted and lost. But butter will float as a single lump and be preserved.

Sri Ramakrishna also spoke of living life as diving into water: "Gather all the information and then plunge in. Suppose a pot has dropped in a certain part of a lake. Locate the spot and dive there.... [Spiritual] discipline is said to be rightly followed only when one plunges in. You may say, even though you dive deep you are still in danger of sharks and crocodiles, of lust and anger. But dive after rubbing your body with turmeric powder; then sharks and crocodiles will not come near you. The turmeric is discrimination and renunciation."

Detachment is necessary; not zombie-like indifference, but self-disciplined and self-contained non-responsiveness arising from understanding the true nature of all things and the true nature of ourselves. That which is around us is not to be hated or despised, but seen as a passing show while we keep our awareness focussed on the inner reality of our true, divine Self. John Blofeld has written about his life in pre-Communist China where he knew many Taoists. Some lived far away from cities in quiet hermitages, but others lived right in Beijing and lived ordinary lives, yet were always centered within, always solitary inside, and at the same time often with others. This is the ideal of Lao Tzu. And here is how the Gita describes one who lives according to his ideals:

52. STEALING THE ABSOLUTE

"Karma yogis perform action only with the body, mind, intellect, or the senses, forsaking attachment, performing action for self-purification. He who is steadfast, having abandoned action's fruit, attains lasting peace. He who is not steadfast, attached to action based on desire, is bound. Renouncing all actions with the mind, the embodied one sits happily as the ruler of the city of nine gates, not acting at all, nor causing action.... Those whose minds are absorbed in That, whose Selves are fixed on That, whose foundation is That, who hold That as the highest object, whose evils have been shaken off by knowledge, attain the ending of rebirth.... Even here on earth rebirth is conquered by those whose mind is established in evenness. Brahman is without fault and the same to all; therefore they are established in Brahman. One should not exult when encountering what is liked, and one should not be repulsed when encountering the disliked. With firm intellect, undeluded, the knower of Brahman is established in Brahman. He whose Self is unattached to external contacts, who finds happiness in the Self, whose Self is united to Brahman by yoga, reaches imperishable happiness.... He who is able to endure here on earth, before liberation from the body, the agitation that arises from desire and anger is steadfast, a happy man. He whose happiness is within, whose delight is within, whose illumination is within: that yogi, identical in being with Brahman, attains Brahmanirvana.... Released from desire and anger, with thoughts controlled, those ascetics who know the Self find very near to them the bliss of Brahmanirvana" (Bhagavad Gita 5:11-13; 17; 19-21; 23-24, 26).

We can see from this that the Bhagavad Gita is truly a universal scripture, embracing and illumining the teachings of all the masters of wisdom.

Open its apertures, be busy about its affairs, and one's whole life is beyond redemption. Wu: "Open the passages! Multiply your activities! And to the end of your days you will remain helpless." Mabry: "If you spend your life filling your senses and rushing around 'doing' things you will be beyond hope." If allow ourselves to become confused and lost in this vast world, literally forgetting ourselves, how will we ever find our way out and back close to the Mother? It is almost hopeless, and involves lifetimes of wasted effort, overwhelmed with the Great Fear.

He who can see the small is clear-sighted; he who stays by gentility is strong. Wu: "To see the small is to have insight. To hold on to weakness is to be strong." Legge: "The perception of what is small is (the secret of) clear-sightedness; the guarding of what is soft and tender is (the secret of) strength." The material universe is immense, immeasurable, and our spirit is like the tiniest point of light. How easy to lose track of it! It seems small and weak in a huge, powerful world, but if we keep our awareness centered in it we will find true sight, true wisdom and true internal strength.

Use the light, and return to clear-sightedness. Thus cause not yourself later distress. This is to rest in the Absolute. There it all is in the proverbial nutshell. Thank you, Master Lao Tzu.

53. Brigandage

If only I had the tiniest grain of wisdom, I should walk in the Great Way, and my only fear would be to stray from it.

The Great Way is very smooth and straight; and yet the people prefer devious paths.

The court is very clean and well garnished, but the fields are weedy and wild, and the granaries are very empty!

They wear gorgeous clothes, they carry sharp swords, they surfeit themselves with food and drink, they possess more riches than they can use! They are the heralds of brigandage! As for Tao, what do they know about it?

(Tao Teh King 53–Wu translation)

If only I had the tiniest grain of wisdom, I should walk in the Great Way. We must not forget that Tao means Way. In other philosophies, walking in a "way" means following a prescribed order of thought and action that was formulated by some external authority. It is a process of conformity and intellectual profession. Not so here. Walking the Tao is living in the perfect consciousness that is the Tao, of manifesting the inherent Truth and Reality of the universe itself. The Tao has no basis but itself. No ideas or verbal formulations can establish or explain it. No one who "follows" in any manner understands the Tao, much less expresses It. What is needed is even a tiny grain of wisdom. That living seed will reveal itself as the Tao, for the Tao is not perceived as an object separate from anything.

And my only fear would be to stray from it. There is a healthy fear: the fear of deviating from the Tao and losing It. For if the Tao is lost, what remains to us? Nothing.

The Great Way is very smooth and straight; And yet the people prefer devious paths. Our evolutionary path has taken us through many forms in which we have only been parts of something, never a self-sufficient whole. Therefore being part of a herd is deeply conditioned in us. Consequently, however independent-minded we may potentially be, the habit of identifying with others and being part of an association is not just hard to break, it is systemic in our subconscious and therefore totally reflexive. We run with the herd without giving it a thought, even if the running is internalized and basically intellectual/emotional. Since the Path that is the Tao is only walked by a single person at a time, those who need company and support are at a marked disadvantage all the way. Because of this people are strongly attracted to devious, roundabout and ultimately futile paths, for all paths except the Tao are exactly that: futile. We live multitudes of wasted lives as a result.

When I was first in India a man told me the story of a man who went into the astral world and saw a gigantic heap of bones. When he asked what they were he was told that those were the bones of the lives in which he had remembered and sought God. This impressed him very much and he began to think that he might not be appreciating himself enough. All those bones! Then he saw an even bigger mountain of bones. These, he was told, were the bones of the lives in which he did not remember or seek God. Suddenly things were back in perspective!

A person's mind is like a mirror. If the mirror is bent or distorted in any way it relays a bent or distorted image. So naturally those with flawed minds pursue only flawed paths. This is why Sri Ramakrishna often said: "The mind is everything." For practically speaking it is.

The court is very clean and well garnished, But the fields are weedy and wild, And the granaries are very empty! That which is artificial, the creation of man, is well kept and impressive, but that which is of nature, that which is of life itself, is neglected and sterile. Such are those who are alienated from the Tao. Enemies of the Tao, they are enemies of themselves.

53. BRIGANDAGE

They wear gorgeous clothes, they carry sharp swords, they surfeit themselves with food and drink, they possess more riches than they can use! They are the heralds of brigandage! As for Tao, what do they know about it? Everything looks admirable, but they are embodiments of dishonesty and deceit. In time they shall bring themselves and all society down into the muck and chaos of all that oppose the Tao, the True Way. Such people are forerunners of death and destruction. We who like to boast of our "high standard of living" should pause and reconsider the way along which we find ourselves rushing and being rushed.

54. The Individual and the State

Who is firmly established is not easily shaken.
Who has a firm grasp does not easily let go.
From generation to generation his ancestral sacrifices shall be continued without fail.
Cultivated in the individual, character will become genuine.
Cultivated in the family, character will become abundant.
Cultivated in the village, character will multiply.
Cultivated in the state, character will prosper.
Cultivated in the world, character will become universal.
Therefore: According to (the character of) the individual, judge the individual; according to (the character of) the family, judge the family; according to (the character of) the village, judge the village; according to (the character of) the state, judge the state; according to (the character of) the world, judge the world.
How do I know this is so? By this.
(Tao Teh King 54)

Who is firmly established is not easily shaken. This seems quite obvious, but Lao Tzu's purpose is to tell us that the only way to not be easily shaken by the vagaries of life is to previously become inwardly firm and stable. Life is lived from the inside out, so the interior condition of the individual will determine the state of his outer life.

Who has a firm grasp does not easily let go. When our ideals and principles are not products of whim or shallow observation, but rather are based on a deep and intelligent insight, we will not easily be moved from our convictions and purpose.

From generation to generation his ancestral sacrifices shall be continued without fail. Not only will the settled and insightful individual be stable and continuing through the years, because he will impart these qualities to his children by example, they, too, will continue steadfast and immovable. Neither he nor his family will be without roots.

Cultivated in the individual, character will become genuine. The forest is green because each individual tree is green. In the same way integrity and personal worth are present only when consciously and wisely cultivated by the individual. When a person is self-motivated and self-disciplined his good qualities will be both authentic and enduring.

Cultivated in the family, character will become abundant. When all the members of a family are united in the pursuit of virtue they will support and strengthen one another so that their collective goodness will increase steadily.

Cultivated in the village, character will multiply. If the same is true of a village, then the countryside will be benefited by their example and virtue will become sought after, for virtue, like vice, can be contagious.

Cultivated in the state, character will prosper. An entire people can attain a level of righteousness unthought of by common men. There have been times in history when entire countries have been renowned for their virtue. For example, everyone who has studied English history knows that during the reign of the King Saint Edward the Confessor in the eleventh century, honesty was so prevalent that if a person dropped their purse on a road they could go back weeks later and find it there undisturbed. Countries have been renowned for kindness and hospitality. Thailand was commonly called The Land of Smiles.

Cultivated in the world, character will become universal. This incredible ideal is even possible worldwide, because if it can be so with a family, a town and a country it can be so with an entire planet.

Therefore: According to (the character of) the individual, judge the individual; according to (the character of) the family, judge the family; according to (the character of) the village, judge the village; according to (the character of) the state, judge the state; according to (the character of) the world, judge the world. This is a bedrock principle of personal wisdom. Character is everything. I know this is so because I grew up in a small town of four hundred and fifty people in which character was the measure of the individual. Money meant nothing, literally. Integrity alone mattered. I lived in this atmosphere for years and have never forgotten it, or seen it anywhere else. But if it could be there it can be anywhere. So I know Lao Tzu is not just dreaming or theorizing.

Mabry's translation implies that it is possible through the two virtues mentioned at the beginning: being established and having a firm grasp.

How do I know this is so? By this. Wu translates this: "How do I know about the world? *By what is within me.*" This is the key to it all. The individual ultimately determines the world. This must be realized.

55. THE CHARACTER OF THE CHILD

One who is steeped in Virtue is akin to the new-born babe.
Wasps and poisonous serpents do not sting it, nor fierce beasts seize it, nor birds of prey maul it.
Its bones are tender, its sinews soft, but its grip is firm.
It has not known the union of the male and the female, growing in its wholeness, and keeping its vitality in its perfect integrity.
It howls and screams all day long without getting hoarse, because it embodies perfect harmony.
To know harmony is to know the Changeless. To know the Changeless is to have insight.
To hasten the growth of life is ominous.
To control the breath by the will is to overstrain it.
To be overgrown is to decay.
All that is against Tao, and whatever is against Tao soon ceases to be.
(Tao Teh King 55–Wu translation)

One who is steeped in Virtue is akin to the new-born babe. A new-born child is only peripherally, even minimally, aware of the material world, but still dwells mostly in the higher consciousness of the subtle worlds. A new-born has no idea about anything, no opinions or classifications of things. Nor has it ambitions and aims. As it is, so it is.

One who is perfected in virtue is very similar, though of course in a higher, more spiritually meaningful way. In a sense, a new-born is an idiot, but a virtuous person most certainly is not. So we must not exaggerate the similarities of piety with earthly things.

Wasps and poisonous serpents do not sting it, nor fierce beasts seize it, nor birds of prey maul it. It has often been seen that infants may have a kind of providential protection, particularly in being safe or immune from various forms of harm that would certainly befall someone else. During my first days in India I was fortunate to come into contact with a remarkable yogi who shared a great deal of esoteric knowledge with me. One time he spoke of the fact that holy protecting spirits (devas) surround a child until the age of three. Proof of this has certainly been seen throughout the ages. And I have myself seen this to be true about the highly virtuous of whatever age.

Its bones are tender, its sinews soft, But its grip is firm. Continuing with the likeness to an infant, this indicates that a virtuous person is gentle in all his ways and is harmless. Yet he is really strong, possessing great self-disciplinary power, courage, and invincible will.

It has not known the union of the male and the female, growing in its wholeness, and keeping its vitality in its perfect integrity. Chastity is an essential trait of the virtuous. Retaining his inherent powers through celibacy, he is established in the consciousness of the One. Through preservation of his innate powers through continence he is a perfect image and likeness of the Divine.

It howls and screams all day long without getting hoarse, because it embodies perfect harmony. Active to a degree often far more than ordinary people, working uninterruptedly, the virtuous are not exhausted, but accomplish more than anyone else. We see this in the lives of the saints over and over, including those that were in very poor health. Why? Because they embody the perfect harmony that results from following the divine law and purpose in a complete manner.

55. The Character of the Child

To know harmony is to know the Changeless. To know the Changeless is to have insight. This perfect order in the mind and heart of the virtuous enables him to know the Highest, and in that knowledge to possess understanding of all things relevant to him. This is why even simple saints have stunned the glib and worldly with their direct, unpremeditated wisdom.

To hasten the growth of life is ominous. Mabry: "Trying to extend one's life-span is dangerous and unnatural." Byrn: "To unnaturally try to extend life is not appropriate." False Taoists through the centuries have been known for their attempts at extending life and even attempting to attain physical immortality. Often their methods have been virtually vampiristic: robbing others of their life essence to increase theirs. At the same time this may merely mean that trying to expand life in the sense of possessions, influence, etc. is unwise and leads to collapse of the egocentric. As Solomon observed: "Pride goeth before destruction, and an haughty spirit before a fall" (Proverbs 16:18).

To control the breath by the will is to overstrain it. Mabry: "To manipulate one's energy with the mind is a powerful thing." Byrn: "To try and alter the life-breath is unnatural." Breath control and cultivation of exotic modes of breathing are a part of the "Taoist magic" intent on bodily immortality. But wise yogis in India have counseled aspirants against unnatural breathing methods considered authentic pranayama. One illustrative incident comes naturally to mind. One time when I was going through a list of various disciplines and asking Sri Ma Anandamayi if they were worthwhile for me or not, I just said the single word "pranayama." Immediately Ma gave a kind of sitting jump and loudly said: "No." Years later in Benares she spoke to me at length about the delusive character of false or misguided pranayama, which only gives an illusion of spiritual benefit that eventually evaporates, leaving the yogi an empty shell. (There is such a thing as real, beneficial pranayama, but this is not the place to begin such a subject. See *Soham Yoga, the Yoga of the Self.*)

To be overgrown is to decay. Mabry: "But whoever possesses such strength invariably grows old and withers." To artificially alter one's strength or physical function by the false "Taoist" methods (obviously not known to Lao Tzu or certainly not approved of by him), is to eventually pay the price by rapid degeneration or loss.

Once a friend telephoned and told me to be sure and watch the upcoming television broadcast of a top-rated interview show. I did, and saw three people who were claiming that they had discovered the secret of physical rejuvenation and possible immortality. They made amazing claims but talked around and around it, not telling what it was. The next day my friend called and asked if I had watched the program. When I said I had, she told me that she knew the three very well, that their secret rejuvenation method was a singularly repulsive form of group sex. (Being a lady, she did not describe it.) They had created a sex cult with quite a few members. However, she told me, both of the men were wearing wigs because they had become prematurely bald, and the woman had undergone several cosmetic surgeries. Lao Tzu knew.

All that is against Tao, and whatever is against Tao soon ceases to be. Mabry: "This is not the way of Tao. All those who do not follow the Tao will come to an early end." Byrn: "Changing the natural is against the way of the Tao. Those who do it will come to an early end."

Lao Tzu continually counsels moving with and accommodating the natural tides. In this way we are in harmony with the Tao and therefore with the principle of true immortality. To "stick in our own oar" is to disrupt the harmony and therefore our synchronization with the Tao.

56. Beyond Honor and Disgrace

> He who knows does not speak; he who speaks does not know.
> Fill up its apertures, close its doors, dull its edges, untie its tangles, soften its light, submerge its turmoil–this is the Mystic Unity.
> Then love and hatred cannot touch him.
> Profit and loss cannot reach him.
> Honor and disgrace cannot affect him.
> Therefore is he always the honored one of the world.
> (Tao Teh King 56)

In this section of the Tao Teh King we are given a description of the worthy seeker of the Tao.

He who knows does not speak; he who speaks does not know. There is an old proverb: "He who knows tells it not; he who tells knows it not." The Kena Upanishads says: "If you think that you have understood Brahman well, you know it but slightly, whether it refers to you [the individual Self] or to the gods. So then is it to be investigated by you [the pupil] [even though] I think it is known. I do not think that I know it well; nor do I think that I do not know it. He who among us knows it, knows it and he, too, does not know that he does not know. To whomsoever it is not known, to him it is known: to whomsoever it is known, he does not know. It is not understood by those who understand it; it is understood by those who do not understand it" (2.1-3).

This is often true of lesser things when a wise person does not want to get entangled in exposition of unresolvable ideas or situations. But it is supremely true in relation to the Tao. The Absolute is beyond words and concepts. Therefore to say anything about It is to speak nonsense. Also by speaking we can find ourselves drawn into useless talk, especially by those that love to contradict and argue.

Sri Ramakrishna said: "What Brahman is cannot be described in words. Everything has been polluted, like food that has touched the tongue–that is, everything has been described in words. But no one has been able to describe Brahman. It is therefore unpolluted." Being beyond the reach of ignorant human mind and speech, the Tao is pure and should be left in peace. So the worthy seeker does not babble on about the Tao, but abides in interior silence where alone the Tao can be found and experienced.

Fill up its apertures. Mabry: "So shut your mouth." Byrn: "Stop talking." In relation to the Unspeakable, silence alone is wisdom and speaking is folly. Silence is absolutely necessary for those who are seeking to know and become one with the Tao.

Close its doors. Mabry: "Guard your senses." Why? "The troubling senses forcibly carry away the mind of even the striving man of wisdom. Restraining all these senses, he should sit in yoga, intent on me. Surely, he whose senses are controlled–his consciousness stands steadfast and firm" (Bhagavad Gita 2:60-61). The senses draw us outward while the Reality, the Tao is inward. Certainly when we attain the perfect vision we will find the Tao is both inside and outside because It is everything. But until then we must guard ourselves because: "When the mind is led about by the wandering senses, it carries away the understanding like the wind carries away a ship on the waters" (Bhagavad Gita 2:67).

Dull its edges. Mabry: "Blunt your sharpness." Feng and English: "Temper your sharpness." We have all acquired a lot of sharp edges and points in past lives and now is the time to blunt them lest we hurt ourselves and others. Interaction with others must be both sparing and of a calm and peaceful character. Not only should there be no conflict, there should be no drawing out of ourselves into useless communication and interchange.

Untie its tangles. Mabry: "Untangle your affairs." "As it is written in the book of the words of Esaias the prophet, saying, The voice of one crying in the wilderness, Prepare ye the way of the Lord, make his paths straight. Every valley shall be filled, and every mountain and hill shall be brought low; and the crooked shall be made straight, and the rough ways shall be made smooth; and all flesh shall see the salvation of God" (Luke 3:4-6). Unless our minds, hearts and lives are not made straight and unencumbered by things of earthly experiences, as well as the ups and downs that reflect a consciousness dominated by the ever-changing material cosmos, perception of the Tao will elude us.

Soften its light. Mabry: "Soften your glare." Mildness is a trait in complete compatibility with the Tao. A Taoist in a very real sense subscribes to the philosophy of Goldilocks: not Too Much, not Too Little, but Just Right. This sentence advocates the principle, not of mere "moderation" but of exact balance which renders something more effective than any other "measure."

Submerge its turmoil. Wu: "Unite the world into one whole." Feng and English: "Be at one with the dust of the Earth." These are rather different translations, but both are wisdom. Certainly unity implies union with the least as well as the greatest of the universe. Nothing can be left out, and certainly nothing should be disdained.

This is the Mystic Unity. Wu: "This is called the Mysterious Whole." The state of Wholeness is both an interior and exterior condition, as the Tao embraces both inside and outside.

Then love and hatred cannot touch him. Chan: "Therefore it is impossible either to be intimate and close to him or to be distant and indifferent to him." The real idea is that nothing can really be "in relation" to him since he has transcended "thingness" and there is no longer an ego to think "they like me" or "they dislike me." For the Me of one who is united with the Tao is beyond the possibilities of any such mental states. Which is why, returning to the first statement, a knower of the Tao keeps silent.

Profit and loss cannot reach him. Since nothing is either "mine" or "not mine" to a knower of the Tao, the concept of profit and loss or gaining and losing just does not apply. Freedom from all anxiety over gaining and keeping possessions is his.

Honor and disgrace cannot affect him. Neither the opinion of those ignorant of the Tao nor their treatment of the perfected Taoist can have any meaning for him. Again, the ego being dissolved there is no one to react to opinion or actions on the part of others.

Therefore is he always the honored one of the world. Feng and English: "This therefore is the highest state of man." Byrn: "This makes them the most noble of all under the heavens." All three are certainly true. The knower of the Tao may be seen on the earth, but he never "walks on the earth" in his consciousness. In India there is a devotional song that says: "When I take refuge in Thee, the world vanishes." So it is with the knower of the Tao. He lives and moves in the Tao, mere appearances being of no import to him.

57. The Art of Government

Rule a kingdom by the Normal.
Fight a battle by (abnormal) tactics of surprise.
Win the world by doing nothing.
How do I know it is so?

Through this:
The more prohibitions there are,
The poorer the people become.
The more sharp weapons there are,
The greater the chaos in the state.
The more skills of technique,
The more cunning things are produced.
The greater the number of statutes,
The greater the number of thieves and brigands.

Therefore the sage says:
I do nothing and the people are reformed of themselves.
I love quietude and the people are righteous of themselves.
I deal in no business and the people grow rich by themselves.
I have no desires and the people are simple and honest by themselves.

(Tao Teh King 57)

Rule a kingdom by the Normal. "Normal" here means ordinary and natural, acting according to the nature of things, not making them more or less and not bending their innate purpose to accomplish something else. In Taoism nature is never to be violated, but rather evoked, appreciated and used to make things even more normal.

Whether the kingdom is a country or a single human being, the nature of both must be discerned and built upon, increased and evolved. Ruling is itself normal, but only when normal means produce normal ends. On the individual level the first step is to know what we really are and all the aspects or components that make up a human being. Yoga alone reveals this. So yogi-kings and yogi-adepts must follow the same laws.

For nearly twenty years I was fortunate to have the acquaintance and friendship of the Raja of Solan, who was usually called Yogi Bhai, Brother Yogi, because of his profound yet natural/normal piety and humility. He was wise and unassuming, yet possessing the qualities of a true king which he had transmuted into the personality of a spiritual potentate. He was a master of himself. Though he always discharged his political duties conscientiously, his heart dwelt increasingly in the inner kingdom of spirit. The older he grew the more venerable he became, the more worthy of honor. When he left this world it was a very sad thing for me, because he was an inspiration as an example of the yoga life. After his (seeming) passing from this world I was attending an annual spiritual conference, the Samyam Sapta, at the Anandamayi Ashram in Brindaban. Yogi Bhai had attended these conferences unfailingly for the last few decades of his life. In fact, I had first met him at such a conference in Dehra Dun many years before. As I was standing in the road outside the ashram, to my absolute astonishment Yogi Bhai came walking out of the gate! There was no mistaking him, his way of dressing, and his jaunty mode of walking with a cane that was a little too tall for him (a trait of later years). Briskly he walked across a small lane and into the gate of another ashram. That gate was made of plaster-covered bricks, and was about four feet thick. Yogi Bhai did not emerge on the other side. I realized that he was showing to me that those who live in the spirit while in the body will never die even when the body is dropped.

Fight a battle by (abnormal) tactics of surprise. Wu: "You fight a war by exceptional moves." And by doing so you violate the nature of things, including human nature which, when it is purged of impurity and distortion, is incapable of initiating conflict much less the carnage of war. So Lao Tzu is warning his readers that "war" of any kind on any level is a mistake. If a goal cannot be attained by peaceful, natural means, by following our own higher nature, then it is a bad goal and bad for us if achieved. Therefore: "One acts according to one's own prakriti [nature]–even the wise man does so" (Bhagavad Gita 3:33).

Win the world by doing nothing. Wu: "You win the world by letting it alone." This means that by living in complete harmony with the world, integrating our true nature with its true nature, the world will be ours–not in the sense of a possession but in the sense of a helpful friend. We should never attempt to manipulate or control the world, though we can benefit the world if we adopt the principles that are in accordance with it. The prime purpose of the world is the evolution of the sentient beings living within it. So to seek our evolution and eventual liberation through yoga practice is to align ourselves with the fundamental nature of the world, to become a part of it in order to transcend it. For the world is a rung in the evolutionary ladder, a means for our growth if we will still our minds and hearts and open ourselves to understand what and why the world really is.

The more prohibitions there are, the poorer the people become. We are creatures of action, not inaction. Therefore it is detrimental to approach life with a Don't Do This And Don't Do That attitude. Our every resolve should be positive. For example, we should not determine: "I will not tell lies," but: "I will always tell the truth." It is not enough to never harm anyone or anything; instead we must always help others and foster the welfare of all things we encounter. Therefore we must always make positive resolves and live accordingly. People become weak by not doing, so prohibitions weaken them. But inspiration to act will make them strong. And it is so with our faculties and powers.

The more sharp weapons there are, the greater the chaos in the state. Cultivating the ability for conflict is to throw ourselves into confusion. For harmony alone is the way of the Tao and therefore of healthy life. Making provision for conflict and the injury of others is an act of intention whose inner impulses will eventually come about. The more means we create of defending ourselves, the more we will have to turn around in aggression on others, making them defend themselves against us. The more poison we accumulate, the more likely someone will die of poisoning. There is a personal form of disarmament that we must engage in thoroughly if we would be at peace. The more defenses we have the less peace will be ours. That is why Jesus counseled us to be "harmless as doves" (Matthew 10:16).

The more skills of technique, the more cunning things are produced. Long ago I heard a comedian say: "When they invented pay telephones, my grandfather invented slugs." The more clever or "slick" ways a culture or person has, for sure the more underhanded and dishonorable things will be done. One example is the constant use of loopholes or omissions in the laws to get what a person wants. The more laws there are, the more ways of evading them will be figured out. Again, it is a matter of a negative approach. Laying down a prohibition and prescribing a punishment is planting the seed of disobedience and transgression. Here, too, the law that whatever we sow we will reap applies. To try to block people from doing wrong is virtually an assurance that they will do wrong. The attempt to control is to guarantee anarchy. This is especially seen in the bringing up of children.

The greater the number of statutes, the greater the number of thieves and brigands. The more Don'ts we create, the more they will be done!

I do nothing and the people are reformed of themselves. If a ruler or administrator is exemplary, so will the people they rule or administer be. An example is better than talk any day. Often the perseverance and patient endurance of good and meek people has reformed wrongdoers who became ashamed of their mistreatment or disrespect shown toward the virtuous.

I love quietude and the people are righteous of themselves. Being what we should be is a positive force that can help others also "be" themselves.

57. THE ART OF GOVERNMENT

Being peaceful and harmonious ourselves is the way to foster peace and harmony around us.

I deal in no business and the people grow rich by themselves. Few things are more harmful than the constant drive and push to expand the economy and increase the GNP. The economy becomes like the arrogant frog who kept inhaling and making herself bigger and bigger until she burst. In many cases more is not better. The constant insistence on expansion brings about collapse. I knew one of the most successful investment advisors in the country. He told me that the government trying to manipulate the economy was a ticket to sure disaster. He said that the only way to fix an ailing economy was to let it alone and give people the chance to correct things unhindered. Meddling and coercing becomes an addiction to both individuals and governments. And suffering is the result.

I have no desires and the people are simple and honest by themselves. The bottom line of this entire section is that good is contagious; therefore if enough people cultivate personal goodness with wisdom it will certainly bring about an increase in the public welfare without an artificial program of some sort.

58. Unobtrusive Government

When a government is unobtrusive, the people are simple and honest. When a government is suspicious and strict, the people are discontented and sneaky.

Blessings are rooted in misery. Misery lurks behind blessing.

Where does it ever end? There is no such thing as "normal." What seems normal is only an illusion, and what seems good is finally revealed to be monstrous. The people's confusion has lasted a very long time.

Therefore the Sage is honest, but not judgmental. Strong, but not injurious to others. Straightforward, but not reckless. Bright, but not blinding.

(Tao Teh King 58 Mabry's translation)

When a government is unobtrusive, the people are simple and honest. When a government is suspicious and strict, the people are discontented and sneaky. Feng and English: "When the country is ruled with a light hand the people are simple. When the country is ruled with severity, the people are cunning." This really does not need much of a commentary, except to point out that it can be applied to various aspects of life, not just government, but to the way parents order their family life, the way organizations order their administration, and the way religious institutions carry on their activities. For example, the more obsessed with sin and hell a church is, the more secretly corrupt are the members. Even in my early teen years I saw that the more noise churches made, the more "hallelujah, glory, glory" they were and the more they fumed and fulminated against "sin" the more secretly corrupt they were.

An acquaintance of mine told me that he knew a very immoral man who was constantly traveling on corporate business. The man was really what is now called a sex addict. He told my friend that when he would come to a town he would get the local newspaper(s) and check where the fundamentalist revival meetings were being held, especially the "holy roller" kind. He said that he had a one hundred percent success rate in picking up a woman for sex at a "Holy Ghost revival." "I never spent the night alone," he boasted.

Emotional religion is based squarely on ego and sensuality. This is not just in Christianity; in every religious tradition where there is intense emotionality, there is intense undercover sexuality. Despite the reputation of "tantrics," in the context of Hinduism the singing, dancing and shouting Vaishnavas are the foulest of all the religious sects. In *Raja Yoga* Vivekananda wrote: "All over the world there have been dancing and jumping and howling sects, who spread like infection when they begin to sing and dance and preach; they also are a sort of hypnotists. They exercise a singular control for the time being over sensitive persons, alas! often, in the long run, to degenerate whole races. Ay, it is healthier for the individual or the race to remain wicked than be made apparently good by such morbid extraneous control. One's heart sinks to think of the amount of injury done to humanity by such irresponsible yet well-meaning religious fanatics. They little know that the minds which attain to sudden spiritual upheaval under their suggestions, with music and prayers, are simply making themselves passive, morbid, and powerless, and opening themselves to any other suggestion, be it ever so evil. Little do these ignorant, deluded persons dream that whilst they are congratulating themselves upon their miraculous power to transform human hearts, which power they think was poured upon them by some Being above the clouds, they are sowing the seeds of future decay, of crime, of lunacy, and of death. Therefore, beware of everything that takes away your freedom. Know that it is dangerous, and avoid it by all the means in your power."

Blessings are rooted in misery. Misery lurks behind blessing. Where does it ever end? Feng and English: "Happiness is rooted in misery. Misery lurks beneath happiness. Who knows what the future holds?" There is no denying that conflict often produces the most advancement, even in the individual. Persecuted people have told me that they were benefitted by the persecution for it made them strong and defined. Once I saw several people on television telling of the horrors of Japanese imprisonment during the Second World War. They unanimously said they were glad for the experience, which deepened their spiritual life. In *The Third Man* Harry Lime says: "In Italy, for thirty years under the Borgias, they had warfare, terror, murder and bloodshed, but they produced Michelangelo, Leonardo da Vinci and the Renaissance. In Switzerland, they had brotherly love, they had five hundred years of democracy and peace–and what did that produce? The cuckoo clock." This is the contradictory nature of human life which at best is uncertain. (Actually, the Swiss never made cuckoo clocks. They originated in the Black Forest area of Germany. Still, it is a good quotation.)

There is no such thing as "normal." What seems normal is only an illusion, and what seems good is finally revealed to be monstrous. The people's confusion has lasted a very long time. This is certainly drastic, especially the statement that what seems good is always found to be terrible. Nevertheless, Yogananda often said that "normal" and "sane" did not mean much, because crazy people with the same craziness get together and declare those who differ from them as officially abnormal and insane. And it cannot be denied that people throughout history have been in the grip of confusion.

Therefore the Sage is honest, but not judgmental. Strong, but not injurious to others. Straightforward, but not reckless. Bright, but not blinding. The wise person never injures another, so though he may speak honestly he will not do so in a condemnatory or censorious way. Yogananda had a very interesting way of showing a person his faults. He would say: "I knew a man [woman] who…" and then would describe their foibles. And that was all. He would not comment and say they were at fault. But the person he was describing got the idea and reformed, but were never embarrassed or hurt. For example, Brother Bimalananda told the members of our monastery that he loved ice cream and discovered that there was always ice cream in the refrigerator at the Encinitas ashram. So he ate some every day. Then one evening when the monks were gathered in the Master's room he said: "I knew a boy so greedy he would eat ice cream every day just because it was there. And it was not his, either." That was the end of that! And young Joe Carbona (Brother Bimalananda) appreciated the Master's tact. I have read that the founder of the Thai Forest Tradition, Acharya Mun, did the same thing very often.

In the twelfth chapter of *Autobiography of a Yogi*, Yogananda wrote about his guru, Sri Yukteswar: "Amazing it was to find that a master with such a fiery will could be so calm within. He fitted the Vedic definition of a man of God: 'Softer than the flower, where kindness is concerned; stronger than the thunder, where principles are at stake.'" I was continually amazed at the tremendous care Anandamayi Ma took to spare the feelings of others, sometimes saying or doing things that would alleviate their anxieties years in the future. She did this in many ways, and always effectually. During my first trip to India, in my last interview with her she very casually mentioned that I should not feel bad or worry if in America I had to relax a certain minor discipline. Confident it would never come about, I actually forgot she said it. But when I had to compromise and began to feel ashamed, Ma's words came to mind and removed my discomfort. When a week or so after this interview I bade farewell to Ma, she told me two things I should do. Somehow I only remembered one and successfully managed to do it. Then I began to feel sad that she had not said anything about my returning to India. One day in conversation with one of my yoga students I said to him with a grieving heart, "Unfortunately, Ma never…" and like a lightning strike suddenly I could see the scene of my farewell and remembered her very last words to me: "And come back in the winter." That was the second thing I should do! And by November I was back in India.

The great saints never hurt our inner eyes with their light, but instead heal us with that light. As Swami Brahmananda, the great disciple of Sri Ramakrishna often said: "We have nothing to give but blessings."

59. BE SPARING

In managing human affairs, there is no better rule than to be sparing.

To be sparing is to forestall; to forestall is to be prepared and strengthened; to be prepared and strengthened is to be ever-victorious; to be ever-victorious is to have infinite capacity; he who has infinite capacity is fit to rule a country, and the Mother (principle) of a ruling country can long endure.

This is to be firmly rooted, to have deep strength, the road to immortality and enduring vision.

(Tao Teh King 59)

In managing human affairs, there is no better rule than to be sparing. Wu: "There is nothing like frugality." Bigger and more are usually not better, despite popular opinion. There is a frugality that comes from both stinginess and obstructionism, but there is also a prudent frugality in which resources are conserved in order to continue using them in the future. As I cited earlier, a wise adage from the past is: "Eat it up; wear it out; make it do or do without." Though we think of frugality as economic, it can be applied in many areas of human life. Actually frugality and moderation are never far apart.

To be sparing [frugal] is to forestall; to forestall is to be prepared and strengthened; to be prepared and strengthened is to be ever-victorious; to be ever-victorious is to have infinite capacity; he who has infinite capacity is fit to rule a country, and the Mother (principle) of a ruling country can long endure. Frugality prevents depletion or bankruptcy and is a foresight that ensures continuity and strength and therefore mastery of a situation. I met a man that from his teen years had been investing safely. He told me that he would calculate how much he could afford to lose, and would invest only that amount. If things went badly he was still solvent and had nearly all his former gains. If things went well, then he was better off than before. Lao Tzu is advocating this approach for it fits people to take on more and greater responsibilities successfully. His interest is not economic development but insurance against the worries and possible entanglements brought about by financial collapse. Peace of mind is his intention.

This is to be firmly rooted, to have deep strength, the road to immortality and enduring vision. When moderation and prudence are observed in all areas of life, then as the master says, great strength and security will result for the moderate and prudent. Since, as Sri Ramakrishna observed, if you can weigh salt you can weigh sugar, cultivation of material wisdom can assist in developing spiritual wisdom and thereby be able to take the path to immortality and enduring vision: essential traits of a happy and worthwhile outlook and life.

60. Governing a Big Country

Govern a big country as you would fry a small fish.

Approach the world with the Tao and evil will have no power. Not that evil has no power, but it will not harm people.

Not that evil is not harmful, but the Sage is dedicated to not harming people–even evil people.

When no one hurts another, all will eventually return to the good.

(Tao Teh King 60–Mabry translation)

Govern a big country as you would fry a small fish. Perhaps this means that the governing of a large country should not intimidate or overwhelm us, but that we should approach it as simply, directly and easily as it is to fry a small fish.

Approach the world with the Tao and evil will have no power. Not that evil has no power, but it will not harm people. When life is lived according to the divine plan (Tao) evil will not be able to work harm. Those in harmony with the Tao live in a completely other world, though they seem to be in this world with everyone else. Just as a magnet cannot pick up brass, so those who live in perfect rectitude are simply on a different wave length from evil forces and they cannot harm them, cannot even touch them, really. This is seen continually, but it is not noticed, so the lesson is rarely learned.

Often negative occultists have done their evil best to harm others through psychic means but were unable to do so. Aleister Crowley decided to kill Bishop Charles Leadbeater of the Liberal Catholic Church with black magic. After a while the bishop wrote to Crowley asking him to stop, since he had to spend at least ten minutes every month deflecting Crowley's curses. Infuriated at the idea that it only took ten minutes to dispel what he considered powerful spells, Crowley desisted. I have witnessed similar situations in which occultists bragged about the mayhem they were going to work on a particular person, but could not do a thing. One of my friends, a Coptic Orthodox bishop, came under the notice of a local magician who boasted that he would soon be dead as a result of his magical workings. When his magic did not affect the bishop, he resorted to putting arsenic in his food, but he put so much in it virtually singed the bishop's nose! So he did not eat it. Meanwhile, at a public meeting the magician was telling his followers that in the morning they would be reading about the bishop's death. But they did not.

Not that evil is not harmful, but the Sage is dedicated to not harming people–even evil people. For every action there is an equal and opposite reaction. Though a scientific statement, this applies equally well to karma. The Yoga Sutras say that a person perfected in harmlessness cannot be harmed by others. A person who truly loves everyone is particularly shielded. Jesus, the embodiment of divine love, made it very clear to his disciples (and later to Pilate) that he was willing to suffer and die for the welfare of others, but that if he had not been willing, then nothing on earth could touch him. ("Thinkest thou that I cannot now pray to my Father, and he shall presently give me more than twelve legions of angels?" (Matthew 26:53). "Then saith Pilate unto him, Speakest thou not unto me? knowest thou not that I have power to crucify thee, and have power to release thee? Jesus answered, Thou couldest have no power at all against me, except it were given thee from above" (John 19:10-11.)

When no one hurts another, all will eventually return to the good. This is a truth that not many groups or nations have cared to try out. However on a small scale it is seen over and over that it is true and can be relied on. Good is contagious. This, too, is rarely tried out.

61. Big and Small Countries

> A great country is like the lowland toward which all streams flow. It is the Reservoir of all under heaven, the Feminine of the world. The Feminine always conquers the Masculine by her quietness, by lowering herself through her quietness.
>
> Hence, if a great country can lower itself before a small country, it will win over the small country; and if a small country can lower itself before a great country, it will win over the great country.
>
> The one wins by stooping; the other by remaining low.
>
> What a great country wants is simply to embrace more people; and what a small country wants is simply to come to serve its patron.
>
> Thus, each gets what it wants. But it behooves a great country to lower itself.
>
> (Tao Teh King 61–Wu translation)

A great country is like the lowland toward which all streams flow. It is the Reservoir of all under heaven, the Feminine of the world. The Feminine always conquers the Masculine by her quietness, by lowering herself through her quietness. "Great" does not just refer to size, but to the character of a major county. Such a country is receptive not aggressive, welcoming all outside influence that proves worthy, and willing to adopt (and adapt) that which is superior. This has been a characteristic trait of India throughout its history. Therefore it could continually advance in civilization and in richness of culture. The Indians were open to outside elements and yet able to maintain their distinctive character while assimilating and making them their own. Another example is Chinese Buddhism, which is an evolutionary recreation of the Buddhism originally brought to China, and permeated with the genius of Chinese culture.

The Divine Feminine prevails by the same kind of openness. She receives and recreates all things for their betterment. This is not passivity, but intense activity whose openness can be mistaken for weak acquiescence. But it is really a working of power. The Feminine does not play a "Yes, Dear," role in relation to the Masculine. Rather, she transforms the Masculine by receiving it completely and evolving it into a form that is a development of its inherent qualities: qualities that would have lain dormant otherwise, and thus the Masculine would never have been fully itself. The Feminine does not absorb, she receives, transmutes and gives a rebirth to all things. Thus she is the Mother of All.

Hence, if a great country can lower itself before a small country, it will win over the small country; and if a small country can lower itself before a great country, it will win over the great country. "Lower itself" is not a very good translation, nor would "humble itself" be acceptable. Rather, Lao Tzu means a large country should exhibit positive condescension in the sense of respectful accommodation and regard for a smaller nation. It should be like a brother or even a father–certainly more than a friend–which shares a common interest and outlook with the smaller country. Empires have been built in this way by the wise.

The one wins by stooping; the other by remaining low. Mabry: "Therefore, by being humble, one gains. And the other, being humble already, also gains." Whether the larger assimilates the smaller or they remain separate with the larger assisting and even fostering the lesser which comes to depend on it, both are mutually benefited and both win by such an arrangement. Of course Lao Tzu is assuming that both are being honest and open with one another without underhanded or ulterior motives. I mention this because in its heyday the British Empire continually strove to extend itself by pretending to be of a fostering and protecting character to various nations. In fact, they liked using the word "protectorate," though eventual control and even tyrannical domination was their purpose.

What a great country wants is simply to embrace more people; and what a small country wants is simply to come to serve its patron. This is meant in a totally positive way, so it is not cynical as it might seem to us living in a morass of political fraud throughout the world.

Lao Tzu in no way opposes the desire of a country to extend its influence either through increasing its population or becoming a leader and trendsetter in a purely cultural sense. There is an empire of government and an empire of moral or cultural influence. No matter how the Soviet Union inveighed against the Decadent West and the United States in particular, on every level their politicians and the common citizens engaged in an almost desperate imitation of everything Western and especially American. Right in Moscow at the height of the Cold War there was a beauty shop called (in Russian) American Woman. I well remember seeing a special program about "youth" in the Soviet Union complete with interviews of teenagers (obviously privileged children of the leaders of the Communist Party) who had flip hairdos (the girls, that is) and were ham radio fans and demonstrated their skill in performing American popular music. There was even a time when a pair of blue jeans made in America could easily be sold in Russia for the equivalent of one hundred dollars. Even today America "rules," despite the continual sneering and outright hostility that is so chic among the envious in Europe and the Middle East.

And it is only good practical sense for smaller or less influential countries to desire the benefits of friendship with the powerful and affluent countries.

Thus, each gets what it wants. But it behooves a great country to lower itself. Mabry: "Thus, both needs are satisfied And each gets what it wants. Remember, the great country should always humble itself." Byrn: "Both large and small countries benefit greatly from humility." If humility and sincere benevolence would dominate our "world scene" we could live in a very different and better world.

62. The Good Man's Treasure

The Tao is the hidden reservoir of all things.
A treasure to the honest, it is a safeguard to the erring.
A good word will find its own market. A good deed may be used as a gift to another.
That a man is straying from the right path is no reason that he should be cast away.
Hence, at the Enthronement of an Emperor, or at the installation of the Three Ministers, let others offer their discs of jade, following it up with teams of horses; it is better for you to offer the Tao without moving your feet!
Why did the ancients prize the Tao? Is it not because by virtue of it he who seeks finds, and the guilty are forgiven? That is why it is such a treasure to the world.
(Tao Teh King 62–Wu translation)

The Tao is the hidden reservoir of all things. Though it contains all, the Tao is not only just unseen, it is hidden from what a Christian hymn calls "earth-dimmed vision." The Tao in this aspect is referred to in a mantra that is recited daily by Hindus:

Purnamidah, purnamidam,
   purnat purnamudachyate;

62. THE GOOD MAN'S TREASURE

Purnasya purnamadaya,
   purnam ewawashishyate.

Purna means total, full and complete, which is what our English term "perfect" used to mean, rather than just without fault. In this verse, the word "Complete" (Purna) refers to the Tao. Here, as best I can, is a translation into English:

This is the Complete; That is the Complete.
   The Complete has come out of the Complete.
If we take the Complete away from the Complete,
   Only the Complete remains.

Let us say it another way: the Absolute is the Tao; the Relative is the Tao. The Relative has emanated from the Absolute. Yet if we "take away" either of these and consider only the one or the other, we will find that each is the Tao; even more, we will discover that the Absolute is the Relative, and the Relative is the Absolute. For both are the Tao.

A treasure to the honest, it is a safeguard to the erring. The Tao fosters and even enriches the honest and true. The more we vibrate in harmony with the Tao, the more we have access to its abundance and the more it empowers and guides us. The Tao is benevolent to all. Certainly it responds to the wise and virtuous but it is a protector of those that stray from the path of the Tao. Despite all the chaos and suffering in the world, still its basic construction ensures eventual evolution and escape from earthly bondage and eventual freedom into boundless life.

A good word will find its own market. A good deed may be used as a gift to another. Good will lead us to its appreciation. Extensive as degradation can be in society, yet that which is good will be recognized and even honored. Doing good is the greatest gift we can give to the world, even though the deed may be small. It is the vibration of goodness that purifies and corrects both us and the world around us.

That a man is straying from the right path is no reason that he should be cast away. In the Liturgy of the Liberal Catholic Church we find these words: "O Lord, thou hast created man to be immortal and made him to be an image of thine own eternity; yet often we forget the glory of our heritage and wander from the path which leads to righteousness. But thou, O Lord, hast made us for thyself and our hearts are ever restless till they find their rest in thee. Look with the eyes of thy love upon our manifold imperfections and pardon all our shortcomings, that we may be filled with the brightness of the everlasting light and become the unspotted mirror of thy power and the image of thy goodness; through Christ our Lord. Amen." There is no mention of casting away or cutting off of anyone, because Bishops Wedgwood and Leadbeater knew from their study of Indian scriptures that it is the inviolable nature of a human being to evolve into Christhood. So although someone may be living in a foolish or negative way, he is a sleeping god of infinite value and never to be cast away. In truth, he cannot be cast away.

Hence, at the Enthronement of an Emperor, or at the installation of the Three Ministers, let others offer their discs of jade, following it up with teams of horses; it is better for you to offer the Tao without moving your feet! Feng and English: "But remain still and offer the Tao." Certainly the greatest gift that can be given to a society is a life lived in perfect conformity with the Tao and the offering of knowledge of the Tao to any who will listen.

Why did the ancients prize the Tao? Is it not because by virtue of it he who seeks finds, and the guilty are forgiven? That is why it is such a treasure to the world. Mabry: "Why did the Sages of old value the Tao so much? Because when you seek, you find and when you sin, you are forgiven. That is why the Tao is the greatest treasure of the Universe." Legge: "Why was it that the ancients prized this Tao so much? Was it not because it could be got by seeking for it, and the guilty could escape (from the stain of their guilt) by it? This is the reason why all under heaven consider it the most valuable thing." The Tao can be attained; and in that attainment all defilement and guilt are dissolved, for they are illusions and only the Tao inside and outside us is real. How great is the Tao!

63. Difficult and Easy

Accomplish do-nothing. Attend to no-affairs. Taste the flavorless.

Whether it is big or small, many or few, requite hatred with virtue.

Deal with the difficult while yet it is easy; deal with the big while yet it is small.

The difficult (problems) of the world must be dealt with while they are yet easy; the great (problems) of the world must be dealt with while they are yet small.

Therefore the Sage by never dealing with great (problems) accomplishes greatness.

He who lightly makes a promise will find it often hard to keep his faith.

He who makes light of many things will encounter many difficulties.

Hence even the Sage regards things as difficult, and for that reason never meets with difficulties.

(Tao Teh King 63)

Accomplish do-nothing. Attend to no-affairs. Mabry: "Do without doing. Work without forcing." Feng and English: "Practice non-action. Work without doing." Blackney: "Act in repose. Be at rest when you work." This is much clearer in the statements of the Bhagavad Gita: "He who perceives inaction in action and action in inaction–such a man is wise among men, steadfast in yoga and doing all action" (Bhagavad Gita 4:18). "Having abandoned attachment, he acts untainted by evil as a lotus leaf is not wetted by water" (Bhagavad Gita 5:10). Remaining in the consciousness of the Self which is one with the Tao, the wise man neither touches anything nor is touched by anything. Action does not shape or condition him in any way. Thus he creates no karmic bonds for himself, but is free.

Taste the flavorless. Mabry: "Taste without seasonings." Blackney: "Relish unflavoured things." We should experience things as they truly are in their essence without any overlay or "flavoring" in the form of attitude, judgment, desire, attraction or aversion. That is, we should see a thing exactly as it is and know it to be exactly what it is without our mind getting in the way to classify, condition and react to it and create a false impression for us to react to and make a muddle of everything. We must see and live according to reality, not according to the desire or fantasy of our egos, which is the way of nearly all people. Self-deception is the keynote of their lives.

Whether it is big or small, many or few, requite hatred with virtue. Blackney: "Great or small, frequent or rare, requite anger with virtue." Whatever the degree, hatred and anger should be reacted to with positivity, not in kind. In this way we protect ourselves and others from being drawn into the whirlpool of negative emotion and drowned. We also protect the universe by not perpetuating or increasing destructive vibrations.

Deal with the difficult while yet it is easy; deal with the big while yet it is small. The difficult (problems) of the world must be dealt with while they are yet easy; the great (problems) of the world must be dealt with while they are yet small. Both the individual and society need to be vigilant and detect the beginning of problems and deal with them before they get much beyond the seed stage. Then private and public life will be ordered and peaceful.

Therefore the Sage by never dealing with great (problems) accomplishes greatness. The greatness he will accomplish is in the form of orderliness and mastery of life.

63. Difficult and Easy

He who lightly makes a promise will find it often hard to keep his faith. Feng and English: "Easy promises make for little trust." We all know about this and should guard against it. For like the old adage says: "Loose lips sink ships" in private life as well as in war.

He who makes light of many things will encounter many difficulties. Feng and English: "Taking things lightly results in great difficulty." Chan: "He who takes things too easily will surely encounter much difficulty." Refusing to face the real state of things, our life runs into chaos. The "no sweat" or "go with the flow" policy is self-defeating. There are people who will not face anything if they can avoid it. I had an aunt and a cousin (her daughter) who lived this way all their lives and made a mess of everything. They had a kind of moral laziness that continually sabotaged them. My cousin died young and tragically as a result of her self-blinding ways.

Hence even the Sage regards things as difficult, and for that reason never meets with difficulties. Feng and English: "Because the sage always confronts difficulties, he never experiences them." Byrn: "The master expects great difficulty, so the task is always easier than planned." The Boy Scout motto "Be Prepared" is wisdom for life. Those who prepare for the worst and meet difficulties head-on will make them turn out for the best. Heedless living is a curse that devastates individuals and societies.

64. Beginning and End

What is at rest is easy to maintain.
What has not yet happened is easy to plan.
That which is fragile is easily shattered.
That which is tiny is easily scattered.
Correct problems before they occur.
Intervene before chaos erupts.

A tree too big around to hug is produced from a tiny sprout. A nine-story tower begins with a mound of dirt. A thousand-mile journey begins with your own two feet.

Whoever tries will fail. Whoever clutches, loses. Therefore the Sage, not trying, cannot fail. Not clutching, he cannot lose.

When people try, they usually fail just on the brink of success. If one is as cautious at the outset as at the end, one cannot fail.

Therefore the Sage desires nothing so much as to be desireless.
He does not value rare and expensive goods.
He unlearns what was once taught.
He helps the people regain what they have lost, to help every being assume its natural way of being, and not dare to force anything.

(Tao Teh King 64–Mabry translation)

What is at rest is easy to maintain. Lin Yutang: "That which lies still is easy to hold." When our mind and life are at rest in the awareness of our spirit-self, they are easy to control and direct.

64. Beginning and End

What has not yet happened is easy to plan. Lin Yutang: "That which is not yet manifest is easy to forestall." Looking ahead and planning what we wish to bring about before interfering conditions can arise, we shall be successful in shaping our life. Further, if we are aware of problems that could arise and take measures to prevent them we will be free of troubles.

That which is fragile is easily shattered. Legge: "That which is brittle is easily broken." If our thought and actions are not flexible and accommodating, they will be shattered to our disappointment and even grief. Failure only can result.

That which is tiny is easily scattered. When negative thoughts, things and situations are just beginning, are only hints, then is the time to deal with them, for they can be easily dispersed. That is why Solomon said: "Take us [Let us catch] the foxes, the little foxes, that spoil the vines" (Song of Solomon 2:15), before the vineyards would be destroyed by them.

Correct problems before they occur. Again, we need to look ahead and see what difficulties might come and set about either preventing them or preparing to meet and overcome them.

Intervene before chaos erupts. Lin Yutang: "Check disorder before it is rife." The moment we see a hint of chaos or disorder we must step in and stop its progress without delay or hesitation.

A tree too big around to hug is produced from a tiny sprout. A nine-story tower begins with a mound of dirt. A thousand-mile journey begins with your own two feet. Wu: "A journey of a thousand leagues starts from where your feet stand." Big things start out being small. If we deal with them from the start, we will be able to either eliminate them or make them develop into what we want them to become.

Whoever tries will fail. Whoever clutches, loses. Therefore the Sage, not trying, cannot fail. Not clutching, he cannot lose. Byrn: "If you rush into action, you will fail. If you hold on too tight, you will lose your grip." This is too obvious to need any comment.

When people try, they usually fail just on the brink of success. If one is as cautious at the outset as at the end, One cannot fail. Wu: "With heedfulness in the beginning and patience at the end, nothing will be spoiled." Many times I have seen projects that were going very well suddenly ruined by the very people working on them. The secret is to be careful every step of the way, to prevent delays and most of all not to rush anything. Steady and sure must be the policy. Then success will result.

Therefore the Sage desires nothing so much as to be desireless. For desire causes rush and carelessness. In fact, nothing destroys like desire, which in a myriad ways brings ruin. Therefore success in anything is guaranteed by not desiring or being attached to a certain goal. Flexibility and accommodation are necessary at all times. Letting things develop without forcing is a wise policy.

He does not value rare and expensive goods. Nor does he value rare and expensive results! Rather, the wise man is willing to let things be natural and humble rather than impress and awe any observers. Simplicity and moderation is a mark of wisdom.

He unlearns what was once taught. Feng and English: "He learns not to hold on to ideas." There is a great deal every one of us must unlearn before we can really learn the true nature and state of things. Much of what we have been told from childhood is errant nonsense. Every so often our minds need a good clearing out. Buddha said that one of the major obstacles to wisdom was clinging to ideas rather than examining and eliminating that which is not in harmony with truth and inner development.

He helps the people regain what they have lost, to help every being assume its natural way of being, and not dare to force anything. The wise man does not presume to indoctrinate and direct people, but shows them the way to find the wisdom that has always been within them. Real spiritual awakening is a process of remembering. When I first read the Bhagavad Gita I felt that my own soul was speaking to me. I did not learn a single thing: I remembered what I had forgotten. Truth is not learned but is recognized. Enlightenment is the natural state of every one of us. We do not force it or even attain it, but we recognize it. Our blind eyes are opened and we see what has always been there. We "come to ourself" in the truest sense. We uncover that which has been present all along but hidden.

65. The Grand Harmony

In ancient times those who followed the Tao did not try to educate the people. They chose to let them be.

The reason people become hard to govern is that they think they know it all.

So, if a leader tries to lead through cleverness, he is nothing but a liability. But if a leader leads, not through cleverness, but through goodness, this is a blessing to all.

To be always conscious of the Great Pattern is a spiritual virtue.

Spiritual virtue is awesome and infinite and it leads all things back to their Source. Then there emerges the Great Harmony.

(Tao Teh King 65–Mabry translation)

In ancient times those who followed the Tao did not try to educate the people. They chose to let them be. The universe and everything in it is evolving, and the evolutionary impulse is from within moving outward. Evolution never comes from without but from within, though an external factor can provoke an internal response that brings about evolutionary unfoldment. Knowing this, those in harmony with the Tao did not try to change others by external worlds or deeds, but simply kept living according to the Tao and by their silent presence in the world produced favorable conditions for the natural growth of others. They were like the leavening which causes bread to rise. They had a profound effect on others, but it was completely internal. So they benefitted them by not interfering with them. Invisibly they assisted in their growth.

The reason people become hard to govern is that they think they know it all. Blackney: "The more the folk know what is going on, the harder it becomes to govern them. For public knowledge of the government is such a thief that it will spoil the realm." This is certainly not in harmony with "the right to know" that the media attributes to people in general. Having information in no way imparts the intelligence and insight to draw right conclusions. There is no denying that in the intervening centuries between Lao Tzu and the present day there has been an opening of consciousness that has certainly rendered most people more capable of understanding what is going on in the world than at his time. Nevertheless, humanity has a long way to go, and until then it is beneficial for us to seriously consider what past leaders have had to say about public life.

So, if a leader tries to lead through cleverness, he is nothing but a liability. But if a leader leads, not through cleverness, but through goodness, this is a blessing to all. Anyone with good sense should know this is true, but in this country we have endured the presidency of corrupt and morally vile men who, we were assured daily, were capable of being worthy presidents because their personal life had no effect on their political life. Those who wanted to deny decency and personal responsibility gladly took to this gospel of evil, but no one with open eyes and ears failed to see that the opposite was true. Each aspect of our life affects all the others because they are essentially one. To ascribe to the possibility, much less the desirability, of moral schizophrenia is itself insane. Yet we have seen in other leaders the value of goodness which guided their endeavors.

To be always conscious of the Great Pattern is a spiritual virtue. Lao Tzu certainly believed in moral absolutes. The Great Pattern of which he speaks is the Natural Law so shrilly and even hysterically denied by the forces that advocate chaos and evil as a way of life. How well do I remember seeing Robert Bork grilled about his belief in Natural Law. Since fools will always do as they please with no regard to realities, it is our duty to ignore them and order our own lives to conform to that Law which is indeed a divine law. Those who do not know or who ignore the divine plan for each one of us cannot live a truly human life. But we can do so and, as Lao Tzu just said, through that be a blessing to all.

Spiritual virtue is awesome and infinite and it leads all things back to their Source. Then there emerges the Great Harmony. Feng and English: "Primal Virtue is deep and far. It leads all things back toward the Great Oneness." Here we have it stated clearly. *Spiritual* virtue is needed, for by its very nature it leads us back to our divine Source, into unity with God. We should prize spiritual virtue above all in ourselves and others. For it leads to the Infinite. What is spiritual virtue? The master yogi, Patanjali, in Yoga Sutras 2:30 says it consists of these ten principles:

1. Ahimsa: non-violence, non-injury, harmlessness
2. Satya: truthfulness, honesty
3. Asteya: non-stealing, honesty, non-misappropriativeness
4. Brahmacharya: sexual continence in thought, word and deed as well as control of all the senses
5. Aparigraha: non-possessiveness, non-greed, non-selfishness, non-acquisitiveness
6. Shaucha: purity, cleanliness
7. Santosha: contentment, peacefulness
8. Tapas: austerity, practical (i.e., result-producing) spiritual discipline
9. Swadhyaya: introspective self-study, spiritual study
10. Ishwarapranidhana: offering of one's life to God

"He that hath ears to hear, let him hear"(Matthew 11:15).

66. The Lords of the Ravines

> How did the great rivers and seas become the lords of the ravines? By being good at keeping low. That was how they became lords of the Ravines.
>
> Therefore in order to be the chief among the people, one must speak like their inferiors.
>
> In order to be foremost among the people, one must walk behind them.
>
> Thus it is that the Sage stays above, and the people do not feel his weight.
>
> Walks in front, and the people do not wish him harm.
>
> Then the people of the world are glad to uphold him forever.
>
> Because he does not contend, no one in the world can contend against him.
>
> (Tao Teh King 66)

How did the great rivers and seas become the lords of the ravines? By being good at keeping low. That was how they became Lords of the Ravines. Once again we see that humility and self-effacement are the secret of advancement and wide influence.

Therefore in order to be the chief among the people, one must speak like their inferiors. Wu: "Therefore, the Sage reigns over the people by humbling himself in speech." Feng and English: "If the sage would guide the people, he must serve with humility." Byrn: "If you want to be the ruler of people, you must speak to them like you are their servant."

66. The Lords of the Ravines

In order to be foremost among the people, one must walk behind them. Wu: "And leads the people by putting himself behind." Byrn: "If you want to lead other people, you must put their interest ahead of your own." We must learn to sincerely put others first and at the same time be an example for them to see and follow of their own accord.

Thus it is that the Sage stays above, and the people do not feel his weight. Mabry: "That way when the sage takes a position of power the people will not feel oppressed." Byrn: "The people will not feel like they are being manipulated, if a wise person is in front as their leader." Freedom of thought and deed results from the example of a wise person.

[He] walks in front, and the people do not wish him harm. Mabry: "And when the Sage leads the people will not think he is in the way." Blackney: "His station is ahead of them To see they do not come to harm." The wise one neither pushes from behind nor pulls from in front.

Then the people of the world are glad to uphold him forever. Because he does not contend, no one in the world can contend against him. Mabry: "Because he refuses to compete, The world cannot compete with him." Never a burden, the sage only uplifts and inspires. Therefore those around him are always in favor of his worthy words and actions. He does not lead them, but they model themselves after his example because they wish to be like him. This is the highest form of leadership.

67. The Three Treasures

All the world says that my Tao is great, but seems queer, like nothing on earth. But it is just because my Tao is great that it is like nothing on earth! If it were like anything on earth, how small it would have been from the very beginning!

I have Three Treasures, which I hold fast and watch over closely. The first is Mercy. The second is Frugality. The third is Not Daring to Be First in the World.

Because I am merciful, therefore I can be brave. Because I am frugal, therefore I can be generous. Because I dare not be first, therefore I can be the chief of all vessels.

If a man wants to be brave without first being merciful, generous without first being frugal, a leader without first wishing to follow, he is only courting death!

Mercy alone can help you to win a war. Mercy alone can help you to defend your state. For Heaven will come to the rescue of the merciful, and protect him with its Mercy.

(Tao Teh King 67–Wu translation)

All the world says that my Tao is great, but seems queer, like nothing on earth. But it is just because my Tao is great that it is like nothing on earth! If it were like anything on earth, how small it would have been from the very beginning! Because humanity lives in ignorance the way a fish lives in water, the Tao seems to be a fantasy and folly, even insanity. But it is really the antidote to those things, being not just wisdom but Reality.

67. The Three Treasures

Those who can only understand matters in the context of this world can only be bewildered at hearing of the Tao.

Many people say: "I don't see that" when they cannot understand. The Tao is too great to see with earthly eyes. Only that which is small can be seen by those immersed in worldly illusions and ignorance. So if we could see it, it would be small indeed and therefore not really the Tao. The only way to see the Tao is to expand our consciousness far beyond its present boundaries. This is what yoga is all about.

I have Three Treasures, which I hold fast and watch over closely. The first is Mercy. The second is Frugality. The third is Not Daring to Be First in the World.

Because I am merciful, therefore I can be brave. Since there is no violence in the heart of a truly merciful person he is fearless even though keenly aware of danger and of the evil that is in the world and which often prevails. Also, being merciful he knows that he has not sown enmity but only kindness, goodness and mercy. Therefore that is what he shall reap.

Because I am frugal, therefore I can be generous. Since he has kept his resources the wise man has a store from which he can draw to help others. Further, because he is frugal it is not his habit to be extravagant and give more than is needed or practical. Therefore his generosity is genuine and not an inflated show.

Because I dare not be first, therefore I can be the chief of all vessels. The wise man is free from overweening ambition and the need to maintain an inflated position in society. Therefore he is full control of his life and chief of all within it.

If a man wants to be brave without first being merciful, generous without first being frugal, a leader without first wishing to follow, he is only courting death! Disaster alone can follow trying to act virtuously without being oneself grounded in virtue.

Mercy alone can help you to win a war. Mercy alone can help you to defend your state. For Heaven will come to the rescue of the merciful, and protect him with its Mercy. Perhaps Jesus had this passage in mind when he perfectly encapsulated it: "Blessed are the merciful: for they shall obtain mercy" (Matthew 5:7).

68. The Virtue of Not-Contending

The brave soldier is not violent.
The good fighter does not lose his temper.
The great conqueror does not fight.
The good user of men places himself below others.
This is the virtue of not-contending, is called the capacity to use men, is reaching to the height of being mated to Heaven, to what was of old.
(Tao Teh King 68)

The brave soldier is not violent. The good fighter does not lose his temper. Wu: "A good soldier is never aggressive." Byrn: "The best warriors do not use violence." Mabry: "The best fighter is not driven by anger." War is a terrible thing, yet entire nations are often forced into armed conflict by aggressive countries. Lao Tzu does not condemn those who are not the aggressor, but gives his wise observations concerning the situation.

First he tells us that a worthy soldier does not like violence and does not lose his coolness of mind in the heat of battle when it is "natural" to become angry. Nor does he harbor enmity toward those he fights against.

The great conqueror does not fight. Wu: "The best way of conquering an enemy is to win him over by not antagonizing him." Mabry: "The true conqueror wins without confrontation." Byrn: "The best tacticians try to avoid confrontation." Lao Tzu now tells us that the greatest conqueror is one that uses reason and wise, honest and uncompromising diplomacy to convince his potential enemies of the way to peace and understanding.

Feng and English have a different translation: "A good winner is not vengeful." It is unfortunately usual that the winners of a war punish the conquered and oppress them terribly. This has come to be expected, so a victor who does not act in this way is considered either weak or foolish. No one seems to recognize the presence of goodness. It is also usual for the defeated to feel humiliated and degraded if the conqueror does not maltreat them! This is a sad proof of how much the character of the human race has become corrupted and distorted.

The good user of men places himself below others. Wu: "The best way of employing a man is to serve under him." Byrn: "The best leaders become servants of their people." This has been seen in the actions of great warriors. In our time (or nearly so) General Douglas MacArthur was a prime example of such conduct. The United States may have "conquered" Japan, but General MacArthur saved Japan, giving it the best constitution in the world, even better than that of his own country. When he left Japan, multitudes of people came to bid him farewell, many of them with signs expressing their love and appreciation. Many shed tears at the departure of their true friend and benefactor.

This principle of Lao Tzu is also seen in the lives of the true saints of India. Swami Sivananda was the loving servant of all humanity. Paramhansa Yogananda was unfailingly humble and caring toward all people, including those who were disrespectful and even inimical to him. In my own visits to India I have witnessed remarkable instances of humility and sacrifice for others on the part of the saints. Of them many can say the words of the hymn: "For his love has been so gracious, it has won my heart at last." This was especially true of Yogananda who has rightly been given the title Premavatar, Incarnation of Love, by those who lived with him.

This is the virtue of not-contending, is called the capacity to use men, is reaching to the height of being mated to Heaven, to what was of old. Wu: "This is called the virtue of non-striving! This is called using the abilities of men! This is called being wedded to Heaven as of old!" Mabry: "I say there is much good in not competing. I call it using the power of the people. This is known as being in tune with Heaven, like the Sages of old." Byrn: "This is called the virtue of non-competition. This is called the power to manage others. This is called attaining harmony with the heavens." The fundamental idea of all these different translations is that those who do not force, do not struggle (contend) with others or the elements of life, themselves are following the eternal pattern of Divine Heaven, which forces nothing but resolves all things through gradual evolution. Realizing that people must evolve for there to be lasting beneficial change, the wise person works for that alone and never resorts to the other means which, being in violation of the divine order and the nature of all things, cannot but fail and in the end work harm.

69. Camouflage

There is the maxim of military strategists: I dare not be the first to invade, but rather be the invaded. Dare not press forward an inch, but rather retreat a foot.

That is, to march without formations, to roll up the sleeves, to charge not in frontal attacks, to arm without weapons.

There is no greater catastrophe than to underestimate the enemy. To underestimate the enemy might entail the loss of my treasures.

Therefore when two equally matched armies meet, it is the man of sorrow who wins.

(Tao Teh King 69)

There is the maxim of military strategists: I dare not be the first to invade, but rather be the invaded. Dare not press forward an inch, but rather retreat a foot. Mabry: "The military has a saying: 'I would rather be passive, like a guest than aggressive, like a host. I would rather retreat a foot than advance an inch.'" Legge: "A master of the art of war has said, 'I do not dare to be the host (to commence the war); I prefer to be the guest (to act on the defensive). I do not dare to advance an inch; I prefer to retire a foot.'" Master Lao Tzu is not advocating that we should be passive and without initiative, but in relation to others we should never be aggressive or invasive, attempting to shape their thought or life. A good example of this is the traditional Eastern Orthodox way of establishing a church in a non-orthodox area. A missionary goes there, takes up residence and simply lives from day to day. If anyone shows interest he speaks to them about Orthodoxy. But if after some time (the recommended time is three years) no one has shown serious interest in becoming part of the Orthodox Church he moves on to another place or returns home. Lao Tzu would approve totally.

That is, to march without formations, to roll up the sleeves, to charge not in frontal attacks, to arm without weapons. Wu: "This is called marching without moving, rolling up one's sleeves without baring one's arms, capturing the enemy without confronting him, holding a weapon that is invisible." Mabry: "This is called going forward without instigating, engaging without force, defense without hatred, victory without weapons." That is really all there is to this: live peacefully and unobtrusively, friendly to all but respectful of them by never interfering or trying to influence them. If asked, opinion and help can be given, but only to the degree requested and with nothing more than continued good will.

There is no greater catastrophe than to underestimate the enemy. To underestimate the enemy might entail the loss of my treasures. Legge: "There is no calamity greater than lightly engaging in war. To do that is near losing (the gentleness) which is so precious." Often people push in and meddle in other people's lives because they think those people are malleable and inferior to them in understanding. This can have very surprising and unpleasant results as the pushed may not just push back, but punch back. Also, we should not underestimate those we think need our guidance or instruction.

Therefore when two equally matched armies meet, it is the man of sorrow who wins. Wu: "Therefore, when opposing troops meet in battle, victory belongs to the grieving side." Legge: "Thus it is that when opposing weapons are (actually) crossed, he who deplores (the situation) conquers." Chan: "Therefore when armies are mobilized and issues joined, the man who is sorry over the fact will win." Since inevitably conflicts will arise, even if only from the side of others, the truly wise one in the matter is the one who regrets it and considers it a loss and a detriment. Often the wise one must apologize to the foolish in order to restore order.

The sum of it all is to live in self-containment and self-effacement, being the peacemaker even if not the cause of conflict.

70. They Know Me Not

>My teachings are very easy to understand and very easy to practice, but no one can understand them and no one can practice them.
>In my words there is a principle.
>In the affairs of men there is a system.
>Because they know not these, they also know me not.
>Since there are few that know me, therefore I am distinguished.
>Therefore the Sage wears a coarse cloth on top and carries jade within his bosom.
>(Tao Teh King 70)

My teachings are very easy to understand and very easy to practice, but no one can understand them and no one can practice them. Wu: "My words are very easy to understand, and very easy to practice: But the world cannot understand them, nor practice them." Why is this? Because minds warped and ravaged by the world and its currents are neither able to understand the truths of the Tao nor able to practice them. First there must be a complete overhauling and renewal of the consciousness. And how will that be done? Only by yoga practice. Until a person is a yogi, all he can hope for are momentary flashes of understanding and inspiration. But for realization of the Tao, not just knowledge about It, steadiness of mind and will are necessary, and these can only be gained through yoga.

In my words there is a principle. Wu: "My words have an Ancestor." Legge: "There is an originating and all-comprehending (principle) in my words." Chan: "My doctrines have a source (Nature)." Jesus said: "The words that I speak unto you, they are spirit, and they are life" (John 6:63). Lao Tzu tells us that his very words both come from and embody the Tao. Knowing the Tao himself, the words of Lao Tzu had the power to impart consciousness itself and comprehension of the Tao. The words of a sage can enlighten the disciple that is purified and prepared. This was seen again and again in the daily life of Swami Sivananda.

In the affairs of men there is a system. Wu: "My deeds have a Lord." Mabry: "My deeds are but service." Legge: "And an authoritative law for the things (which I enforce)." Chan: "My deeds have a master (Tao)." Everything goes according to cosmic law (ritam). Those who contravene that law court chaos and disaster. Those who conform to that law attain order and success. So the first step in practical spiritual life is to learn the fundamental and unchangeable laws of physical, mental and spiritual life. Where are they to be found? The Bhagavad Gita is the most perfect exposition of the Science of Life. The eleven major Upanishads of which the Gita is a practical digest, are also a source of the laws of spirit-consciousness. The laws of interior life and conscious evolution are found in the Yoga Sutras of Patanjali.

Because they know not these, they also know me not. Wu: "The people have no knowledge of this. Therefore, they have no knowledge of me." It is impossible to know the Infinite without knowing our way through the labyrinth of the finite. There is no hope of knowing the Tao if we do not know the way things work in the outer and inner worlds. Aspiration means nothing if there is no knowledge of how to realize it.

Since there are few that know me, therefore I am distinguished. Wu: "The fewer persons know me, the nobler are they that follow me." Mabry: "And since so few understand me, then such understanding is rare and valuable indeed." "Then said one unto him, Lord, are there few that be saved? And he said unto them, Strive to enter in at the strait gate: for many, I say unto you, will seek to enter in, and shall not be able" (Luke 13:23-24). "Enter ye in at the strait gate: for wide is the gate, and broad is the way, that leadeth to destruction, and many there be which go in thereat: because strait is the gate, and narrow is the way, which leadeth unto life, and few there be that find it" (Matthew 7:13-14).

Large numbers are to be found outside true knowledge, few only are those who are true knowers (gnostics). Those who look for a large group to join will find many, but none of them will find the truth. Those who are willing to be only one of a few or even to be totally alone in their seeking have a chance at seeking and finding.

There is a story of a famous guru a century or so back in Western India who was kidnapped by a gang. They treated him very respectfully but demanded that each of his disciples pay them one rupee each as ransom. Since the guru was said to have hundreds of disciples, this would net them a lot of money. But the guru pointed out that the disciples might not trust them to let him go so easily, so they should release him and let him collect the ransom himself. To this they readily agreed, saying they would come for the ransom in one month. At the end of a month they came to him and received three and one-half rupees. "Because," he explained to them, "I only have three true disciples, and one other is half a disciple. The rest are not my disciples at all." Groupies abound; disciples are rare.

"Rare and valuable indeed" are those who know the Way (Tao) and walk it. Many are involved in religion and philosophy, but few are those who are moving toward enlightenment. Rare in truth are those who truly teach the way, rarer still are those that begin walking on the way, and rarest are those that persevere unto the end and become themselves the Tao.

Therefore the Sage wears a coarse cloth on top and carries jade within his bosom. Wu: "Therefore, the Sage wears coarse clothes while keeping the jade in his bosom." Mabry: "Therefore the Sage wears common clothes and hides his treasures only in is heart." Legge: "It is thus that the sage wears (a poor garb of) hair cloth, while he carries his (signet of) jade in his bosom." Feng and English: "Therefore the sage wears rough clothing and holds the jewel in his heart." This is absolutely true. The flashy, charismatic glitter gurus are only surface show. What you see is all you will ever get. The genuine sages live, look, act and teach simply, often deliberately veiling themselves so only those who have inner sight will recognize them. The ignorant either cannot see them or sneer at them in contempt. But those that possess at least some wisdom see their glory. How many times have spiritually blind people asked me: "What do you see in N.?" "What do you get from going to N.?" and suchlike. God told Samuel: "The Lord seeth not as man seeth; for man looketh on the outward appearance, but the Lord looketh on the heart" (I Samuel 16:7). When Goliath saw David "he disdained him" (I Samuel 17:42). So are the ignorant and the doomed to wander.

71. Sick-Mindedness

Who knows that he does not know is the highest.
Who (pretends to) know what he does not know is sick-minded.
And who recognizes sick-mindedness as sick-mindedness is not sick-minded.
The Sage is not sick-minded. Because he recognizes sick-mindedness as sick-mindedness, therefore he is not sick-minded.
(Tao Teh King 71)

Who knows that he does not know is the highest. Wu: "To realize that our knowledge is ignorance, this is a noble insight." Socrates said: "The only true wisdom is in knowing you know nothing." And similarly: "To know, is to know that you know nothing. That is the meaning of true knowledge." This is not cynicism or self-satirization, but an awareness of how infinite knowledge is and how tiny, even trivial, our knowledge is. To know is to be; so to know the Tao is to be the Tao. Until that knowledge is attained by us we are ignorant; and the wise know that. The important thing to realize is that although our present knowledge is ignorance, we are destined to become knowers. Knowledge is not an unattainable thing, but is our destiny and even our nature.

The wise know that mere intellectual knowledge is ultimately nothing, valueless. But they also know that true knowledge is everything and must be sought for assiduously. The greatest philosopher of India,

Shankaracharya, spent his life teaching the absolute necessity of jnana: knowledge of Reality, of Brahman, the Absolute. It is also the process of reasoning by which the Ultimate Truth is attained, the knowledge by which one is aware of one's identity with Brahman. What a glorious and exalted viewpoint! That alone marks out the possessor of wisdom.

Who (pretends to) know what he does not know is sick-minded. It is truly a mental-spiritual sickness to try and deceive others in claiming that we know something when we do not know it at all. The worst are the false gurus that pretend to be enlightened (or even a divine incarnation) and gain disciples through their pretence, teaching ignorance rather than knowledge.

Wu: "To regard our ignorance as knowledge, this is mental sickness." It is mental illness to fool ourself into thinking that the ideas that pop into our wandering minds are true, even divine, knowledge. Did you ever know people that believed their dreams were revelations of truth? I have. I have known people whose minds were completely out of their control, running here and there and spewing out utter foolishness that they believed were channeled messages from God.

Feng and English: "Ignoring knowledge is sickness." To ignore, reject or willfully forget the truth is a psychological aberration. Even worse is to know what is the truth but to deliberately act and speak contrary to it, either to deceive ourselves or others. For example, people in delusive religions become hysterical, hostile and even violent when someone does not believe as they do. They will often ask people: "What do you think of…?" and name their pet delusion or deluder. No matter how gently or diplomatically you indicate that you do not believe, they will "go ballistic." Why? *They know it is nonsense, completely false*, but because they want it to be true they have brainwashed themselves about it. Yet they know it is false. To protect their hypocrisy they attack you. Watch out.

And who recognizes sick-mindedness as sick-mindedness is not sick-minded. What about the old "judge not" cant that I have heard from nearly every scoundrel and hypocrite I have ever met? It is deceitful nonsense. Those who see the truth of things are continually accused of being judgmental and negative. May I give an example? Once a woman told me that all forms of nuclear defense were unnecessary, including the "Star Wars" project that at the time was a favorite for such people to denounce. Why, I asked her, were such programs unnecessary, even wrong? "Because," she said, "the Tibetan lamas knew how to vaporize nuclear warheads by their will power alone." Now, I had never heard of such a thing being claimed by Tibetan teachers. And I pointed out to her that it could not be expected that the nations of the world would accept that assertion unless the lamas proved to them they could do such a thing, and would be around to do it if any attack occurred. She began screaming at me that it was people like me who caused war in the world and who were preventing the world peace that could so easily be achieved. Her behavior was truly insane. This is the way of the sick-minded. Be aware of it and do not mistake it. And do not deal with it. Depart in peace.

Wu: "Only when we are sick of our sickness shall we cease to be sick." How true this is. Only when we vigorously reject our own folly for what it is will we possibly become wise.

Mabry: "Only someone who realizes he is ill can become whole." Byrn: "Only by recognizing that you have an illness can you move to seek a cure." Acknowledgement of the true situation is essential for a healthy and worthy future. "Positive thinking" is not lying to oneself and others about the true nature of things. Only honesty can pave the way for correction and improvement. Finally, those who do not realize or admit they are ill cannot be healed by God, much less by human beings. Only when they accept the truth can benefit come to them. Otherwise *they* are the embodiment of negativity and destructiveness. As Saint Paul said: "From such turn away" (II Timothy 3:5).

The Sage is not sick-minded. Because he recognizes sick-mindedness as sick-mindedness, therefore he is not sick-minded. There is a very important implication in this statement: Those who can recognize sick-mindedness are not sick-minded themselves and have the ability to avoid sick-mindedness. The "no judgement" people are themselves sick-minded. *Krino* means to condemn and wish harm to someone, not just be aware of their real nature or condition. If there was no judgment all criminals would be allowed to do as they please and there would be neither police nor judges and juries. Would anyone sane want much a society? But the "don't judge" people are sick-minded and therefore hate truth, being evil themselves.

Wu: "The Sage is not sick, being sick of sickness; This is the secret of health." I knew a man who never had smoked a single cigarette. The reason? His mother was a chain smoker who had him clean out her ashtrays when he was growing up. Seeing its nastiness, he grew to loathe smoking, so never engaged in it himself. Those who are repulsed by wrongdoing are safe from doing wrong themselves. When Paramhansa Yogananda was daily going to Pacific Palisades to supervise the creation of the Lake Shrine, he asked one of the young residents of the ashram to skip school and come with him. "Call up and tell them you are sick," he told the boy. "But I am not sick!" the boy protested. "Yes, you are," said the Master, "You are sick of the world." Such sickness is a guarantee of present and continued health.

Byrn: "The Master is whole because he sees his illnesses and treats them, and thus is able to remain whole." Only the proficient yogi is capable of recognizing, facing and curing his negative mental traits.

Blackney: "The Wise Man has indeed a healthy mind; he sees an aberration as it is and for that reason never will be ill." Indeed so.

72. On Punishment (1)

> When the people no longer fear your power, it is a sign that a greater power is coming.
> Interfere not lightly with their dwelling, nor lay heavy burdens upon their livelihood. Only when you cease to weary them, will they cease to be wearied of you.
> Therefore, the Sage knows himself, but makes no show of himself; loves himself, but does not exalt himself. He prefers what is within to what is without.
> (Tao Teh King 72–Wu translation)

When the people no longer fear your power, it is a sign that a greater power is coming. Mabry: "When people lose their fear of power then great power has indeed arrived." Immediately there comes to mind the modern film version of *The Island of Dr. Moreau*. Despite his pretenses of love for the animals he is trying to turn into human beings, Dr. Moreau controls them through intense pain when they "misbehave." At one point some of these altered animals are speaking with him, and one asks him: "Father, if there is no pain, is there no law?" For breaking Dr. Moreau's "law" always brought pain.

In both religious and civil life the threat of punishment in some form of pain, physical or psychological, is considered necessary to keep people in line and obeying the law. Civil life is perhaps too complex to quickly make a worthy and not merely theoretical statement regarding the threat of pain, but I can confidently say that such a threat is only needful in a religion when it is false, hypocritical, coercive and an infraction of the judgment and freedom of the members. Certainly when there is no longer fear among the members we can know that a higher and greater power has come into function, in both civil and religious life, on the part of the official structure and in the hearts of the people.

So Lao Tzu is telling all those in power (including parents) that only when there is no fear is there justice, right and truth. I am acquainted with a totally pacifist church which holds as a cardinal principle that children must never be caused pain in any form. They are never spanked, shaken, shouted at or "talked to" in any threatening or coercive manner. Rather, the reason for the rules are carefully and rationally explained to them, confident that they have a higher nature that will respond. And it is so. Never have I seen such happy, loving and obedient children in the West as those in that church. I have seen the same thing in India where, at least in the truly religious households, children are respected and treated as intelligent and innately good. I have seen for myself that Lao Tzu is speaking correctly in this verse.

Interfere not lightly with their dwelling, nor lay heavy burdens upon their livelihood. Only when you cease to weary them, will they cease to be wearied of you. This principle should be kept in mind in all aspects of our interaction with people. Interference is never right, though intervention may be. But if it is necessary, we must not forget the wise Biblical injunctions: "Fathers, provoke not your children to wrath: but bring them up in the nurture and admonition of the Lord" (Ephesians 6:4). "Fathers, provoke not your children to anger, lest they be discouraged" (Colossians 3:21).

Therefore, the Sage knows himself, but makes no show of himself; loves himself, but does not exalt himself. He prefers what is within to what is without. Knowing it is likely that the civil rulers will ignore his wisdom, but realizing that the principles he sets forth will be adopted by the wise in their personal life, Lao Tzu now speaks of the Sage and lists sagely traits for us to apply to ourselves.

The English speak of a person who "keeps himself to himself," and that is a quality of a true sage. He knows himself and knows his value as part of the life of the Tao, but he does not declaim it or push himself forward and attract the attention of the heedless. He lets them be at peace and so is at peace himself.

He loves himself as he loves the Tao, but he does not put himself above others, for they, too, are part of the Tao, even if they know it not. But he knows it and respects them and leaves them to find it out on their own.

The sage is intent on the inward life, knowing that it is more real than the outer life, plus he knows that the outer proceeds from the inner and that we must first conceive our thoughts, words and deeds inwardly and then project them outwardly in conformity with the inner order, the Way of the Tao that is Itself the Way. The sage always sees things with the inner eye and analyzes them according to the principles of inner realities. Thus his outer life is a perfect reflection and manifestation of his inner, true life.

73. On Punishment (2)

> A soldier who has the courage to fight will eventually be killed. But one who has the courage not to fight will live.
>
> In these two, one is good and the other harmful. Who knows why Heaven allows some things to happen? Even the Sage is stumped sometimes.
>
> The way of Heaven: Does not compete, but is good at winning. Does not speak, yet always responds; Does not demand, but is usually obeyed; Seems chaotic, but unfolds a most excellent plan.
>
> Heaven's net is cast wide and though its meshes are loose, nothing is ever lost.
>
> (Tao Teh King 73–Mabry translation)

A soldier who has the courage to fight will eventually be killed. But one who has the courage not to fight will live. This is not about military endeavor, but about the individual who has realized the necessity for personal transformation, something that seems to require long and intense struggle. But Lao Tzu is going to introduce to us a different and more successful perspective.

The person who jumps right into hand-to-hand combat with ego and its negative forces from many past lives is certainly courageous, but because his basic approach is erroneous, combatting inimical forces with personal enmity which by its nature is egoism masquerading as nobility, he will be defeated and his efforts "killed" by complete reversal.

But he who has the courage to follow the path of nature and not force, the way of Tao and not the way of the world, will not only live, he will be victorious.

There are two ways to approach our inner purification and restructuring. One way is negative, expressing itself as: "I am going to overcome this and fight it with all my strength," or the positive way: "I am only and always going to do the right in the future." The positive way invoked the person's inner, divine nature. Such a one says: "By finding my true Self, all that is negative and harmful in my life sphere will dissolve and melt away." Instead of saying: "I will never lie again," he says: "From now on I will always speak the truth." He never says: "I will not," but "I will." This is very important and is the difference between wasted effort and ultimate failure and true success. It is the way of Swami Sivananda of Rishikesh who formulated the motto: "Be Good. Do Good." It is entering into our essential being that is needed, not engaging in all forms of "doing" that only cover up our inner being.

In these two, one is good and the other harmful. Who knows why Heaven allows some things to happen? Even the Sage is stumped sometimes. One of the obstacles in spiritual transformation is the habit of looking outward at externals and stewing over them. "Why?" can be the path away from any discovery of truth. Lao Tzu is not telling us to be passive or indifferent, but to not bother with that which is none of our business. The philosopher Epictetus urged people to study their life and determine what they could influence or change in their life and what they could not. Then all their energy and attention should be focussed on what was in the scope of their will and action. Everything else should be accepted or ignored. So rather than trying to figure out the things over which we have no control, we should put all our attention on what we can control and change. It is a simple principle, but who thinks of it?

The way of Heaven: Does not compete, but is good at winning. Does not speak, yet always responds. Does not demand, but is usually obeyed. Seems chaotic, but unfolds a most excellent plan. Now Lao Tzu is going to tell us the way of Heaven which is the way of Spirit, of our own true Self. We need to take each phrase in turn.

Does not compete, but is good at winning. Actually, those who compete do not win in the long run. Those who do not pay attention to what others are doing, but mind their own business and invest their time completely in their own perfection will always win without even entering the contest. That is why Jesus taught: "Seek ye first the kingdom of God, and his righteousness; and all these things shall be added unto you" (Matthew 6:33). Put your mind and heart on the one thing, the Life of the Tao, and everything else will come to you effortlessly.

Two examples in Jesus' life of those who did not have the right idea are Saint Peter, who liked to ask: "What shall this man do?" about others. As a consequence when under pressure he failed. The other was Martha, the sister of Lazarus and Mary Magdalene. "[Jesus] entered into a certain village: and a certain woman named Martha received him into her house. And she had a sister called Mary, which also sat at Jesus' feet, and heard his word. But Martha was cumbered about much serving, and came to him, and said, Lord, dost thou not care that my sister hath left me to serve alone? bid her therefore that she help me. And Jesus answered and said unto her, Martha, Martha, thou art careful and troubled about many things: but one thing is needful: and Mary hath chosen that good part, which shall not be taken away from her" (Luke 10:38-42). (Notice that Martha did not reprimand Mary, she reprimanded Jesus: "Lord, do You not care?" So she blamed Jesus, not Mary.)

Jesus also said: "Seek, and ye shall find" (Matthew 7:7). Those who seek in the world for the things of the world shall indeed find just that and keep finding it over and over through constant rebirth until such seeking is stopped. The wise stop it right now.

Does not speak, yet always responds. Those who do not occupy themselves with speaking, but keep silent and listen, will be able to respond to the inner call of their own Self and the upward call of the Tao.

Does not demand, but is usually obeyed. Just as the proximity of fire can kindle fire in something nearby, in the same way the presence of a sage can stimulate others to wisdom and righteousness without a word of teaching. Coming into the presence of a master has transformed many people. I met people in India who had reformed criminals (some of them organized crime bosses) when they just entered into a room where the holy one was. Just a sight of them was enough to change their lives forever. I have known yogis whose silent company could cure addictions and negative habit patterns. I well remember when I had decided to slack off and delay taking up the yoga life. All I had to do was look into the eyes of Swami Bimalananda, a great disciple of Yogananda, to be freed from that foolishness. Whenever my "fire" would burn low and be in danger of going out, Sri Daya Mata (in those days Sister Daya) need only enter the room and I would "flame on" again. Yogananda used to tell people: "Change yourself and you will change thousands." But he meant a total change, not a token one.

Seems chaotic, but unfolds a most excellent plan. "You must be nuts!" These words or some like them have been addressed to the wise throughout the history of humanity. Ignorant people consider the wise foolish and stupid. "That makes no sense" is a common statement of condemnation when such people encounter truth, especially the truth of eternal verities.

When Yogananda decided to start a vegetarian café at the Hollywood center, several restauranteurs offered to help him, but when he told them his ideals regarding the preparation and serving of the food they insisted he would fail. But he did not. Eventually every day people would be standing along the west wall waiting for a table. After he had made a success of the Hollywood café, one day at the Encinitas hermitage he went with Sister Meera (whom I heard tell about this) to look at a ramshackle two-car garage on the property that everyone felt should be torn down. He stood in the center and looked carefully around and then remarked: "Yes. This will make a very good café." When Meera protested, he told her: "Wait and see." And she did: in time as many people were served there every year as at the Hollywood café.

The Hollywood center was born when Sister Meera went with Yogananda to the southeast corner of Sunset and Edgemont in Hollywood. At that time there were no buildings around, but only a decrepit park where homeless drunks lived and slept. It was considered a bad part of town by everyone. But not by Yogananda. He stood and looked around and told her: "This will make a very good center." "But no one will ever come to this place" she protested "they will be afraid to!" "You see only with your two eyes," Yogananda told her, "but I see with my one eye of intuition that one day there will be three huge buildings on the other three corners, and this fourth will be our center where many will come." When I moved next door to the Hollywood center in 1961, the big Kaiser Foundation had been built right across the street. On the other two corners were extensive one-story business buildings that were empty. Before I went to India at the end of November of 1962, Yogananda's prophecy had come true and there were two multi-story buildings on those corners.

Saints and masters embody the counsel of Saint Paul: "Let no man deceive himself. If any man among you seemeth to be wise in this world, let him become a fool, that he may be wise. For the wisdom of this world is foolishness with God" (I Corinthians 3:18-19). And the wisdom of God is foolishness to the world.

"Choose you this day whom ye will serve" (Joshua 24:15).

Heaven's net is cast wide and though its meshes are loose, nothing is ever lost. Lin Yutang: "The heaven's net is broad and wide with big meshes, yet letting nothing slip through."

The ways of heaven, the Tao, are found throughout the universe, and human beings consider them either non-existent or defective. But its laws, its meshes, gather up all in time and bring them to the Eternal Abode, the Tao.

74. On Punishment (3)

> When the people are no longer afraid of death, why scare them with the specter of death?
> If you could make the people always afraid of death, and they still persisted in breaking the law, then you might with reason arrest and execute them, and who would dare to break the law?
> Is not the Great Executor always there to kill? To do the killing for the Great Executor is to chop wood for a master carpenter, and you would be lucky indeed if you did not hurt your own hand!
> (Tao Teh King 74–Wu's translation)

Just what Lao Tzu had in mind when he wrote this section I do not know, but I can certainly say that exoteric religion East and West traffics in fear created by threats they make to those who do not follow their dictates or dogmas. Every word written here can be applied to them.

When the people are no longer afraid of death, why scare them with the specter of death? Mabry: "If people do not fear death how can you threaten them with it?" The purpose of authentic religion is to remove fear. Therefore a religion that makes its adherents fear that disobedience or disbelief will result in their death, or that death will result in great suffering in this world or in some form of hell, is a domain of demons and not divine truth. Because their religion is false and feeble they have no other way to bolster their authority than fear of punishment and pain (often the same thing), as well as promises of rewards and pleasure on earth and in heaven for those who "trust and obey."

If you could make the people always afraid of death, and they still persisted in breaking the law, then you might with reason arrest and execute them, and who would dare to break the law? Feng and English: "If men live in constant fear of dying, and if breaking the law means that a man will be killed, who will dare to break the law?" This is the specious reasoning of exoteric religion, but humans being what they are look for an out and usually find or fabricate one. Nevertheless many are terrified into compliance with the demands of their religion. When growing up I continually heard members of the church saying that if there was no immortality of the soul or no hell there would be no reason to follow the ways of our religion. When I would suggest that God is worthy of our love and that should be our motivation, I was always dismissed with contempt. After some years I dismissed the false religion and them.

Is not the Great Executor always there to kill? To do the killing for the Great Executor is to chop wood for a master carpenter, and you would be lucky indeed If you did not hurt your own hand! Chan: "There is always the master executioner (Heaven) who kills. To undertake executions for the master executioner is like hewing wood for the master carpenter. Whoever undertakes hewing wood for the master carpenter rarely escapes injuring his own hands." Those who take the role of judge and jailer, claiming to speak for God, meting out condemnation, punishment and even death to the recalcitrant, will themselves feel the ax in time. That is not a threat: just a statement of law, the law of Karma. "For with what judgment ye judge, ye shall be judged: and with what measure ye mete, it shall be measured to you again" (Matthew 7:2).

75. Punishment (4)

When people are hungry, it is because their rulers eat too much tax-grain.

Therefore the unruliness of hungry people is due to the interference of their rulers. That is why they are unruly.

The people are not afraid of death, because they are anxious to make a living. That is why they are not afraid of death.

It is those who interfere not with their living that are wise in exalting life.

(Tao Teh King 75)

When people are hungry, it is because their rulers eat too much tax-grain. Wu: "Why are the people starving? Because those above them are taxing them too heavily. That is why they are starving." This is certainly true in many instances.

Therefore the unruliness of hungry people is due to the interference of their rulers. That is why they are unruly. Civil disobedience often results from government interference that is unjust, foolish and destructive. I am sorry to say that famines have been engineered by governments that wanted to prove that without them the people could not survive. Their friends in high places ignored the fact that the people were not surviving at all! The wife of a former governor of Madras State during the British Raj told me that her husband had engineered famines in the Madras State that brought about the deaths of tens of thousands of Indians. One time he collaborated with the governor of Bombay State to sell rotten rice (her words) to the Madras State. In this way the Bombay State governor got rich and thousands died of starvation in Madras State. And the British Raj told the world: "If we were not here things would be much worse, even impossible!" And a foolish, gullible world believed it. The much vaunted poverty of India was a result of one thousand years of exploitive tyranny: seven hundred years of Moslem domination and three hundred years of British domination. It took nearly fifty years to recover from this blight, but today India is well on its way to becoming a major economic force in the world. Jai Hind!

The people are not afraid of death, because they are anxious to make a living. That is why they are not afraid of death. Wu: "Why do people make light of death? Because those above them make too much of life. That is why they make light of death. The people have simply nothing to live upon! They know better than to value such a life!" Feng and English: "Why do the people think so little of death? Because the rulers demand too much of life." Governments often create poverty so the people will be so desperate in their struggle to live that they will either be distracted from the evils of those governments or too busy barely living that they have no time or inclination to protest, much less rid themselves of such a government. Some Russian friends told me that in the heyday of the Soviet Union the people used to say: "If the Soviet government was put in charge of the Sahara desert, within a week there would be a shortage of sand." Stupidity and cunning often combine to perpetuate what Lao Tzu is discussing.

It is those who interfere not with their living that are wise in exalting life. Mabry: "Therefore, it seems that one who does not grasp this life too tightly is better off than one who clings." Feng and English: "Having little to live on, one knows better than to value life too much." There seems to be no consensus among translators as to the meaning of these words, so apparently we can choose which we prefer. There certainly is a difference between living and life. As I read once long ago: "Most people make a living, but very few make a life."

76. HARD AND SOFT

When man is born, he is tender and weak; at death, he is hard and stiff. When the things and plants are alive, they are soft and supple; when they are dead, they are brittle and dry. Therefore hardness and stiffness are the companions of death, and softness and gentleness are the companions of life.

Therefore when an army is headstrong, it will lose in a battle.

When a tree is hard, it will be cut down.

The big and strong belong underneath.

The gentle and weak belong at the top.

(Tao Teh King 76)

When man is born, he is tender and weak; at death, he is hard and stiff. When the things and plants are alive, they are soft and supple; when they are dead, they are brittle and dry. Therefore hardness and stiffness are the companions of death, and softness and gentleness are the companions of life. Feng and English: "Therefore the stiff and unbending is the disciple of death. The gentle and yielding is the disciple of life." A major principle of Taoism is the insistence on flexibility and the ability to "roll with the punches" rather than punch back and compound the conflict. In the Taoist view life is pliable and death, or that which breeds death, is hard and unyielding. "Blessed are the meek: for they shall inherit the earth" (Matthew 5:5), is the same view. It did not originate with Jesus, for the Psalm says: "The meek shall inherit the earth; and shall delight themselves in the abundance of peace" (Psalms 37:11). According to the Aquarian Gospel the Essenes were well acquainted with the Taoist writings, and the psalmist may have been also. (Not all of the psalms were written by David). There is a great deal of mistaken thought and action that arises from a misapplied insistence on standing up and being firm about principles that are purely personal rather than truly matters of justice and righteousness. The principle of forgiveness and returning good for evil is purely Taoist in the context of this section of the Tao Teh King. So is: "The letter killeth, but the spirit giveth life" (II Corinthians 3:6).

Therefore when an army is headstrong, it will lose in a battle. Wu: "Therefore, a mighty army tends to fall by its own weight, just as dry wood is ready for the axe." Any individual or group which exalts their "standards" or ideas of "right" above good sense and respect for others will also lose and fall. "Here I stand," insisted Martin Luther and look at the spiritual blight he ushered into the world. Nailing personal ideas to doors as Luther did is not the way to bring either wisdom or right.

When a tree is hard, it will be cut down. This is why both spiritual and political movements come and go. When they become "giants of the forest" their death warrant is already made out.

The big and strong belong underneath. Wu: "The mighty and the great will be laid low." Mabry: "The strong and rigid are broken and laid low." This can be understood in two legitimate ways. One is that the great and powerful should be the servants of the people, they should be the support and burden-bearers for those of lesser power than they. The other is that such people will, if they do not cultivate humility, flexibility and care for those "beneath" them, themselves be broken and brought low.

The gentle and weak belong at the top. Wu: "The humble and the weak will be exalted." Mabry: "The soft and weak will always overcome." Here again we find that the meek and humble will eventually rise, even if only after tremendous suffering and upheaval. Also that it is those who are mild and aware of their own frailty that have the moral strength needed to be leaders and governors.

All the preceding can be applied to the inner polity of the seeker for enlightenment. Each one of us is a kingdom and often various of our

76. Hard and Soft

aspects clamor for the pre-eminence and control—even tyranny. Just as a state should be ordered rightly, so must we be. Therefore Lao Tzu is a master teacher of both governments and individuals who seek to be united with the Tao and embody its traits perfectly.

77. Bending the Bow

The Tao (way) of Heaven, is it not like the bending of a bow? The top comes down and the bottom-end goes up, the extra (length) is shortened, the insufficient (width) is expanded. It is the way of Heaven to take away from those that have too much and give to those that have not enough.

Not so with man's way: he takes from those that have not and gives it as tribute to those that have too much.

Who can have enough and to spare to give to the entire world? Only the man of Tao.

Therefore the Sage acts, but does not possess, accomplishes but lays claim to no credit, because he has no wish to seem superior.

(Tao Teh King 77)

The Tao (way) of Heaven, is it not like the bending of a bow? The top comes down and the bottom-end goes up, the extra (length) is shortened, the insufficient (width) is expanded. It is the way of Heaven to take away from those that have too much and give to those that have not enough. The Virgin Mary said in prophetic inspiration: "[God] hath shewed strength with his arm; he hath scattered the proud in the imagination of their hearts. He hath put down the mighty from their seats, and exalted them of low degree. He hath filled the hungry with good things; and the rich he hath sent empty away" (Luke 1:51-53). According to the Aquarian Gospel she studied the teachings of Lao Tzu in Egypt at the Essene community in Zoan. And this passage from Saint Luke's gospel confirms that.

Just before going to India for the first time in 1962, I had the great good fortune to meet and hear Sri A. B. Purani, the administrator of the renowned Aurobindo Ashram of Pondicherry, India. From his lips I heard the most brilliant expositions of Vedic philosophy, and nothing in my subsequent experience has equaled them. In one talk he told the following story that fits right in with this section of the Tao Teh King:

In ancient India there lived a most virtuous Brahmin who was considered by all to be the best authority on philosophy. One day the local king ordered him to appear before him. When he did so, the king said: "I have three questions that puzzle and even torment me: Where is God? Why don't I see him? And what does he do all day? If you can't answer these three questions I will have your head cut off." The Brahmin was appalled and terrified, because the answers to these questions were not just complex, they were impossible to formulate. In other words, he did not know the answers. So his execution date was set.

On the morning of the execution day the Brahmin's young son appeared and asked the king if he would release his father if he, the son, would answer the questions. The king agreed, and the son asked that a container of milk be brought to him. It was done. Then the boy asked that the milk be churned into butter. That, too, was done.

"The first two of your questions are now answered," he told the king. The king objected that he had been given no answers, so the son asked: "Where was the butter before it was churned?" "In the milk," replied the king. "In what part of the milk?" asked the boy. "It was everywhere in the milk," answered the king. "Just so, agreed the boy, "and in the same way God is within all things and pervades all things." "Why don't I see him, then?" pressed the king. "Because you do not 'churn' your mind and refine your perceptions through meditation. If you do that, you will see God. But not otherwise. Now let my father go." "Not at all," insisted the king. "You have not told me what God does all day."

"To answer that," said the boy, "we will have to change places. You come stand here and let me sit on the throne." The request was so audacious the king complied, and in a moment he was standing before the enthroned Brahmin boy who told him: "This is the answer. One moment you were here and I was there. Now things are reversed. God perpetually lifts up and casts down every one of us. In one life we are exalted and in another we are brought low–oftentimes in a single life this occurs, and even more than once. Our lives are completely in his hand, and he does with us as he wills."

Everything in this world is both a raising up and a wearing down. Equilibrium is always being sought, so the opposite is also being produced at all times. And so it goes in a never-ending cycle. However things were at the end of a creation cycle, the same situation is manifested at the beginning of the next cycle. Not only is not a single atom ever lost from the universe, no movement goes unfinished or goes without a counter-movement. As Anandamayi Ma often said: "Getting implies losing."

Not so with man's way: he takes from those that have not and gives it as tribute to those that have too much. Mabry: "This is not the way of men, however, for they take from those who have little to increase the wealth of the rich." Legge: "It is not so with the way of man. He takes away from those who have not enough to add to his own superabundance." I think we all know this is simple truth about every era of recorded history. What I told earlier about the governor of Madras State is a horrible example. His wife who told me about this was the embodiment of sorrow and discontent. She smoked cigarettes and drank alcohol through most of her waking hours. What she had told me explained everything. The guilt she felt at not having revealed all this at the time was tormenting her every moment of her life. I doubt if she ever found any peace.

Who can have enough and to spare to give to the entire world? Only the man of Tao. Wu: "Who except a man of the Tao can put his superabundant riches to the service of the world?" Mabry: "So who is it that has too much and offers it to a needy World? Only someone who knows the Tao." This is true both materially and spiritually, though we usually only think of those whose abundant wisdom can be given to thousands and millions. Nevertheless, in India I have met several multimillionaires of a genuine spiritual character who perpetually gave monetary assistance to a vast number of people. One Bengali family had created the largest charitable trust in India. They lived only a few degrees from the poverty level, giving everything else for the welfare of others. Those who dedicate their lives to the spiritual uplift and enlightenment of others by their example can continue to do so for centuries and even millennia after they leave this world.

Therefore the Sage acts, but does not possess, accomplishes but lays claim to no credit, because he has no wish to seem superior. Wu: "Therefore, the Sage does his work without setting any store by it, accomplishes his task without dwelling upon it. He does not want his merits to be seen." Mabry: "Therefore, the Sage works anonymously. He achieves great things but does not wait around for praise. He does not want his talents to attract attention to him." Legge: "Therefore the (ruling) sage acts without claiming the results as his; he achieves his merit and does not rest (arrogantly) in it: he does not wish to display his superiority." As I have said, I have known many who acted thus both in the material and spiritual spheres. My beloved Swami Sivananda was a never-failing source of material and spiritual good. Yet humility was a dominant trait in him. It can be done. Lao Tzu is not just theorizing.

78. Nothing Weaker than Water

> In the whole World nothing is softer or weaker than water. And yet even those who succeed when attacking the hard and the strong cannot overcome it because nothing can harm it.
> The weak overcome the strong. The soft conquers the hard. No one in the world can deny this yet no one seems to know how to put it into practice.
> Therefore the Sage says "One who accepts a people's shame is qualified to rule it. One who embraces a condemned people is called the king of the Universe." True words seem paradoxical.
> (Tao Teh King 78–Mabry translation)

In the whole World nothing is softer or weaker than water. And yet even those who succeed when attacking the hard and the strong cannot overcome it Because noting can harm it. Lin Yutang: "There is nothing weaker than water but none is superior to it in overcoming the hard, for which there is no substitute." Here again we have the constant theme of Lao Tzu as to the wisdom of flexibility and accommodation. Though others may think of us as water, "weak as water" being a common expression, yet if we persist in our determination to be soft and flexible we shall eventually prevail. Many times it is simply a matter of karma: overcoming the negative karmas of others with our positive karma. But not in the sense of conquering or vanquishing, but of clearing up and healing. Harmlessness is the way to become invulnerable and unharmed.

The weak overcome the strong. The soft conquers the hard. No one in the world can deny this yet no one seems to know how to put it into practice. Certainly he who does know how to put this wisdom of Lao Tzu into practice is the greatest of sages and a blessing to the entire world. One of the great problems of humanity is knowing the right principles but having no insight as how to apply them.

Therefore the Sage says "One who accepts a people's shame is qualified to rule it. One who embraces a condemned people is called the king of the Universe." True words seem pardoxical. Legge: "Therefore a sage has said, "He who accepts his state's reproach, is hailed therefore its altars' lord; to him who bears men's direful woes they all the name of King accord." Chan: "Therefore the sage says: He who suffers disgrace for his country is called the lord of the land. He who takes upon himself the country's misfortunes becomes the king of the empire. Straight words seem to be their opposite." Byrn: "Therefore the Master says: "Only he who is the lowest servant of the kingdom is worthy to become its ruler. He who is willing to tackle the most unpleasant tasks is the best ruler in the world." Blackney: "Because of this the Wise Man says that only one who bears the nation's shame is fit to be its hallowed lord; that only one who takes upon himself the evils of the world may be its king. This is paradox." Lin Yutang: "Who bears himself the sins of the world is king of the world."

As you see, nearly every translation I have consulted has given different but valuable perspective on this verse. Two facts are affirmed in these translations:

1) The wise can take upon themselves the ills of a nation, often by being persecuted by those for whom they suffer or by identifying with those faults. There is here a very definite idea of a kind of mediator with heaven on the behalf of the people, one who sorrows for their evils and folly and may even give his life for them.

2) Truth–true wisdom–often seems to be contradictory or paradoxical; though clear it seems to be confused and nonsensical. To most people Lao Tzu was just a goofy and disagreeable old man. No one but the

gate keeper minded when he left to never be seen or heard of again. But millions through the centuries have revered and even worshipped him.

All praise be to the great master-teachers of the world, and may we be master-students of their wisdom.

79. Peace Settlements

Patching up a great hatred is sure to leave some hatred behind. How can this be regarded as satisfactory?

Therefore the Sage holds the left tally, and does not put the guilt on the other party.

The virtuous man is for patching up; the vicious is for fixing guilt.

But "the way of Heaven is impartial; it sides only with the good man."

(Tao Teh King 79)

Patching up a great hatred is sure to leave some hatred behind. How can this be regarded as satisfactory? Mabry: "When enemies are reconciled, some resentment invariably remains. How can this be healed?" Blackney: "How can you think it is good to settle a grievance too great to ignore, when the settlement surely evokes other piques?" It is certainly true that wherever passion and moral violence have resulted in wrongdoing, any correction of the situation is certain to create hatred and resentment in the guilty wrongdoers. It is unavoidable and cannot be left open to question.

This question asked by Lao Tzu is actually a test question. There are those who try to frighten off others from doing the right because it might "hurt" someone or "make trouble" or "make things worse." I grew up with this moral cowardice that is also bullying of the virtuous. This is in the class of the "Well, which is worse…?" question intended to present far-fetched consequences of doing right that to the foolish may appear as much worse than fulfilling one's moral obligations. The askers of these kind of questions are reprehensible in the extreme, confusers and destroyers of those they influence. "But what would you do if...?" they love to challenge others. They are the kind of people that when I was very young had come up with the assertion that there is no black or white, just shades of gray. Fiddlesticks!

As a man once told me, behind a big front there is a big back. Like the fox without a tail they are attempting to hide their own culpability, terrified that someone will see them for what they truly are. Of course their favorite is the "judge not lest ye be judged" challenge. But oh, how they judge and hate those that "judge." If there is anyone in the world that should be avoided it is these moral cowards whose guilt has forced them into such modes of hateful defense. Hating themselves they hate others, including those that would agree with them that nothing should be done if offense and complaint would be the result.

Wisdom and truth, however, say this: "Different is the good, and different, indeed, is the pleasant. These two, with different purposes, bind a man. Of these two, it is well for him who takes hold of the good; but he who chooses the pleasant, fails of his aim. Both the good and the pleasant approach a man. The wise man, pondering over them, discriminates. The wise chooses the good in preference to the pleasant. The simple-minded, for the sake of worldly well-being, prefers the pleasant" (Katha Upanishad 1:2:1-2).

Therefore the Sage holds the left tally, and does not put the guilt on the other party. Legge: "Therefore (to guard against this), the sage keeps the left-hand portion of the record of the engagement, and does not insist on the (speedy) fulfilment of it by the other party." Chan: "Therefore the sage keeps the left-hand portion (obligation) of a contract and does not blame the other party." The wise man's response in Mabry's translation asks: "How can this be healed?" Certainly rectification is the goal and not inciting more conflict. As the saying goes, it often is not what we do but the way in which we do it. So although facts must be faced, every reasonable attempt must be made to avoid genuine injury to anyone while acknowledging that the blustering of the guilty and resentful cannot be avoided no matter what is or is not done in the matter.

The virtuous man is for patching up; the vicious is for fixing guilt. Chan: "Virtuous people attend to their left-hand portions, While those without virtue attend to other people's mistakes." Byrn: "A virtuous person will do the right thing, and persons with no virtue will take advantage of others." Blackney: "The virtuous man promotes agreement; the vicious man allots the blame." There is no avoiding that the good will cooperate and attempt to set everything right while the bad will assign guilt and make personal attacks on the guiltless. That is their (very revealing) choice. They must be free to do so and the good must be free to act as is right: good, though unpleasant to those in the actual wrong.

There are people who are always jumping at the chance to declare their innocence. I knew an entire family who no matter how small or insignificant something was, would have a race with one another in exclaiming: "It's not *my* fault!" T. H. White in *The Elephant and the Kangaroo* writes about people who were so far gone down that path that they would even say: "It's not my fault; I did it." Sociopaths especially assign blame on others for their own actions and words. A little boy in the previously-mentioned family liked to excuse himself by declaring: "Well, he/she made me mad!" And it was accepted as an excuse.

But *"the way of Heaven is impartial; it sides only with the good man."* Byrn: "The Tao does not choose sides, the good person receives from the Tao because he is on its side." There is a Vedic hymn that begins *Ritam cha Satyam*: Right and Truth.

Heaven is impartial because it needs nothing and has no interest at all. Order and Truth are its very nature, so it is always favorable to the orderly and the truthful. The purpose of the universe is evolution and those that are evolving find themselves in harmony with it and are blessed. It is not that the Tao is on our side, but that we are on the Tao's side, as Byrn renders it. We are for the Tao and the Tao is for us. A perfect and fruitful partnership, indeed.

80. The Small Utopia

It is best to have small communities with few people.
Although they have goods and equipment in abundance few of them are even used.
They have great love of life, and are content to be right where they are.
Although they have boats and carriages, there is no place they particularly want to go.
And although they have access to weapons and machineries of war, they have no desire to show them off.
Let people return to simplicity, working with their own hands. Then they will find joy in their food, beauty in their simple clothes, peace in their living fulfillment in their tradition.
And although they live within sight of neighboring states and their roosters and dogs are heard by one another, the people are content to grow old and die without having gone to see their neighbor states.
(Tao Teh King 80–Mabry translation)

In these days of "global village" thinking and obsession throughout the world with annual increase in "the gross national product," these words of Lao Tzu seem very strange in varying degrees, depending on one's background.

It is best to have small communities with few people. This I know to be true, because I lived as a child and young adult in a wonderful peaceful and friendly (even loving) town of only four hundred and fifty people. I have also spent time in small "third world" countries where life was far better on all levels than in the "developed" and "leading" countries. Human values were much more developed and prized there than anywhere else. Some of the very small, "postage stamp" European countries are admirable in the same way.

Although they have goods and equipment in abundance few of them are even used. This I have also seen as wisdom. Here in America I visited a family that had a most close relationship with one another, both adults and children. It was wonderful. They had the only black-and-white television set I had seen in decades and they never turned it on. Instead they truly lived together and communicated with one another. Every evening all of them, grandparents, parents and children sat together until bedtime and talked, laughed and had fun and spoke about serious things as well. My uncle John Burke bought a car in the nineteen-twenties. He and my aunt Florence were satisfied with it and never got another. People thought they were strange and behind the times when they were really just contented and sensible. Someone loaned my maternal grandmother a television set. In a few weeks she asked them to take it back because there was nothing worth watching on it, and continued reading in the evenings as she had always done. This is genuine freedom and happiness.

They have great love of life, and are content to be right where they are. Although they have boats and carriages, there is no place they particularly want to go. There are some that travel to learn and genuinely expand their minds, but most people travel out of boredom, restlessness, discontent and even habit.

And although they have access to weapons and machineries of war, they have no desire to show them off. Remember the huge parades of war machines and weapons that the Soviets so loved? And the parade of red Toyota trucks filled with thugs and machine guns that the Taliban affected? I had the privilege of meeting the former President of Costa Rica who led his country in total disarmament in 1948 and writing it into their constitution the following year. The keys to the army headquarters were given to the Minister of Education so it could be used as a school. The money that would have been the military budget has been so intelligently invested that the infant mortality rates, life expectancy and literacy rates of Costa Rica are equal and in some instances better than those of most "developed" countries.

Let people return to simplicity, working with their own hands. Then they will find joy in their food, beauty in their simple clothes, peace in their living fulfillment in their tradition. Legge: "I would make the people return to the use of knotted cords (instead of the written characters). They should think their (coarse) food sweet; their (plain) clothes beautiful; their (poor) dwellings places of rest; and their common (simple) ways sources of enjoyment."

In the first phrase Legge's translation is referring to the quipu, an arrangement of cords and knots that in several civilizations were used to keep records and send messages. We may be horrified at Lao Tzu's advocacy of illiteracy. Who would read the Tao Teh King? Or is it that they would not need to, but instead would be living the Tao?

Someone once told me of the king of a small country who was approached by outsiders who offered to bring literacy to his people. "You want to ruin us and our culture," he told them. When we think of the wandering minstrels, musicians and storytellers and the prevalent folk theater that have vanished from nearly all literate and modern countries, we see what he meant.

One time in Benares (Varanasi) I ate in a very large restaurant that was filled with customers. There was only one waiter, and he could not read or write. He would just come to a table and the people would state what they wanted (at our table there were ten or more). Then he would relay the orders in the kitchen and later bring to each customer the very thing he had ordered. Since I was used to waiters and waitresses bringing just three or four items to a table and asking who ordered what, I was impressed. I was even more impressed back in America when I heard some barely literate people from rural Kentucky discussing the family history of people they were not even related to, citing the names of who had married whom for generations.

80. The Small Utopia

Simplicity is the way to health and happiness. Dr. Josef Lenninger, by far the most brilliant physician I have known, told me that once a young European prince had come to live with his family for several weeks. When he first came he had many health problems, but when he left after sharing their simple food and way of life he was perfectly healthy, prompting Dr. Lenninger's father to comment: "We are the real princes; we eat only what is healthy and strengthening."

And although they live within sight of neighboring states and their roosters and dogs are heard by one another, the people are content to grow old and die without having gone to see their neighbor states. Wu: "Though there may be another country in the neighborhood so close that they are within sight of each other and the crowing of cocks and barking of dogs in one place can be heard in the other, yet there is no traffic between them, and throughout their lives the two peoples have nothing to do with each other." I know of modern countries where people do not go even a few miles from where they were born, and it hurts them not a bit. One man told me that his father "married a foreigner," a woman from a village ten miles away from his place of birth. I have seen from studying the history of homogenized countries which today lead the world that there was a time when their culture was as rich and varied as though there were many small countries within one. Cultural "sophistication" is not so valuable as we are told to think, and "provincialism" is not so disadvantageous as we have been assured. See how the nations of the world are losing their distinct character through cultural uniformity and the "melting pot" experience. And has contentment, happiness and personal worth increased? We know it has not.

81. The Way of Heaven

True words are not fine-sounding; fine-sounding words are not true.

A good man does not argue; he who argues is not a good man.

The wise one does not know many things; he who knows many things is not wise.

The Sage does not accumulate (for himself). He lives for other people, and grows richer himself; he gives to other people, and has greater abundance.

The Tao of Heaven blesses, but does not harm.

The Way of the Sage accomplishes, but does not contend.

(Tao Teh King)

True words are not fine-sounding; fine-sounding words are not true. Wu: "Sincere words are not sweet, Sweet words are not sincere." Mabry: "True words are not beautiful. Beautiful words are not true." Blackney: "As honest words may not sound fine, fine words may not be honest ones." This is a fact, but one that is usually ignored on all levels of life. If a card house of plausibility is constructed, then no one cares very much whether or not it will really prove workable. And when it does not, people do not seem to mind very much. This is glaringly evident in politics, especially government budgets and programs. But it is equally true in religious, philosophical, practical and personal life. "Alka-Seltzer tastes great!" That little gem of prevarication clued me in when I was only three or four years old that advertising was falsehood. But a cousin of mine, when she was only six or seven years old, could talk me in and out of anything. "Sounds great!" is part of the Great Alka-Seltzer Con of life. We must be on our guard, but without being cynical or fearful.

A good man does not argue; he who argues is not a good man. Legge: "Those who are skilled (in the Tao) do not dispute (about it); the disputatious are not skilled in it." Byrn: "Wise men don't need to debate; men who need to debate are not wise." People who are in the wrong love to argue and wrangle because it is very near to the idea that the strongest wins and the winner is right. Argumentation destroys right understanding and right attitude. The cleverest and most glib will win and thereby "prove" their position is right. I know of a spiritual radio station that adamantly refuses to broadcast debates because they are just vehicles of egotistical declaration of personal ideas and never produce any true benefit. People just cheer for the side they like and then argue as to who won the debate. Debates are very close to the "My dad can beat up your dad" attitude.

Legge's translation implies that the Tao cannot even be spoken about, so those who know the Tao know they cannot argue about It. Byrn's translation indicates that wise people are secure in their wisdom and do not need to challenge or change other people's opinions. On the other hand, the weak and insecure cannot manage without controversy and strong-arm intellectual tactics.

The wise one does not know many things; he who knows many things is not wise. Wu: "The wise are not erudite, The erudite are not wise." Mabry: "The wise are not necessarily well-educated. The well-educated are not necessarily wise." Legge: "Those who know (the Tao) are not extensively learned; the extensively learned do not know it." Feng and English: "Those who know are not learned. The learned do not know." Chan: "A wise man has no extensive knowledge; He who has extensive knowledge is not a wise man." Byrn: "Wise men are not scholars, and scholars are not wise."

Intellectuality has no correlation with wisdom. As Yogananda pointed out, most "scholars" and "experts" have what he called "intellectual indigestion." Paramhansa Nityananda told people: "You were born with a brain, not a book," meaning that native intelligence is needed, and in many instances excessive study prevents the arising of good sense. Lao Tzu is not being anti-intellectual but is against getting ideas from sources other than one's own intelligence and integrity. In other words, formal study requires intellectual digestion and processing.

The Sage does not accumulate (for himself). He lives for other people, and grows richer himself; he gives to other people, and has greater abundance. This is because the Tao does the same. It is inexhaustible goodness in all aspects of existence. Those who have united consciously with the Tao become egoless and intent on the welfare of others, tap the inner and outer wealth and abundance of the Tao and are the Tao to the world.

The Tao of Heaven blesses, but does not harm. Wu: "The Way of Heaven is to benefit, not to harm." Even the pains and struggles of life are part of the Tao's blessing, and only good can come of them and other problems if we allow it to be so. The fact is, suffering and struggle come from transgression of the Tao, not as punishment but as a means of our learning and self-correction. For example, life does not pass us by, but we pass by life. This we must learn. It may hurt, but eventually will become healing.

The Way of the Sage accomplishes, but does not contend. Wu: "The Way of the Sage is to do his duty, not to strive with anyone." Mabry: "The Sage's way is to work, yet not to compete." The wise do not bother poking into other people's lives, but quietly and contentedly live their own life the best they can, because they are secure, intelligent and wise. They are self-contained and self-sufficient like the Tao. They never compare themselves with others to see if they are ahead of them or behind. They simply are what they are, and therefore they advance and evolve. They do not change the world; they change themselves. And then the world is changed. For the world is the Tao. That is the sum and substance of the matter.

DID YOU ENJOY READING THIS BOOK?

Thank you for taking the time to read *The Tao Teh King for Awakening*. If you enjoyed it, please consider telling your friends or posting a short review at Amazon.com, Goodreads, or the site of your choice.

Word of mouth is an author's best friend and is much appreciated.

Get your FREE Meditation Guide

Sign up for the Light of the Spirit Newsletter and get *Ten Simple Tips to Improve Your Meditation Today.*

Get free updates: newsletters, blog posts, and podcasts, plus exclusive content from Light of the Spirit Monastery.

Visit: http://ocoy.org/newsletter-registration

Glossary

Avatar(a): A fully liberated spirit (jiva) who is born into a world below Satya Loka to help others attain liberation. Though commonly referred to as a divine incarnation, an avatar actually is totally one with God, and therefore an incarnation of God-Consciousness.

Avyakta(m): Unmanifest; invisible; when the three gunas are in a state of equilibrium' the undifferentiated.

Bhagavad Gita: "The Song of God." The sacred philosophical text often called "the Hindu Bible," part of the epic Mahabharata by Vyasa; the most popular sacred text in Hinduism.

Brahman: The Absolute Reality; the Truth proclaimed in the Upanishads; the Supreme Reality that is one and indivisible, infinite, and eternal; all-pervading, changeless Existence; Existence-knowledge-bliss Absolute (Satchidananda); Absolute Consciousness; it is not only all-powerful but all-power itself; not only all-knowing and blissful but all-knowledge and all-bliss itself.

Bhava: Subjective state of being (existence); attitude of mind; mental attitude or feeling; state of realization in the heart or mind.

Buddhi: Intellect; intelligence; understanding; reason; the thinking mind; the higher mind, which is the seat of wisdom; the discriminating faculty.

Chidakasha: "The Space (Ether) of Consciousness." The infinite, all-pervading expanse of Consciousness from which all "things" proceed; the subtle space of Consciousness in the Sahasrara (Thousand-petalled Lotus). The true "heart" of all things. Brahman in Its aspect as limitless knowledge; unbounded intelligence. This is a familiar concept of the Upanishads. It is not meant that the physical ether is consciousness. The Pure Consciousness (Cit) is like the ether (Akasa), an all-pervading continuum.

Darshan: Literally "sight" or "seeing;" vision, literal and metaphysical; a system of philosophy (see Sad-darshanas). Darshan is the seeing of a holy being as well as the blessing received by seeing such a one.

Dharma: The righteous way of living, as enjoined by the sacred scriptures and the spiritually illumined; law; lawfulness; virtue; righteousness; norm.

Dharmic: Having to do with dharma; of the character of dharma.

Dwandwa(s): The pairs of opposites inherent in nature (prakriti) such as pleasure and pain, hot and cold, light and darkness, gain and loss, victory and defeat, love and hatred.

Guna: Quality, attribute, or characteristic arising from nature (Prakriti) itself; a mode of energy behavior. As a rule, when "guna" is used it is in reference to the three qualities of Prakriti, the three modes of energy behavior that are the basic qualities of nature, and which determine the inherent characteristics of all created things. They are: 1) sattwa–purity, light, harmony; 2) rajas–activity, passion; and 3) tamas–dullness, inertia, and ignorance.

Hiranyagarbha: Cosmic intelligence; the Supreme Lord of the universe; also called Brahma, cosmic Prana, Sutratma, Apara-brahman, Maha-brahma, or karya-brahman; Samasti-sukshma-sarirabhimani (the sum-total of all the subtle bodies); the highest created being through whom the Supreme Being projects the physical universe; cosmic mind.

Ishwara: "God" or "Lord" in the sense of the Supreme Power, Ruler, Master, or Controller of the cosmos. "Ishwara" implies the powers of omnipotence, omnipresence, and omniscience.

Jnana: Knowledge; knowledge of Reality–of Brahman, the Absolute; also denotes the process of reasoning by which the Ultimate Truth is attained. The word is generally used to denote the knowledge by which one is aware of one's identity with Brahman.

Jnanendriyas: The five organs of perception: ear, skin, eye, tongue, and nose.

Kaivalya: Transcendental state of Absolute Independence; state of absolute freedom from conditioned existence; moksha; isolation; final beatitude; emancipation.

Kama: Desire; passion; lust.

Karma: Karma, derived from the Sanskrit root *kri*, which means to act, do, or make, means any kind of action, including thought and feeling.

It also means the effects of action. Karma is both action and reaction, the metaphysical equivalent of the principle: "For every action there is an equal and opposite reaction." "Whatsoever a man soweth, that shall he also reap" (Galatians 6:7). It is karma operating through the law of cause and effect that binds the jiva or the individual soul to the wheel of birth and death. There are three forms of karma: sanchita, agami, and prarabdha. Sanchita karma is the vast store of accumulated actions done in the past, the fruits of which have not yet been reaped. Agami karma is the action that will be done by the individual in the future. Prarabdha karma is the action that has begun to fructify, the fruit of which is being reaped in this life.

Krishna: An avatar born in India about three thousand years ago, Whose teachings to His disciple Arjuna on the eve of the Great India (Mahabharata) War comprise the Bhagavad Gita.

Kshatriya: A member of the ruler/warrior caste.

Kundalini: The primordial cosmic conscious/energy located in the individual; it is usually thought of as lying coiled up like a serpent at the base of the spine.

Lila: Play; sport; divine play; the cosmic play. The concept that creation is a play of the divine, existing for no other reason than for the mere joy of it. The life of an avatar is often spoken of as lila.

Mahashakti: The Great Power; the divine creative energy.

Mahat Tattwa: The Great Principle; the first product from Prakriti in evolution; intellect. The principle of Cosmic Intelligence or Buddhi; universal Christ Consciousness, the "Son of God," the "Only Begotten of the Father," "the firstborn of every creature.

Maya: The illusive power of Brahman; the veiling and the projecting power of the universe, the power of Cosmic Illusion. "The Measurer"–a reference to the two delusive "measures," Time and Space.

Mulaprakriti: Avyaktam; the Root [Basic] Energy from which all things are formed. The Divine Prakriti or Energy of God.

Muni: "Silent one" (one observing the vow of silence–mauna); sage; ascetic.

Nirguna: Without attributes or qualities (gunas).

Nirguna Brahman: The impersonal, attributeless Absolute beyond all description or designation.

Nitya: Eternal; permanent; unchanging; the ultimate Reality; the eternal Absolute. Secondarily: daily or obligatory as in Nityakarma.

Pradhana: Prakriti; causal matter.

Prakriti: Causal matter; the fundamental power (shakti) of God from which the entire cosmos is formed; the root base of all elements; undifferentiated matter; the material cause of the world. Also known as Pradhana. Prakriti can also mean the entire range of vibratory existence (energy).

Prana: Life; vital energy; life-breath; life-force; inhalation. In the human body the prana is divided into five forms: 1) Prana, the prana that moves upward; 2) Apana: The prana that moves downward, producing the excretory functions in general. 3) Vyana: The prana that holds prana and apana together and produces circulation in the body. 4) Samana: The prana that carries the grosser material of food to the apana and brings the subtler material to each limb; the general force of digestion. 5) Udana: The prana which brings up or carries down what has been drunk or eaten; the general force of assimilation.

Purna: Full; complete; infinite; absolute; Brahman.

Rajas: Activity, passion, desire for an object or goal.

Rajasic: Possessed of the qualities of the raja guna (rajas). Passionate; active; restless.

Ramakrishna, Sri: Sri Ramakrishna lived in India in the second half of the nineteenth century, and is regarded by all India as a perfectly enlightened person–and by many as an Incarnation of God.

Rita(m): Truth; Law; Right; Order. The natural order of things, or Cosmic Order/Law. Its root is ri, which means "to rise, to tend upward." It is said to be the basis for the Law of Karma.

Saguna: Possessing attributes or qualities (gunas).

Saguna Brahman: Brahman with attributes, such as mercy, omnipotence, omniscience, etc.; the Absolute conceived as the Creator, Preserver, and Destroyer of the universe; also the Personal God according to the Vedanta.

Sahaja: Natural; innate; spontaneous; inborn.

Sankalpa: A life-changing wish, desire, volition, resolution, will, determination, or intention–not a mere momentary aspiration, but an empowering act of will that persists until the intention is fully realized. It is an act of spiritual, divine creative will inherent in each person as a power of the Atma.

Sanskrit: The language of the ancient sages of India and therefore of the Indian scriptures and yoga treatises.

Satsang(a): Literally: "company with Truth." Association with godly-minded persons. The company of saints and devotees.

Sattwa: Light; purity; harmony, goodness, reality.

Sattwa Guna: Quality of light, purity, harmony, and goodness.

Sattwic: Partaking of the quality of Sattwa.

Satya Loka: "True World," "World of the True [Sat]", or "World of Truth [Satya]." This highest realm of relative existence where liberated beings live who have not entered back into the Transcendent Absolute where there are no "worlds" (lokas). From that world they can descend and return to other worlds for the spiritual welfare of others, as can those that have chosen to return to the Transcendent.

Shakti: Power; energy; force; the Divine Power of becoming; the apparent dynamic aspect of Eternal Being; the Absolute Power or Cosmic Energy; the Divine Feminine.

Shankara: Shankaracharya; Adi (the first) Shankaracharya: The great reformer and re-establisher of Vedic Religion in India around 500 B.C. He is the unparalleled exponent of Advaita (Non-Dual) Vedanta. He also reformed the mode of monastic life and founded (or regenerated) the ancient Swami Order.

Tamas: Dullness, darkness, inertia, folly, and ignorance.

Tamasic: Possessed of the qualities of the tamo guna (tamas). Ignorant; dull; inert; and dark.

Tapasya: Austerity; practical (i.e., result-producing) spiritual discipline; spiritual force. Literally it means the generation of heat or energy, but is always used in a symbolic manner, referring to spiritual practice and its effect, especially the roasting of karmic seeds, the burning up of karma.

Upanishads: Books (of varying lengths) of the philosophical teachings of the ancient sages of India on the knowledge of Absolute Reality. The upanishads contain two major themes: (1) the individual self (atman) and the Supreme Self (Paramatman) are one in essence, and (2) the goal of life is the realization/manifestation of this unity, the realization of God (Brahman). There are eleven principal upanishads: Isha, Kena, Katha, Prashna, Mundaka, Mandukya, Taittiriya, Aitareya, Chandogya, Brihadaranyaka, and Shvetashvatara, all of which were commented on by Shankara, Ramanuja and Madhavacharya, thus setting the seal of authenticity on them.

Vasudeva: "He who dwells in all things"–the Universal God; the father of Krishna, who is himself also sometimes called Vasudeva.

Veda: Knowledge, wisdom, revealed scripture. See Vedas.

Vedas: The oldest scriptures of India, considered the oldest scriptures of the world, that were revealed in meditation to the Vedic Rishis (seers). Although in modern times there are said to be four Vedas (Rig, Sama, Yajur, and Atharva), in the upanishads only three are listed (Rig, Sama, and Yajur). In actuality, there is only one Veda: the Rig Veda. The Sama Veda is only a collection of Rig Veda hymns that are marked (pointed) for singing. The Yajur Veda is a small book giving directions on just one form of Vedic sacrifice. The Atharva Veda is only a collection of theurgical mantras to be recited for the cure of various afflictions or to be recited over the herbs to be taken as medicine for those afflictions.

Vedic: Having to do with the Vedas.

Vivekananda (Swami): The chief disciple of Sri Ramakrishna, who brought the message of Vedanta to the West at the end of the nineteenth century.

Yuga: Age or cycle; aeon; world era. Hindus believe that there are four yugas: the Golden Age (Satya or Krita Yuga), the Silver age (Treta Yuga), The Bronze Age (Dwapara Yuga), and the Iron Age (Kali Yuga). Satya Yuga is four times as long as the Kali Yuga; Treta Yuga is three times as long; and Dwapara Yuga is twice as long. In the Satya Yuga the majority of humans use the total potential–four-fourths–of their minds; in the Treta Yuga, three-fourths; in the Dwapara Yuga, one half; and in the Kali Yuga, one fourth. (In each Yuga there are those who are using either more or less of their minds than the general populace.) The Yugas move in a perpetual circle: Ascending Kali Yuga, ascending Dwapara Yuga, ascending Treta Yuga, ascending Satya Yuga, descending Satya Yuga, descending, Treta Yuga, descending Dwapara Yuga, and descending Kali Yuga—over and over. Furthermore, there are yuga cycles within yuga cycles. For example, there are yuga cycles that affect the entire cosmos, and smaller yuga cycles within those greater cycles that affect a solar system. The cosmic yuga cycle takes 8,640,000,000 years, whereas the solar yuga cycle only takes 24,000 years. At the present time our solar system is in the ascending Dwapara Yuga, but the cosmos is in the descending Kali Yuga. Consequently, the more the general mind of humanity develops, the more good can be accomplished by the positive, and the more evil can be accomplished by the negative. Therefore we have more contrasts and polarization in contemporary life than previously before 1900.

About the Author

Abbot George Burke (Swami Nirmalananda Giri) is the founder and director of the Light of the Spirit Monastery (Atma Jyoti Ashram) in Cedar Crest, New Mexico, USA.

In his many pilgrimages to India, he had the opportunity of meeting some of India's greatest spiritual figures, including Swami Sivananda of Rishikesh and Anandamayi Ma. During his first trip to India he was made a member of the ancient Swami Order by Swami Vidyananda Giri, a direct disciple of Paramhansa Yogananda, who had himself been given sannyas by the Shankaracharya of Puri, Jagadguru Bharati Krishna Tirtha.

In the United States he also encountered various Christian saints, including Saint John Maximovich of San Francisco and Saint Philaret Voznesensky of New York. He was ordained in the Liberal Catholic Church (International) to the priesthood on January 25, 1974, and consecrated a bishop on August 23, 1975.

For many years Abbot George has researched the identity of Jesus Christ and his teachings with India and Sanatana Dharma, including Yoga. It is his conclusion that Jesus lived in India for most of his life, and was a yogi and Sanatana Dharma missionary to the West. After his resurrection he returned to India and lived the rest of his life in the Himalayas.

He has written extensively on these and other topics, many of which are posted at OCOY.org.

Light of the Spirit Monastery

Light of the Spirit Monastery is an esoteric Christian monastic community for those men who seek direct experience of the Spirit through meditation, sacramental worship, discipline and dedicated communal life, emphasizing the inner reality of "Christ in you the hope of glory," as taught by the illumined mystics of East and West.

The public outreach of the monastery is through its website, OCOY.org (Original Christianity and Original Yoga). There you will find many articles on Original Christianity and Original Yoga, including *Esoteric Christian Beliefs*. *Foundations of Yoga* and *How to Be a Yogi* are practical guides for anyone seriously interested in living the Yoga Life.

You will also discover many other articles on leading an effective spiritual life, including *The Yoga of the Sacraments* and *Spiritual Benefits of a Vegetarian Diet*, as well as the "Dharma for Awakening" series–in-depth commentaries on these spiritual classics: the Upanishads, the Bhagavad Gita, the Dhammapada, and the Tao Teh King.

You can listen to podcasts by Abbot George on meditation, the Yoga Life, and remarkable spiritual people he has met in India and elsewhere, at http://ocoy.org/podcasts/

Reading for Awakening

Light of the Spirit Press presents books on spiritual wisdom and Original Christianity and Original Yoga. From our "Dharma for Awakening" series (practical commentaries on the world's scriptures) to books on how to meditate and live a successful spiritual life, you will find books that are informative, helpful, and even entertaining.

Light of the Spirit Press is the publishing house of Light of the Spirit Monastery (Atma Jyoti Ashram) in Cedar Crest, New Mexico, USA. Our books feature the writings of the founder and director of the monastery, Abbot George Burke (Swami Nirmalananda Giri) which are also found on the monastery's website, OCOY.org.

We invite you to explore our publications in the following pages.

Find out more about our publications at
lightofthespiritpress.com

Satsang with the Abbot
Questions & Answers about Life, Spiritual Liberty, and the Pursuit of Ultimate Happiness

Grounded in the perspective of classic Indian thought, directly taught by such luminaries as Swami Sivananda of Rishikesh and Sri Anandamayi Ma, and blessed with the clarity and originality of thought that can only come from years of spiritual practice (sadhana), Abbot George Burke's answers to inquirers' questions are unique, fresh, and authoritative.

The questions in this book range from the most sublime to the most practical. "How can I attain samadhi? " "I am married with children. How can I lead a spiritual life? " "What is Self-realization? "

In Abbot George's replies to these questions the reader will discover common sense, helpful information, and a guiding light for their journey through and beyond the forest of cliches, contradictions, and confusion of yoga, Hinduism, Christianity, and metaphysical thought.

What Readers say:
"Abbot George speaks as one who knows his subject well, and answers in an manner that conveys an effortlessness and humor that puts one at ease, while, at the same time, a wisdom and sincerity which demands an attentive ear. "—*Russ Thomas*

The Christ of India
The Story of Original Christianity

"Original Christianity" is the teaching of both Jesus of Nazareth and his Apostle Saint Thomas in India. Although it was new to the Mediterranean world, it was really the classical, traditional teachings of the ancient rishis of India that even today comprise Sanatana Dharma, the Eternal Dharma, that goes far beyond religion into realization.

In The Christ of India Abbot George Burke presents what those ancient teachings are, as well as the growing evidence that Jesus spent much of his "Lost Years" in India and Tibet. This is also the story of how the original teachings of Jesus and Saint Thomas thrived in India for centuries before the coming of the European colonialists.

What Readers say:

"Interpreting the teachings of Jesus from the perspective of Santana Dharma, The Christ of India is a knowledgeable yet engaging collection of authentic details and evident manuscripts about the Essene roots of Jesus and his 'Lost years'. ...delightful to read and a work of substance, vividly written and rich in historical analysis, this is an excellent work written by a masterful teacher and a storyteller." –*Enas Reviews*

Yoga: Science of the Absolute
A Commentary on the Yoga Sutras of Patanjali

In *Yoga: Science of the Absolute*, Abbot George Burke draws on the age-long tradition regarding this essential text, including the commentaries of Vyasa and Shankara, the most highly regarded writers on Indian philosophy and practice, as well as I. K. Taimni and other authoritative commentators, and adds his own ideas based on half a century of study and practice. Serious students of yoga will find this an essential addition to their spiritual studies.

What Readers say:

"Abbot George has provided a commentary that is not only deeply informative, making brilliant connections across multiple traditions, but eminently practical. More importantly he describes how they can help one empower their own practice, their own sadhana." —Michael Sabani

Soham Yoga
The Yoga of the Self

An in-depth guide to the practice of Soham sadhana.

Soham (which is pronounced like "Sohum") means: I Am That. It is the natural vibration of the Self, which occurs spontaneously with each incoming and outgoing breath. By becoming aware of it on the conscious level by mentally repeating it in time with the breath (*So* when inhaling and *Ham* when exhaling), a yogi experiences the identity between his individual Self and the Supreme Self.

The practice is very simple, and the results very profound. Truly wondrous is the fact that Soham Yoga can go on all the time, not just during meditation, if we apply ourselves to it. The whole life can become a continuous stream of liberating sadhana. "By the mantra 'Soham' separate the jivatma from the Paramatma and locate the jivatma in the heart" (Devi Bhagavatam 11.8.15). When we repeat Soham in time with the breath we are invoking our eternal being. This is why we need only listen to our inner mental intonations of Soham in time with the breath which itself is Soham.

What Readers say:

"The more I read this book, study it and practice Soham meditation and japa, the more thrilled I am to find this book. It is a complete spiritual path of Yoga."—*Arnold Van Wie*

Dwelling in the Mirror
A Study of Illusions Produced by Delusive Meditation and How to Be Free from Them

"There are those who can have an experience and realize that it really cannot be real, but a vagary of their mind. Some may not understand that on their own, but can be shown by others the truth about it. For them and those that may one day be in danger of meditation-produced delusions I have written this brief study." –Abbot George Burke

In *Dwelling in the Mirror* you will learn:
- different types of meditation and the experiences they produce, and the problems and delusions which can arise from them.
- how to get rid of negative initiation energies and mantras.
- what are authentic, positive meditation practices and their effects and aspects.
- an ancient, universal method of meditation which is both proven and effective.

What Readers say:

"I totally loved this book! After running across many spiritual and self-help books filled with unrealistic promises, this little jewel had the impact of a triple Espresso."—Sandra Carrington-Smith, author of *Housekeeping for the Soul*

The Dhammapada for Awakening
A Commentary on Buddha's Practical Wisdom

The Dhammapada for Awakening brings a refreshing and timely perspective to ancient wisdom and shows seekers of inner peace practical ways to improve their inner lives today.

It explores the Buddha's answers to the urgent questions, such as "How can I find find lasting peace, happiness and fulfillment that seems so elusive?" and "What can I do to avoid many of the miseries big and small that afflict all of us?".

Drawing on the proven wisdom of different ancient traditions, and the contemporary masters of spiritual life, as well as his own studies and first-hand knowledge of the mystical traditions of East and West, Abbot George illumines the practical wisdom of Buddha in the Dhammapada, and more importantly, and make that makes that teaching relevant to present day spiritual seekers.

What Readers say:

"In this compelling book, Abbot George Burke brings his considerable knowledge and background in Christian teachings and the Vedic tradition of India to convey a practical understanding of the teachings of the Buddha. ...This is a book you'll want to take your time to read and keep as reference to reread. Highly recommended for earnest spiritual aspirants" *–Anna Hourihan, author, editor, and publisher at Vedanta Shores Press*

The Gospel of Thomas for Awakening
A Commentary on Jesus' Sayings as Recorded by the Apostle Thomas

"From the very beginning there were two Christianities." So begins this remarkable work. While the rest of the Apostles dispersed to various areas of the Mediterranean world, the apostle Thomas travelled to India, where growing evidence shows that Jesus spent his "Lost Years," and which had been the source of the wisdom which he had brought to the "West."

In *The Gospel of Thomas for Awakening*, Abbot George shines the "Light of the East" on the sometimes enigmatic sayings of Jesus recorded by his apostle Saint Thomas, revealing their unique and rich practical nature for modern day seekers for spiritual life.

Ideal for daily study or group discussion.

What Readers say:

"An extraordinary work of theological commentary, *The Gospel of Thomas for Awakening* is as informed and informative as it is inspired and inspiring".—*James A. Cox, Editor-in-Chief, Midwest Book Review*

The Tao Teh King for Awakening
A Practical Commentary on Lao Tzu's Classic Exposition of Taoism

With penetrating insight, Abbot George Burke illumines the the wisdom of Lao Tzu's classic writing, the Tao Teh King (Tao Te Ching), and the timeless practical value of China's most beloved Taoist scripture for spiritual seekers. With a unique perspective of a lifetime of study and practice of both Eastern and Western spirituality, Abbot George mines the treasures of the Tao Teh King and presents them in an easily intelligible fashion for those wishing to put these priceless teachings into practice.

Illumined with quotes from the Gospels, the Bhagavad Gita, Yogananda and other Indian saints and Indian scriptures.

What Readers say:
"Burke's evident expertise concerning both Western and Eastern spirituality, provides readers with a wide-ranging and intriguing study of the topic. For those who seek spiritual guidance and insight into Lao Tzu's wisdom, this work offers a clear pathway." – *Publisher's Weekly (BookLife Prize)*

The Bhagavad Gita for Awakening
A Practical Commentary for Leading a Successful Spiritual Life

With penetrating insight, Abbot George Burke illumines the Bhagavad Gita's practical value for spiritual seekers. With a unique perspective from a lifetime of study and practice of both Eastern and Western spirituality, Abbot George presents the treasures of the Gita in an easily intelligible fashion.

Drawing from the teachings of Sri Ramakrishna, Jesus, Paramhansa Yogananda, Ramana Maharshi, Swami Vivekananda, Swami Sivananda of Rishikesh, Papa Ramdas, and other spiritual masters and teachers, as well as his own experiences, Abbot Burke illustrates the teachings of the Gita with stories which make the teachings of Krishna in the Gita vibrant and living.

What Readers say:
"This is not a book for only "Hindus" or "Christians." Anyone desiring to better their lives mentally, emotionally, and spiritually would benefit greatly by reading this book."— *Sailaja Kuruvadi*

The Upanishads for Awakening
A Practical Commentary on India's Classical Scriptures

With penetrating insight, Abbot George Burke illumines the Upanishads' practical value for spiritual seekers, and the timelessness of India's most beloved scriptures. With a unique perspective of a lifetime of study and practice of both Eastern and Western spirituality, Abbot George mines the treasures of the Upanishads and presents them in an easily intelligible fashion for those wishing to put these priceless teachings into practice

The teachings of the Upanishads are the supreme expressions of the eternal wisdom, the eternal vision of the ancient rishis (sages) of India. The truths embodied in the Upanishads and their inspired digest-summary, the Bhagavad Gita, are invaluable for all who would ascend to higher consciousness.

What Readers say:
"It is always a delight to see how he seamlessly integrates the wisdom of the West into the East."
–Roopa Subramani

The Bhagavad Gita–The Song of God
A new translation of the most important spiritual classic which India has produced.

Often called the "Bible" of Hinduism, the Bhagavad Gita is found in households throughout India and has been translated into every major language of the world. Literally billions of copies have been handwritten and printed.

The clarity of this translation by Abbot George Burke makes for easy reading, while the rich content makes this the ideal "study" Gita. As the original Sanskrit language is so rich, often there are several accurate translations for the same word, which are noted in the text, giving the spiritual student the needed understanding of the fullness of the Gita.

For those unable to make a spiritual journey to India, a greater pilgrimage can be made by anyone anywhere in the world by simply reading The Holy Song of God, the Srimad Bhagavad Gita. It will be a holy pilgrimage of mind and spirit.

Robe of Light
An Esoteric Christian Cosmology

In *Robe of Light* Abbot George Burke explores the whys and wherefores of the mystery of creation. From the emanation of the worlds from the very Being of God, to the evolution of the souls to their ultimate destiny as perfected Sons of God, the ideal progression of creation is described. Since the rebellion of Lucifer and the fall of Adam and Eve from Paradise flawed the normal plan of evolution, a restoration was necessary. How this came about is the prime subject of this insightful study.

Moreover, what this means to aspirants for spiritual perfection is expounded, with a compelling knowledge of the scriptures and of the mystical traditions of East and West.

What Readers say:

"Having previously read several offerings from the pen of Abbot George Burke I was anticipating this work to be well written and an enjoyable read. However, Robe of Light actually exceeded my expectations. Abbot Burke explicates the subject perfectly, making a difficult and complex subject like Christian cosmology accessible to those of us who are not great theologians."—*Russ Thomas*

A Brief Sanskrit Glossary
A Spiritual Student's Guide to Essential Sanskrit Terms

This Sanskrit glossary contains full translations and explanations of many of the most commonly used spiritual Sanskrit terms, and will help students of the Bhagavad Gita, the Upanishads, the Yoga Sutras of Patanjali, and other Indian scriptures and philosophical works to expand their vocabularies to include the Sanskrit terms contained in them, and gain a fuller understanding in their studies.

What Readers say:

"If you are reading the writings of Swami Sivananda you will find a basketful of untranslated Sanskrit words which often have no explanation, as he assumes his readers have a background in Hindu philosophy. For writings like his, this book is invaluable, as it lists frequently used Sanskrit terms used in writings on yoga and Hindu philosophical thought.

"As the title says, this is a spiritual students' guidebook, listing not only commonly used spiritual terms, but also giving brief information about spiritual teachers and writers, both modern and ancient.

"Abbot George's collection is just long enough to give the meanings of useful terms without overwhelming the reader with an overabundance of extraneous words. This is a book that the spiritual student will use frequently."—*Simeon Davis*

Spiritual Benefits of a Vegetarian Diet

The health benefits of a vegetarian diet are well known, as are the ethical aspects. But the spiritual advantages should be studied by anyone involved in meditation, yoga, or any type of spiritual practice.

Although diet is commonly considered a matter of physical health alone, since the Hermetic principle "as above, so below" is a fundamental truth of the cosmos, diet is a crucial aspect of emotional, intellectual, and spiritual development as well. For diet and consciousness are interrelated, and purity of diet is an effective aid to purity and clarity of consciousness.

The major thing to keep in mind when considering the subject of vegetarianism is its relevancy in relation to our explorations of consciousness. We need only ask: Does it facilitate my spiritual growth–the development and expansion of my consciousness? The answer is Yes.

A second essay, *Christian Vegetarianism,* continues with a consideration of the esoteric side of diet, the vegetarian roots of early Christianity, and an insightful exploration of vegetarianism in the Old and New Testaments.

Available as a free Kindle ebook download at Amazon.com.

Foundations of Yoga

Ten Important Principles Every Meditator Should Know

An in-depth examination of the important foundation principles of Patanjali's Yoga, Yama & Niyama.

Yama and Niyama are often called the Ten Commandments of Yoga, but they have nothing to do with the ideas of sin and virtue or good and evil as dictated by some cosmic potentate. Rather they are determined on a thoroughly practical, pragmatic basis: that which strengthens and facilitates our yoga practice should be observed and that which weakens or hinders it should be avoided.

It is not a matter of being good or bad, but of being wise or foolish. Each one of these Five Don'ts (Yama) and Five Do's (Niyama) is a supporting, liberating foundation of Yoga. An introduction to the important foundation principles of Patanjali's Yoga: Yama & Niyama

Available as a free Kindle ebook download at Amazon.com, as well as in paperback.

Perspectives on Yoga
Living the Yoga Life

"Dive deep; otherwise you cannot get the gems at the bottom of the ocean. You cannot pick up the gems if you only float on the surface." Sri Ramakrishna

Many people come to the joyous and liberating discovery of yoga and yoga philosophy, and then dive no deeper, resting on their first understanding of the atman, Brahman, the goal of yoga, and everything else the classic yoga philosophy teaches about "the way things are."

In *Perspectives on Yoga* author Abbot George Burke shares the gems he has found from a lifetime of "diving deep." This collection of reflections and short essays addresses the key concepts of the yoga philosophy that are so easy to take for granted. Never content with the accepted cliches about yoga sadhana, the yoga life, the place of a guru, the nature of Brahman and our unity with It, Abbot George's insights on these and other facets of the yoga life will inspire, provoke, enlighten, and even entertain.

What Readers say:
"Abbot George eloquently brings the eastern practice of seeking God inwardly to western readers who have been taught to seek God outwardly."—*Bill Braddock*

May a Christian Believe in Reincarnation?

Discover the real and surprising history of reincarnation and Christianity.

A growing number of people are open to the subject of past lives, and the belief in rebirth–reincarnation, metempsychosis, or transmigration–is becoming commonplace. It often thought that belief in reincarnation and Christianity are incompatible. But is this really true? May a Christian believe in reincarnation? The answer may surprise you.

Reincarnation-also known as the transmigration of souls-is not just some exotic idea of non-Christian mysticism. Nor is it an exclusively Hindu-Buddhist teaching.

In orthodox Jewish and early Christian writings, as well as the Holy Scriptures, we find reincarnation as a fully developed belief, although today it is commonly ignored. But from the beginning it has been an integral part of Orthodox Judaism, and therefore as Orthodox Jews, Jesus and his Apostles would have believed in rebirth.

What Readers say:
"Those needing evidence that a belief in reincarnation is in accordance with teachings of the Christ need look no further: Plainly laid out and explained in an intelligent manner from one who has spent his life on a Christ-like path of renunciation and prayer/meditation."—*Christopher T. Cook*

The Unknown Lives of Jesus and Mary
Compiled from Ancient Records and Mystical Revelations

A unique compilation of ancient records and mystical revelations, which includes historical records of the lives of Jesus Christ and his Mother Mary that have been accepted and used by the Church since apostolic times. This treasury of little-known stories of Jesus' infancy, his sojourn in the Orient as recorded in the famous Ladakh Manuscript, and his passion, crucifixion, and resurrection, will broaden the reader's understanding of what Christianity really was in its original form: a far more vibrant and conscious movement than what we see today in its place.

But this book is more than just a collection of ancient texts. Abbot George Burke's illuminating and scholarly commentary adds a further dimension and relevance, and will guide you to a deeper understanding of how, as he puts it, "to manifest the inner Christ that abides within us all.".

What Readers say:

"Abbot George offers a fresh and intelligent interpretation of these texts from his own theological tradition of Hindu-Christian syncretism."—*River Ezell*

Coming Soon

The Odes of Solomon: A Commentary

The Aquarian Gospel for Awakening

www.ingramcontent.com/pod-product-compliance
Lightning Source LLC
Chambersburg PA
CBHW031613160426
43196CB00006B/112